Dennis Green

# DENNIS GREEN

## NO ROOM FOR CRYBABIES

Dennis Green
with Gene McGivern

SPORTS PUBLISHING INC

A Division of Sagamore Publishing

Champaign, IL 61820

Book Research and Development: Nicholas Cooper-Lewter
Editor, Production Manager: Susan M. McKinney
Book Design: Michelle R. Dressen
Dustjacket Design: Deborah M. Bellaire

ISBN:1-57167-175-7

Printed in the United States

*Dedicated to Bus, Anna, Marie, Patti, Jeremy, Vanessa, Billy,
Bobby, Stan, Greg and the rest of my family,
past, present and future.*

---

*I believe I can fly*
*I believe I can touch the sky*
*I think about it every night and day*
*Spread my wings and fly away*

*I believe I can soar*
*I see myself running*
*Through that open door*
*I believe I can fly*
*I believe I can fly*

*There are miracles in life that I must achieve*
*But I know they start inside of me*
*If I can see it*
*Then I can be it*
*If I just believe it*
*There's nothing to it*

*I believe I can fly*

—R. Kelly, composer/artist, 1996

---

# CONTENTS

*Foreword* .................................................................................. vi

*Acknowledgments* ................................................................ vii

*Introduction: Uphill Struggles, Upbeat Spirit* ........................ ix

1    Kickoff in Canton ......................................................... 1

2    Bus and Anna's Baby Boy ........................................... 17

3    Picking Up the Pieces .................................................. 27

4    We Are Playing, We Are Staying .................................. 39

5    Learning the Coaching Business .................................. 51

6    Waking Up the Wildcats ............................................. 61

7    Ghost Chasing .............................................................. 71

8    That Super Season ....................................................... 81

9    Stanford Man ............................................................... 93

10    Coming to Minnesota ................................................ 103

11    Going To War .............................................................. 115

12    Owning Up To a Problem ........................................... 125

13    Don't Believe The Hype .............................................. 139

14    You Only Have One Reputation ................................. 149

15    Can't We All Just Get Along? ..................................... 163

16    NFL Issues .................................................................. 177

17    Observations ............................................................... 189

18    Well Rounded, Well Grounded ................................... 199

19    If It Lasts Until Tomorrow . . . ................................... 211

Dennis Green's Coaching Resume ...................................... 225

# FOREWORD

by Dr. Harry Edwards
Professor, University of California (Berkeley)
Consultant, San Francisco 49ers

Among the many concerns triggering the Black revolt in American sport during the 1960s, none was more provocative than the stark disparity between Black athletes' growing domination of major team sports, at both the collegiate and professional levels, and the utter lack of Black access to decision-making and authority positions—such as head coaches—of these same sports. Football was the premier revenue-producing collegiate sport. In the late 1960s, it was also rapidly emerging as the preeminent televised professional sport. There was tremendous resistance to allowing Blacks so great a forum and spotlight.

There was also a pervasive disinclination to "take a chance" on Black head coaching candidates. An argument could be made that a head coach of a top 10 collegiate or an NFL team ranks behind only the U.S. President as a focus of scrutiny and critical judgment. In a crazy, unpredictable game, members of the White sports establishment were more disposed to hire people that they knew—meaning White head coaching candidates.

And particularly in the NFL when Black candidates were finally considered for head coaching jobs, the overwhelming majority of them—unlike their White counterparts—were former players, if not stars in the league. It was as if Black head coaching candidates required additional credentials and credibility as evidence of their legitimacy and potential coaching competence.

These were the circumstances that confronted Dennis Green in his quest to rise through the occupational and status hierarchy of the football coaching profession. After achieving two head coaching positions in the NCAA division I collegiate ranks and serving as an offensive assistant to Bill Walsh with the San Francisco 49ers, Dennis became head coach of the Minnesota Vikings. One of only four Black head coaches hired over the modern history of the NFL, he is the only one who achieved his position without the benefit of prior experiences as a player in the league.

His journey to membership in one of the sport's most elite fraternities makes for a very good football story. But its relevance as a tale of challenges met extends far beyond the gridiron. Seldom, if ever, are people with the aspirations, energy, and mental toughness to reach such heights of achievement qualified as "angelic." But fewer still have been "crybabies" inclined toward lamenting and whining over the difficulties and challenges of their circumstances and the work that they have chosen. Dennis Green has kept his eyes on the prize and simply forged ahead. And in this saga, there are perhaps lessons for us all.

# ACKNOWLEDGMENTS

Your health and the health of your family are the most important things in the world. Like so many other things in life, your health is something you sometimes can't control. At least we can control how we react to life's adversity.

This book, *No Room For Crybabies,* is all about life's continuous challenges and obstacles. I want my life to be measured not by the pain and hardships I've endured, but by my will to keep moving forward, setting goals, working hard and seeking excellence.

Thank God we're not expected to be perfect—I've never expected that from myself, but I will always keep trying to be my best. I ask of myself the same things I ask of my players and coaches —desire, dedication and determination.

Here's to all the people who helped me make my career and this book possible:

- To all my coaches who taught me when I was a player. I hope you enjoyed coaching me as much as I enjoyed playing for you. Many of my coaching ideas came from my experiences in dealing with the real world as a student-athlete in the 1960s.
- To all the head coaches I served under and people I coached alongside. My years as an assistant coach gave me an opportunity to contribute and feel needed. Thanks to all of my contemporaries for their professionalism and cooperation.
- To all the players and coaches who have been with me in six seasons with the Vikings. Every year we have been in the hunt, and that is the essence of competition. I hope you savor our victories that were considered "must-win," especially when we were counted out yet still came back strong to claim a piece of glory. Our football staffs have always been tough enough and talented enough to get us over the top. My confidence level remains high because of you.
- Thanks to my friends for supporting me, and also thanks to my enemies, who continue to remind me that I must always be tough. My friends know I will stay strong.
- I've appreciated the energy that my co-author Gene McGivern has brought to this book. Who says an Iowa Hawkeye and an

Iowa State Cyclone can't find common ground? We've had a good working relationship in part because Gene understands my background and how it prepared me to deal with my life's challenges. We both have inspirational parents and siblings (he has two sisters and six brothers). Believe me, Gene's background as a Cyclone distance runner came in handy during some of our marathon sessions this summer.

- My special thanks go to Dr. Nicholas Cooper-Lewter for his research, ideas and support in getting this book off the drawing board. We met and became friends because of our mutual understanding and respect. We both left home in 1967 to seek the American dream through academics and athletics—I was off to the University of Iowa, while Nicholas ventured to Ashland College. When you move as many times as I have, you pick you friends carefully, as I have here in Minnesota. Nicholas is among them.

- Thanks to Jim Klobuchar and his book, *Purple Hearts and Golden Memories: 35 Years with the Minnesota Vikings.* I wish more people in the media had his knowledge of the Vikings' history.

I often say that I am the luckiest man alive to have Marie as my wife. She has been with me every step of the way the last few years. I love her with all my heart, and she gave me the encouragement to stick with this book project because, as she put it, "A lot of people want to know how you feel." Our daughter, Vanessa, is going to be like her mother—sugar, spice and everything nice, yet still full of strength and spirit.

Patti and Jeremy: Always know that I love you and I'm doing great. My older children want things to go easier for me, but they understand that I'm a fighter. All my brothers are the best, too—Billy, Bob, Stan and Greg. It seems like just yesterday when we were walking along the road with Mom and Dad, heading to our favorite bridge from which to cast our fishing poles.

To Mom and Dad: I will always love you. Even after all these years, I still think of you every day.

I also thank God for putting me in the position to have my family and friends. In the master plan, I think I'm only halfway there.

—Dennis Green

# INTRODUCTION

## UPHILL STRUGGLES, UPBEAT SPIRIT

*"He came to town with a set of drums, a Super Bowl ring and a silver star.*

*"It struck the locals as an odd collection of hardware, but it shouldn't have. A man who would voluntarily coach for five years at Northwestern has to be driven by rhythms slightly alien to most coaches.*

*"Denny Green. The sheriff's star was strictly symbolic and imaginary. It was something the new Viking coach bestowed on himself in a moment of mock consternation his first day on the job in 1992 . . .*

*"Nobody was going to confuse Dennis Green with John Wayne, or Tom Landry for that matter, or Bud Grant. Green was verbal and jazzy, a guy from the asphalt and the baby boom. He was both a coach and a part-time musician, identities to which he gave almost equal ardor. He was also black. Not much attention was given to that simple but profound fact when he was named to the job by the Vikings' new CEO, Roger Headrick. The times, after all, are filled with the demands of cultural sensitivity. It was considered sensitive not to dwell on Denny Green's heritage and his trailblazing status. In other words, he was a coach first and an African American second. That was true. But there was an enormous significance to his appointment, nonetheless. It was a breakout from the historical patterns in the National Football League, or practically any league."*

—Jim Klobuchar, in his 1995 book
*Purple Hearts and Golden Memories:
35 Years with the Minnesota Vikings,*
introducing Dennis Green to his readers

It's July in Minnesota, footballs will soon replace humidity in the air, and all is well in the world. Now that the mosquitos are biting more often than walleyes in these parts, it must mean that football season is near. Honey, have you seen my purple face paint?

Get some fresh batteries in the remote control and cue the Hank Williams, Jr., Monday Night Football theme song, if you please.

*"Are you ready for some football?"* Dennis Green is always ready.

It's 1997 and if you listen to Twin Cities sports analysts, it's supposed to be a pressure-filled, pivotal season for the sixth-year Minnesota Viking coach. So why does Green seem so relaxed and confident in training camp in the July dog days in Mankato?

Maybe it was the February birth of his daughter, Vanessa, and the support of his wife, Marie. An off-season of good music and good fishing probably didn't hurt. Factor in a productive six months on the Vikings' player personnel side, and you understand why Green is eager for the August 31 regular-season opener to arrive.

Operation 1997 started for Green and his soldiers in mid-July. They loaded up the window air conditioners and headed south on Highway 169 for the dormitory rooms and practice fields of Mankato State University. This is where the Vikings hope to use the previous six months of acquisitions, strategy, and goals as a springboard into the next six months of fury and focus.

Perhaps it was a good omen when in the second week of training camp, one of the team buses en route to a LaCrosse, Wisconsin, scrimmage, had its accelerator stick. The 1997 Minnesota Vikings also look like a team in a hurry to reach its destination. Maybe they get that from their head coach, who was in junior high when both of parents died in a cruel, two-year span.

Green admits he's been hurrying to accomplish things ever since, just in case he meets a similar fate as Mom and Dad.

A few days later, the Viking players waited in the Minneapolis-St. Paul airport gate to board their Northwest Airlines charter flight to Canton, Ohio, for a preseason game vs. Seattle that would officially usher in the 1997 National Football League season. The television monitor anchored above the seating area had a live feed from a Los Angeles courtroom. The verdict in the Carroll O'Connor slander lawsuit was being read.

Viking Robert Smith strained to hear as the rambling, multi-count verdict was being announced. A teammate strolled up and asked, "Isn't that Archie Bunker? What's he on trial for?" With its 6 a.m.-to midnight demands, an NFL training camp makes it difficult to keep up on current events.

It turned out to be a good weekend, for O'Connor, the star of TV's "In the Heat of the Night," and for the Minnesota Vikings, who are trying to survive the heat of the day. O'Connor was found not liable of slander. And the Vikings, who looked sharp in the nationally televised preseason victory in Canton, were surviving some oppressive weather.

After some up-and-down preseason performances, the jury was still out on the Vikings as they came into the regular season. But Green had several reasons to think that, just maybe, this would be a breakthrough season:

- Running back Robert Smith and linebacker Eddie McDaniel are healthy again.
- Quarterback Brad Johnson is ready, the defense is willing, and receiver Cris Carter is able.
- Offensive line ace Randall McDaniel is signed to a new contract.
- The 1997 draft picks showed early promise.
- Some preseason injuries around the league, especially in the NFC Central, contributed further to the expected parity in the 1997 NFL season.
- There were no prolonged training camp holdouts.
- There were no major off-the-field controversies this year, letting the focus stay on football instead of personal issues.

The confident Green, starting his sixth season as Minnesota head coach and 26th season as a football coach, has a plan. As he loves to say, "Plan your work, and work your plan."

In football, like in the Carroll O'Connor slander trial, actions speak louder than words. And throughout his 48 years, Green has been a man of accomplishment. Whether he's raising money for the Boys and Girls Clubs, raising the talent and expectation level on his football team, or raising eyebrows with candid remarks in this autobiography, Green approaches every task with precision and a plan.

There have been few dull moments in the six seasons Green has been the Minnesota Vikings' head coach. On the field, the Vikings are continuing a steady rebuilding process that began in 1992 with an 11-5 record. Green's teams have never finished under .500 in a season. Four of the five teams made the playoffs, and two won the NFC Central Division championship.

In these six years, Green has patiently and deliberately molded his team. All-Pro cornerstones like McDaniel and Carter are still around from the previous regime, but the majority of guys Green will count on in 1997 and beyond are his draft picks and acquisitions. He will succeed or fail with his own personnel.

Off the field, Green is hoping his personal conflicts and battles are behind him. Whatever happens, he's determined not to let critics and pundits set his agenda. Green remains positive, moves forward, and avoids making excuses. He exudes a calm and confidence that convinces you he'll still be the one leading this franchise into the 21st century.

He's already defying a modern trend in head coaching longevity. Of the nine new NFL head coaches hired in 1992, Green is one of three still in his job. Only two current NFL coaches have more seniority in their current positions—Buffalo's Mary Levy and Kansas City's Marty Schottenheimer.

Green has regularly faced off against the best coaches in the game. He's pulled upsets of Lou Holtz while at Northwestern, Stanford and with the Vikings. Two of those even involved football games. The latter situation came in 1996, when Holtz, apparently feeling unappreciated, abruptly resigned at Notre Dame. Half the country had him returning to Minnesota as the Vikings' head coach. Never mind that Green still held that job and had more than two years left on his contract. Green and his players, reeling in a four-game losing streak at the time, took offense to the hype surrounding Holtz. Their anger probably helped them gut out a 16-13 overtime win at Oakland the next Sunday night. The victory was the Vikings' defining moment for 1996. It started a stretch of four wins in five games—they lost to Denver on a tipped pass in the end zone in the final seconds—which propelled them back into the playoffs.

Just as every season has its defining moment, perhaps Green is entering his defining season with the Minnesota Vikings. He thinks his team, as early as this year, will take the next step and join powers like the Dallas Cowboys, San Francisco 49ers and Green Bay Packers as legitimate Super Bowl contenders.

Because he's such a positive thinker, Green hopes that enough good football and good fortune in 1997 could even cause a spinoff effect in three other areas:

1) Make this the year his boss, Roger Headrick, finally gets some long overdue respect. Headrick and Green have shared the role as the media's lightning rod for all Minnesota Vikings ills.

2) Help get the Vikings' long-term stadium needs resolved, or at least get some fair public debate, to ensure a sound financial future.

3) Help the team's on-going ownership fiasco get a positive resolution.

What the heck, maybe Dennis Green will buy the Vikings. Maybe he'll become the Vikings' 30% majority partner the NFL is calling for. He's considered it. Don't underestimate his will. All his life, he's been surprising people who expect him to fall short.

The youngest of five brothers in a working-class neighborhood of Harrisburg, Pennsylvania, Green was just 11 years old when his father died and age 13 when his mother died. He easily could have slipped into despair and succumbed to the evils lurking in his inner-city hangouts. But he's never been a crybaby and never wanted anything but a chance.

His dream of earning a football scholarship began in junior high. He was rewarded with several scholarship offers after he helped his John Harris High team to back-to-back unbeaten football seasons in 11th and 12th grades. He was elected class president as a junior and senior, and was the crew foreman as a 17-year-old in his third-shift job at the airport.

When he left Harrisburg in 1967 for the University of Iowa, he understood what was at stake. He had a plan, and it wasn't limited to football. Green and his peers were among the first wave of African American men in the country in the 1960s to capitalize on athletic ability and receive an opportunity to attend college on full scholarships. Many would be the first in their families to earn college degrees.

Green looked impressive on Iowa's freshman team in 1967 and then won the varsity's starting tailback job in spring practice. He scored the winning touchdown in his first varsity college game as Iowa upset No. 7-ranked Oregon State. He followed that up with 175-yard rushing game at Texas Christian and a two-TD performance at home in a loss to top-10 ranked Notre Dame. An injury in game four ended his season.

Many people thought Green would never get the chance to earn a living in football after he joined 15 black football teammates in the 1969 boycott of spring practice at Iowa. The players earned labels as radicals and troublemakers. Yet Green was the first guy voted back on the Hawkeye squad by the white players, who respected his work ethic and attitude. Green split the starting tailback job as a junior. For his final season, he agreed, for the good of the team, to switch from the more visible spot of running back—a position he played since ninth grade—to wingback. He earned his degree in four years.

Many thought that as an African American, Green could never go far in what had traditionally been a white man's profession of major-college coaching. Yet he paid his dues early, remained patient and capitalized on opportunities when they surfaced. He earned a reputation simply as an excellent coach, not an excellent African American coach.

Nothing was handed to him. He accepted a job in 1972 as a volunteer assistant coach at the University of Iowa. After working 5 a.m. until 1 p.m. each weekday as a laborer to support his first wife, Margie, and children Patti and Jeremy, Green toiled afternoons, evenings and weekends as a Hawkeye coach-in-training. His next season was spent at the University of Dayton in his first full-time football coaching job. He returned to Iowa City in 1974 and spent three seasons as a Hawkeye assistant.

Stanford's head coach in the mid-70s, Bill Walsh, had heard a lot about Green. He was impressed enough in their first face-to-face meeting that he hired Green on the spot. Walsh later brought Green along in 1979 to San Francisco as he began assembling a 49er team that would win three Super Bowl championships in eight years.

Everyone knows that as the 49ers' receiver coach, Green played a lead role in the early development of Jerry Rice and John Taylor. Few know that it was Green who was as responsible as anyone for the 49ers' decision to draft Joe Montana instead of Steve Dils in the 1979 draft.

Green took a risk when he left a 49er team on the verge of its first Super Bowl season in 1980 to become the offensive coordinator of a John Elway-led Stanford team. Even his friends cringed in 1981 when he left Elway and Stanford to become the head coach of the lowly Northwestern Wildcats. But he had a plan. As the first African American head coach in NCAA Division I-A history, Green would carry the burden of an NCAA-record losing streak that would reach 34, and the pressure of carrying the torch for future black coaches. If he failed, as so many others at Northwestern had, perhaps opportunities for other blacks to be head coaches would come slower. And in the worst scenario, if Green couldn't breathe life into Northwestern football, the school might decide to drop the sport, or even find themselves pushed out of the Big Ten Conference.

After an 0-11 initial season that was as pleasant as a kick in the groin, the Wildcats did break through. Green was selected Big Ten Coach of the Year in his second season; amazing when you consider his team won just three out of 11 games. He took the program about as far as anyone could in five years.

In the years after Green returned to the 49ers in 1986, he was discouraged by the lack of opportunity for African Americans to become head coaches in the NFL and in major colleges. He nearly left the coaching profession altogether in 1988 for a management job in advertising and marketing, but hung on and picked up a Super Bowl ring following the 49ers' 1988 championship season.

The right opportunity finally came for Green in the first week of 1989. He left the security of the San Francisco 49er juggernaut to become the head coach at Stanford, a team that won three games the season before. Except for a couple of years under Walsh, the Cardinal program had never quite reached its potential. Even the great John Elway never played in a bowl game during his four seasons there.

Sensing what he called a "country-club atmosphere" in the football program, Green lit a fire under his Stanford players. Everything took off in their second season. History was against him when he took a team into South Bend to face No. 1-ranked Notre Dame—the last time the Irish lost a home football when they were ranked No. 1 was 1951. But Green had a plan, not to mention a 240-pound running back named Tommy Vardell. The Cardinal played like anything but the underdog and overcame a 13-point second-quarter deficit to score a 36-31 victory. In the season finale at Cal, Stanford trailed 25-24 with 12 seconds to play but failed on a two-point conversion and appeared to have lost. Green didn't stop coaching, his players didn't stop executing, Cal made some costly mistakes, and in 12 seconds, Stanford pulled out a 27-25 victory.

An 8-3 regular-season finish and an Aloha Bowl bid followed in 1991, when the Cardinal won six PAC Ten games for the first time since 1970 and forged a seven-game winning streak, the school's longest since 1951. Only a Georgia Tech touchdown in the final 20 seconds in the Aloha Bowl prevented Stanford from posting its first postseason victory since 1978.

Despite a marvelous coaching resume—with Bill Walsh heading his references—Green was not a cinch to become a head coach in the NFL. At the time, only one team in NFL history—the Oakland Raiders with Art Shell—had hired an African American as a head coach. Green's name was regularly on candidate lists, but he quickly grew weary of courtesy interviews and a process he called "ghost chasing."

Eventually, Green's day arrived. Vikings president Roger Headrick, eager to make his mark in his new position, heard glowing references and liked Green's sales pitch and core philosophies. Headrick concluded that this objective outsider—rather than an NFL assistant with strong Minnesota connections—was what the underachieving Vikings needed. So six weeks shy of his 43rd birthday, in January of 1992, Green was hired as the fifth head coach in Minnesota Vikings history and first head coach to come from outside the Vikings family in 25 years.

This was not your father's Viking team that Green inherited. The discipline and pride of the 1970s glory years were in short supply. So were numerous first-, second- and third-round draft picks, due to the costly trade for Herschel Walker. Given what Dallas gained and the Vikings got and gave up, it's generally considered the worst trade in Minnesota pro sports history. Green has been trying to steer a football operation haunted by many such mistakes of the past. The Vikings have been plagued by a dysfunctional ownership structure. You can just picture the Vikings receptionist screening phone calls these days: *"Coach, it's Jerry Maguire on line one... and Jerry Springer on line two."*

After years of infighting and power plays, there's still no majority shareholder, and too often, an absence of loyalty and unity. *(Miss the board meeting? It's OK, pick up your morning newspaper. Somebody already leaked the confidential reports to local newspaper columnists ...)* Green points to two deals cut years ago by former team president Mike Lynn that he says are haunting the current operation, causing a $9 million annual cash drain that handicaps the team's free-agent pursuit. First there's the Vikings' $5 million annual debt payment on the owners' loan that bought out former partners Irwin Jacobs and Carl Pohlad. That includes approximately $2.7 million in interest alone per year. Throw in another $4 million the Vikings believe they overpay in Metrodome rent in comparison to deal struck by the Minnesota Twins.

If you're a pro sports team in the Twin Cities trying to sell your message to a skeptical public, your timing could be better. If the public isn't ticked off at an 80-year-old rich guy named Pohlad, they're irked at a 20-year-old rich kid named Garnett. Try to find someone who doesn't have a gripe one way or another about Met Stadium, Met Center, Memorial Stadium and Metrodome. The Minnesota Timberwolves continued the cycle with the controversial, prolonged Target Center buyout. The local NHL soap opera, involving the emotional loss of a team and the eventual promise of an expansion franchise, has taken a toll on public confidence, too. The Twins' controversial, "Is it a loan, or is it a gift?" stadium plan diminished credibility again.

Now legitimate Vikings stadium issues that deserve careful consideration—and could determine the franchise's long-term viability—have become a political football. Requests for a fairer lease have been ignored by the Metropolitan Sports Facilities Commission. Requests for a reasonable public dialogue on a possible multi-purpose stadium for the future have not been well received in the media or the public.

Green's biggest disappointment in five seasons is the Vikings' inability to turn regular-season success into playoff success. As you'll probably be reminded a few dozen times this season, Green's Vikings are 0-4 in playoff games. Green offers no alibi: "We didn't play well enough to win in those games," he says.

That will remain an issue until Green and the Vikings win a postseason game. But just for fun, consider these facts:

- Don Shula, Tom Landry and Chuck Noll—who combined to coach in 15 Super Bowls—only had five playoff berths combined in their first five seasons as NFL head coach (1-4 combined record).
- Shula (six Super Bowls) and Landry (five Super Bowls) didn't win their first playoff game until their sixth and eighth seasons, respectively, as head coaches in the league.
- Bud Grant was 2-5 in the playoffs in his first six seasons.
- And while it may be apples and oranges, consider that across town, the Minnesota Timberwolves are 0-3 in playoff games under Coach Flip Saunders, and Tom Kelly's Twins are 0-0 in the last six seasons of postseason play.

Under Green's direction, the Vikings have done many things right over the last five seasons:

- They have reached the playoffs four out of five years. (In his last eight seasons in the NFL, Green has worked with teams that made the playoffs seven times.)
- They have one of the best records in December of NFL teams, including a 12-5 record in that pivotal month since 1993.

- They have learned to win in the fourth quarter. The Vikings had lost 10 straight games when trailing after three quarters before an October 4 home game vs. Chicago, in Green's first season. Despite trailing 20-0 after three quarters on that day, Minnesota rallied and posted a 21-20 victory. That was the first of 13 times over five seasons the Vikings have rallied to win in the fourth quarter. Only Miami with 15 and New England with 14 have better comeback records from 1992 through 1996.
- They've held leads well, too. Under Green, they are 34-7 when leading after three quarters.
- They are 26-14 in the Metrodome under Green, including a 16-4 record vs. the NFC Central.
- They are 7-3 vs. the Green Bay Packers since Green arrived.
- Their five-year regular season record of 47-33 includes winning records on grass (13-11), turf (34-21), outdoors (18-15), indoors (28-18) and in temperatures under 40 degrees (5-3).

Green has received extensive national media exposure since he first became a college head football coach in 1981. Throughout his career he's had the distinction of being:

- probably the only guy to be the subject of a six-page profile in *Sports Illustrated* and also be profiled in *Bassin'* magazine because of his love and knowledge of fishing.
- one of the few guests from any profession to appear on both Good Morning America and the Today Show on the same day—after Northwestern ended its NCAA-record losing streak in 1982;
- a four-time guest on ESPN's "Up Close" program, hosted by Roy Firestone and Chris Myers;
- an in-studio analyst on CBS's NFL Today pre-game show;
- interviewed live on numerous occasions by the Fabulous Sports Babe on ESPN Radio;
- signed by the nationally syndicated One-On-One sports network in 1997 to serve as an analyst for a weekly NFL talk show.

Green established a good rapport and relationship with the media in coaching stops at Iowa, Northwestern, Stanford and the 49ers. His phone rings often with questions and requests from the national media.

So why do some in the Twin Cities media make Green feel as unwelcome as a brother-in-law who sells Amway?

Green said the conflict began in 1992, the moment that he, and not Pete Carroll, a local favorite, was introduced as the Vikings coach. That initial press conference was supposed to be a shining moment for Green, who had landed his first NFL head coaching job. But the press conference was marred when a local newspaper columnist who had lobbied for Carroll, embarrassed himself by chastising Viking president Roger Headrick.

When Green preaches to his team about mental toughness, he knows the subject. He has endured media scrutiny and personal attacks in the Twin Cities that would have buried many public figures. Green explains later in this book that while he's made mistakes, he's never sexually harrassed anyone. He feels like he's been a victim of blackmail tactics. He's understandably reluctant to air these sagas on page one of the morning newspaper or on the 10 o'clock newscasts. He's found himself in a no-win situation as he's tried to protect his rights and his privacy. Put yourself in his shoes—have you ever tried to defend yourself against false allegations?

If Green thought his battles with some of his media critics would be different in 1997, consider two media reports from the first weekend of training camp alone:

1) A St. Paul newspaper columnist, discussing Green's resiliency through so much adversity, offers what he calls "a compliment" to Green by saying he's like a "cockroach" who won't go away.

2) Meanwhile, a Twin Cities morning radio show continues its mean-spirited attacks on Green. The station's new "wacky" guy, with a microphone and his first and only media pass in hand, comes to training camp to ambush Green and interrupt a legitimate interview session. The guy asks a crude question—unrelated to football—simply to record a sound bite of Green bouncing him from the premises.

If you're Dennis Green, Clem Haskins or Roger Headrick, such treatment apparently comes with the territory. But ask yourself when was the last time somebody called Paul Molitor "a cockroach," or tried to embarrass Kevin McHale, Tom Kelly, Kirby Puckett or Bill Musselman in public.

Green has been a tireless worker for charity and community issues. Even one of his newspaper critics wrote in 1996 that Green "has gone into the community and done more actual work for good causes than any high-profile coach or manager (in the Twin Cities) in recent decades." Green himself hung out as a kid at the Boys Club in Harrisburg, a place he learned to play chess. Green figures his community time is well spent if he can help a girl or boy learn to appreciate fishing or music or improve their self esteem. One of his mottos is, "Well rounded is well grounded."

Green, an avid drummer, even had a plan to help some talented local musicians get exposure. As executive producer of Savannah Street Music, he put a sizable chunk of his own money into producing an album, titled Sunset Celebration, that included world-renowned trumpeter Doc Severinsen as well as Green on drums. Green invited his brother, Stan, to sing one of the songs on the album and fulfilled Stan's lifelong dream to become a recording artist.

Green feels blessed to be in a position to meet other prominent people. His music interests have afforded him the chance to get to know artists like B.B. King, Ray Charles and Kenny G. He's done charity work with people like Bill Cosby and Gregory Hines. In his role on the NFL Competition Committee, Green has worked alongside the biggest names in pro football. He shares some of his visions in a chapter on the future of the NFL.

Interesting guy, this Dennis Green. I'm glad he's written his life's story and poured so much of himself into the project. I'm glad he speaks so candidly about his struggles and triumphs, on race and sports, and on where the Minnesota Vikings and the NFL might be headed.

*Gene McGivern*

# KICKOFF IN CANTON

*"The Minnesota Vikings in 1997 are a happy football team. Except for maybe the 0-11 year at Northwestern when that team was caught in the losing streak, the teams I've coached have always been upbeat and have enjoyed their jobs.*

*"The Viking players like the way we do things. They lay it on the line, and I think we've won a lot of close games because of that pride and team spirit. The players here like playing in this system and like playing for the head coach and coaching staff they have. It's all upbeat, no crybabies. It's all systems go.*

*"Our philosophy is to work hard, learn and expect to be good. My job is to create the atmosphere where the players know that no one in the organization wants to win more than me. Therefore, I will play the BEST and be fair with the REST.*

*"I know the difference between a party and having a good time. When you enjoy yourself, enjoy what you do, bring a smile, some energy and a positive approach to your job, there's nothing like it."*

—Dennis Green on his team's
preseason mood in 1997

It was exciting to touch down at the Akron-Canton airport on July 25. A police escort was waiting in the landing area to lead our transport of four buses on the 30-minute drive to Canton for our Friday afternoon tour of the Pro Football Hall of Fame.

If you've ever played or coached the game of football, or are a fan who's hooked on the game, you can't help feeling some goosebumps when you walk through the Hall of Fame doors and a touch a bit of history. Even though I never coached against or met many the people enshrined here, I like to believe that I share their passion for competition and excellence. The inductees and players and coaches showcased here share many of the same core philosophies of football and life—like the "three Ds" of desire, determination and dedication that I often speak of. You don't have to be on the same wall to appreciate that you're on the same page with these football legends.

A trip to Canton's Hall of Fame and stadium is both an invigorating and humbling experience. When you're consumed in the daily grind of the NFL, concentrating on that next practice and the next game, you rarely get a chance to sit back and ponder your good fortune. This site is as good a place as any to recall the friendships, the struggles, the joys, the battles and the feelings of the highly emotional game and business of football. In Canton, even Bud Grant cried.

It's also an honor to be selected to play in the National Football League's ceremonial opening preseason game. The national television spotlight pumps up the players and coaches. For young players trying to make the team, it may be their only chance to play in an NFL game on network TV. Even the veterans want to go out and make some big plays to establish momentum for the upcoming season.

This 1997 season will be the first in which a Minnesota Vikings team plays a regular-season game in August—our season starts August 31 in Buffalo. And this July 26 game is the earliest preseason game in franchise history. If the foundation we're trying to build this preseason can take root, and if we can get some better luck on the injury-front, maybe we'll become the first Minnesota Viking team to be playing after January 17 in a season. That has to be our long-range mindset.

While the rest of the team strolls through the exhibits and soaks up the atmosphere, I go to a private meeting room to talk football with the ABC-TV broadcasters on hand for the game. They get a chance to get additional background and insights they will use during the three-hour telecast. Al Michaels, who's always been a fair reporter, lived two miles from the Stanford campus in San Francisco back in my California days. Dan Dierdorf, a guy I played against in the Big Ten when he was an All-America offensive tackle at Michigan, was a great NFL offensive lineman with St. Louis and a guy who's in the Hall of Fame himself. Even though he never played in a Super Bowl, he never doubted his ability to play. Lynn Swann, who was instrumental in the Pittsburgh Steelers' Super Bowl success, still looks as smooth as ever.

Frank Gifford isn't here for this Friday meeting because he's giving the presenter speech for 1997 inductee Wellington Mara. Frank has always been one of the best color commentators. He's going through some tough times personally with all the sensationalism in the national media, but hopefully he will be able to hang in there. Time heals all wounds. I dropped him a card a while back to tell him he was in my thoughts. People like me who have always had the utmost respect for Frank Gifford will always have that respect.

The team's visit is cut short by time constraints, and we boarded the buses for a 40-minute drive back to our hotel in Akron. NFL road trips may seem glamorous, but in reality they're quick business trips with one purpose. We'll catch a couple hours of personal time then have some late Friday night meetings before it's lights out at 11 p.m. After the grueling week of travel and practice we've had, this will be one of the best nights of sleep we'll all get.

Since we started training camp in Mankato, I'm really missing my wife Marie and daughter Vanessa Anna-Marie. One of the advantages of playing a preseason game is you get a short break from training camp and spend Saturday night and Sunday at home. Boy, am I looking forward to that. I also talked to my adult children, Patti, 30, and Jeremy, 26, before I left for the airport early this morning. That's always a good luck charm for me. I talk with them before every game. They both live and work in the Phoenix area, but we try to talk four or five times a week.

Lightning and thunder in the morning give way to a sunny, humid day in Canton. The newly installed astroturf at Fawcett Stadium will be cooking. As the buses wind through the neighborhood and into the stadium, you sense a state fair atmosphere. Some first-tier neighbors rent out their front yards for parking. Cookout grills and tailgate tables dot other lawns. Kids sell lemonade, pop and baked goods for 50 cents. It's like a summerfest for this football-crazed community.

As I stood on the sidelines during warm-up drills, Bruce Springsteen's "Born in the USA" blared on the loudspeakers, adding to the Fourth of July atmosphere. Watching football in this 25,000-seat stadium, which is built into a small valley, provides an intimacy that's unusual for an NFL game. It's like the difference in watching a concert at Guthrie Theater instead of Target Center. The Goodyear Blimp floats high above the stadium, a reminder you're in the NFL corporate fast lane. But at the same time, a small airplane circles the stadium and carries a banner for a used car lot, reminding you that Canton is kind of like the NFL's main street. Large end-zone banners bring a taste of the future to this celebration of the past, advertising the Pro Football Hall's new World Wide Web site.

Coming to Ohio brings back memories of my first paid coaching job, 24 years ago, down the road at the University of Dayton. I earned $6,000 a year and coached quarterbacks, running backs and receivers. I've only coached in this stadium once before, in 1987, when the 49ers played here in the Hall of Fame preseason game. Has it been 10 years already since I sat in the press box alongside fellow San Francisco coaches Mike Holmgren and George Seifert? I never thought I'd be back here someday as an National Football League head coach.

As I begin my sixth year as the Vikings coach, 10th year in the NFL and 26th season in coaching, scenes from my life flash before me. My time with my parents was much too brief, although it planted my seeds for success. I had great support from my brothers, teachers and classmates and was born at the right time to get opportunities beyond my hometown of Harrisburg. Getting a chance to play college football on a scholarship in the Big Ten Conference was special but didn't come without some pain. I endured one of the most frustrating times of my life as a college player after being labeled a radical and an agitator for joining 15 black teammates in a boycott of spring practice. We were caught up in the times of the revolt of the black athlete. I'll never say it was a mistake to stand up for your principles. But the protest—designed to get more respect as individuals from coaches, additional black assistant coaches and better academic counseling—didn't turn out the way any of us hoped. Some guys never got over it. Some legitimate, big-time players never played again. There was a feeling we all were black-balled by a powerful National Football League of 1971 that was comfortable with the status quo. We graduated and are in professional fields now, but most of my black teammates felt their careers could have ended on a better note.

Maybe nobody's playing career ends the way they would like. Everyone has to stop playing some day, for a variety of reasons. But it never is easy. I'm still involved in a game I love. I guess that makes me a survivor.

The sidelines here are cramped. We have 25 more players in uniform than we'd have on a regular-season roster trying to land jobs, yet we're confined to an area half the size of a normal NFL sideline. That's OK—we're trying to build mental toughness in this training camp. Plenty of media and celebrities squeeze onto the sidelines, too, and contribute to the induction weekend hoopla. A crew from NFL Films catches me when I come out for pre-game drills. Before I know what I've agreed to, the tape is rolling and I'm starring in a skit. The premise is that an average fan taps me on the shoulder during a game to suggest a play, and when I give it a try, the play goes for a touchdown. High fives abound. If only it were that easy. NFL Films does a great job of capturing the excitement and inside feel of the game. A lot of people want a piece of your time as a professional coach, but you can't forget your responsibility to help sell your product. That marketing has been one of the reasons the NFL has thrived.

As kickoff draws near, several Canton youths get to march down from their seats on the grassy hill above the corners of the end zone. The kids are part of the NFL's new flag football program titled P.L.A.Y, an initiative to promote the sport for boys and girls in neighborhood recreational settings. The energy and joy the kids display as they work on passing drills remind me that once we step on the field, there's still a lot of little kid in all of us. If the game stops being fun, you know it's time to walk away.

Frank Gifford: *Fawcett Stadium, Canton, Ohio, sold out with 25,000 crammed into this tiny stadium for Hall of Fame Day. We're ready to kick off our 28th season of bringing you NFL football (on ABC-TV).*

Al Michaels: *Didn't the Pro Bowl end about a week ago?*

Dan Dierdorf: *As far as I'm concerned, this day couldn't come soon enough. I'm ready to get started... What better way is there to start any season than to remember your past? That's exactly what happens today on this Saturday in July in Canton, Ohio. We honor the men who have founded the game, built the game, and made the game what it is.*

Al Michaels: *It's Minnesota vs. Seattle, two teams with high hopes, and I think legitimate high hopes. The Vikings were in the playoffs last year but lost to Dallas in a wild-card game. But Brad Johnson is their man. He signed a $15 million contract. He is the quarterback. Dennis Green is the coach. This is Green's sixth year. Dennis Green has (as much) tenure as any coach in the National Football Conference, speaking to the rigors of that business...*

Frank Gifford: *You don't see a lot of patience in this business anymore. There are 11 new head coaches in the NFL this year. I'd call that a pretty shaky profession.*

It's almost time for the National Anthem. They've got all the bases covered today. Handling pre-game field announcing is that boxing-wrestling announcer who's become famous for his "Let's Get Ready to Rummm-ble" introduction. Singing the anthem is the vocal group, The O'Jays. They grew up and began their professional singing career in Canton, and are back to play a concert that night at the Canton Civic Center, their first concert in their hometown in 20 years.

The Vikings win the coin toss and will receive. The Seahawks' kick lands in the hands of our rookie return man, Robert Tate, who comes from my hometown of Harrisburg. He was a legend as a multi-sport star athlete at my alma mater, John Harris High. He had three 1,000-yard rushing seasons and became the first four-sport letterman in school history. After an excellent career as a return man at Cincinnati, we drafted him in the sixth round.

What do you know? Robert took the opening kickoff and returned it 52 yards, making the other John Harris High alum on hand proud.

Al Michaels: *Here's the kick... Tate from the three-yard line... straight up the middle... The Vikings, who were terrible on special teams last year, begin the preseason with a nice runback—all the way to the Seattle 44. That's one area Dennis Green said (they) must improve on—special teams... The Vikings were near the bottom of several NFL statistical areas on special teams last year, and it's amazing they made the playoffs when you look at those numbers."*

It was a pretty good day for the Vikings. The defense got an interception on its first play and scored a touchdown later on a fumble return. Brad Johnson looked sharp, Cris Carter and Jake Reed had some nice catches. Randall Cunningham showed he can still play and gives us a backup quarterback we can win with. So many young guys stepped up big. We built a 21-3 lead and held on to win 28-26. We had way too many penalties but will get that solved as we continue training camp.

Al Michaels: *It's second down and six, there's a fake, here's a pass deep to Carter... makes the catch. That's why Cris Carter ends up in the Pro Bowl year after year, among other reasons... He took care of second-year cornerback Fred Thomas, the way he took him to school. Thomas was called for interference, to boot.*

Frank Gifford: *We're always talking about the height of the Viking receivers. Cris Carter has had a remarkable couple of seasons. He had 96 catches last year and 122 in '95. Warren Moon had it down pat, and now it looks like Brad Johnson has it, too. Hang it up and let him go get it.*

Dan Dierdorf: *Everything he does today will draw a big ovation from the crowd because he played at Ohio State and he's from the state of Ohio.*

Al Michaels: *It's always easy to say a guy's a future Hall of Famer. But Cris Carter is getting into that range now. He's already caught 667 passes. If he has another couple of decent seasons and ends up with 1,000 catches, he gets in (the Hall of Fame).*

Dan Dierdorf: *How many guys over there in the Hall of Fame can say "I was put on waivers in the middle of my career, in the prime of my career." The Eagles and Buddy Ryan had no home for Cris Carter. They felt he could only run the fade route. Minnesota reaped the rewards.*

We came together as a Viking coaching staff back on February 11 after a month that included the playoffs; scouting at the East-West Shrine Game and the Senior Bowl; the Super Bowl; and a one-week winter vacation. We had only one change on our coaching staff, so the continuity is there (offensive line coach Keith Rowen moved into an assistant head coaching job at Oakland; Mike Tice moved from tight ends to offensive line; and Dave Atkins came on board to coach tight ends).

In this first meeting, I reminded our staff of our mission. We must scout and evaluate draft and free-agent possibilities; realistically rank our returning players; determine who we will and will not bring back; and work hard to develop our younger players so they are ready for training camp in July. Our staff confidence level is high and expectations are even higher. I emphasize these five points to my coaches:

- My No. 1 job is to create an atmosphere that encourages and enables you to do your job.
- Your No. 1 job is to get your players to understand our goals and understand the system we'll use to reach our goals.
- Love coming to work.
- Our best chance to win a World Championship is to build on the enthusiasm of what we've done.
- Stick together like glue, even when disagreements arise. The season is only five months away.

What we really tried to do this year was have our 1997 season start after our loss to Dallas in the 1996 postseason playoffs. The off-season no-longer exists in the National Football League—it's now the acquisition season.

First we wanted to sign and retain our very best players, and we did. That meant retaining Randall McDaniel, an eight-time Pro Bowl player; Robert Smith, the leading rusher in the NFL before his season-ending injury occurred; Leroy Hoard, a backup to Robert Smith at running back who will give us the best 1-2 running punch in the NFL; Jeff Brady, a linebacker who's been to a lot of different teams until he found a home with us.

Then we had some other guys who were restricted free agents —David Palmer, David Dixon and Fernando Smith—all those guys we wanted to retain. So in the acquisition phase, we were able to get that accomplished.

Then we moved into the draft phase, involving scouting, traveling to all-star games in Mobile, Alabama, and Palo Alto, California, and attending the scouting combine in Indianapolis. We looked at as many players as we could. We tried to get a realistic evaluation not only of their football talent but a good feel for their development potential and a read on their desire to play. You try to discover things like how they'll handle coming into a lot of money. Can they stay focused on football?

That preparation took us into this year's draft, and I think it came out well for the Minnesota Vikings. We drafted Dwyane Rudd, an All-American linebacker from Alabama, in the first round; Torrian Gray, a strong safety from Virginia Tech—one of the most physical teams in college football in 1996—in the second round; Stalin Colinet, a big, strong defensive end from Boston College who's one of the few players in the NFL to hail from the Bronx, in the third; Antonio Banks, a cornerback from Virginia Tech in the fourth; Tony Williams, an extremely active nose tackle who had 100-plus tackles last season for Memphis State, in the fifth; Robert Tate, from my hometown of Harrisburg where he was an athletic legend; and a sleeper in the seventh round—Matthew Hatchette, a big-time, downfield wide receiver from Langston College, a small Oklahoma school.

After our draft we felt like we had covered our needs, but took one more look at any other fill-in guys who could round out our depth. That's when we signed and brought out of retirement Randall Cunningham, a two-time MVP in the National Football League. He had an outstanding career in Philadelphia. After sitting one year with an injury and being retired last season, Randall has come in and accepted the role as a backup quarterback. We also signed Greg Briggs, a fast, explosive special teams player; Robert Green, the former Bears running back who always hurt us when he played us, and I guy we think is much better suited to running on artificial turf in contrast to the sluggish, slow Soldier Field grass; and Leonard Wheeler, a cornerback who hurt us when he played with Cincinnati.

We also returned the core of the starters who came on strong to finish the 1996 season—proven leaders like Cris Carter, Jake Reed, Brad Johnson, Randall McDaniel and Todd Steussie on offense, and John Randle, Dixon Edwards, Jeff Brady, Dewayne Washington and Orlando Thomas on defense. Plus we will have two key players back from costly 1996 injuries—Robert Smith and Ed McDaniel. Everyone has seen what Robert's potential is as a running back. Eddie is one of the best read-diagnose-attack linebackers around. He will help put us back in the mix as one of the best defenses in the league, which is where we normally are.

Going into the 1997 season, we felt these roster additions would make us a much stronger team. We went into areas where our depth was the weakest, like running back and linebacker, and turned those into positions of strength. I believe we have a chance to make this my best Viking team in my six seasons. We've gone 11-5 once, and won the NFC Central Division twice, but we think this could be even better.

What we set out to do in training camp was to put our players and coaches in a situation where our mental toughness would show itself and in the end be a significant factor in our success. We had to play three of our first four regular-season games on the road at some of the toughest places to win—Buffalo, Chicago and Green Bay. So we knew we'd have to develop the mentality of a road warrior, which means being able to go into a hostile environment and outplay a team from start to finish in front of their fans, family and friends. That's really the only way you can win on the road.

So our training camp was about trying to develop that kind of mental toughness so we would realize how difficult our early schedule would be. We went on three trips in a seven-day span, playing here at the Hall of Fame game plus taking two long bus rides into Wisconsin for scrimmages vs. New Orleans and Kansas City. It was hot and humid, and there were some 5 a.m. wakeups.

As an organization we worked hard on our depth this year. We had to reload when we came here in 1992, we had some talented guys like Chris Doleman, Henry Thomas and Roy Barker, who are still in the NFL but became casualties here because of our salary cap. It's no secret the Vikings haven't been able to be major players in free agency because we can't come close to offering the kind of signing bonuses some teams are willing to play.

There are two ways to rebuild a team. Some people feel you immediately tear the whole program down to rebuild it. But in the NFL you don't have that much time. What we tried to do over my first five years is be competitive while we were rebuilding, fully realizing we missed out on a whole group of players from the Herschel Walker trade. Dallas ended up getting the Vikings' first-, second- and sixth-round picks in 1990; our first- and second-round picks in 1991; and our first-, second- and third-round picks in 1992. We're just now getting over that 1989 trade. But through it all we had to take an attitude of not giving in, not making excuses, not being crybabies. Now we think we've arrived.

For me, being a head coach is a juggling act, because I try to be involved in all aspects. You have to be well organized to make it all work. That's something I've always had a knack for since I was a kid back in Harrisburg organizing the pickup sports games at the playgrounds or making assignments in my night job as a 17-year-old shift foreman at the airport.

When you're a type-A personality like I am, you want to get a lot done in a short period of time. That was probably ingrained in me because my parents died so young. I doubted whether I would live very long, so I've tried to accomplish as much as I can as quickly in life as I can.

I'm not a hectic type, like a lot of type-A guys are. But you definitely do a lot of juggling to keep up with the demands of the job. My passions for family, music, fishing and community work give me plenty of outlets to escape.

I was anxious for the 1997 season to arrive because I feel we are building a winning organization. It starts at the top with Roger Headrick.

He's been steady and consistent as the chief executive officer and president of the Minnesota Vikings. He's been in a tough situation, because like most presidents, he reports to a board of directors. Of course, the Vikings board doesn't see the day-to-day operations like Roger does. Not only does he run the organization with a steady hand, he sometimes has to explain difficult situations. His most significant contribution is that steadiness. He's very supportive of the type of team we've put on the sidelines. Like most people, he wants to win every single game, but he understands it doesn't always happen that way. He knows you have to take the field and do the best you can.

It's always been exciting for me working with the Vikings. We have the opportunity to build a very good football team. To do that you have to be involved in every phase of the game—offense, defense, special teams and personnel. A lot of NFL head coaches want to go even further and fight for exclusive authority in their organizations. Guys like Mike Ditka, Dick Vermeil, Dan Reeves and Bill Parcells were able to get that single authority. But I haven't had, nor do I need, that kind of control. I have a great working relationship with Frank Gilliam, our vice-president of personnel. I've known Frank since 1966; he's one of the guys who recruited me to play at the University of Iowa, and was a long-time Iowa assistant coach. He understands what kind of players it takes to win. That's why, in my six years with the Vikings, we haven't had any disagreements as far as what player we should go after or the team's direction.

I've always tried to have a good mix on my coaching staff of young guys in their first through fourth years and veteran guys who have been in a lot of wars. When you go to play the game, you want to have guys on your sideline who've been there before. You never want your players to think the other team has better coaches than you have. That's one area where we always hold our own. I like to hire guys who will be good teachers and give their guys a lot of confidence.

We haven't tried to assemble one staff and hold them together forever. I've had 13 guys who coached for me during my first five years here that were promoted within football. Guys like Tony Dungy, now the head coach at Tampa Bay; Tyrone Willingham, now head coach at Stanford; and Keith Rowen, assistant head coach for the Oakland Raiders. Four other guys moved up to coordinator jobs around the league.

Like we always say, someone's departure is someone else's opportunity. I like the guys working with me this year. A football staff and a football team get very close. When you assemble a staff, you try to make sure everyone brings something to the table.

Now in his fifth year as our offensive coordinator, Brian Billick brings total knowledge of our system. We've known each other for years, and we worked together at Stanford. He understands exactly what I want offensively, what our system is and what we have to do. It makes it a lot easier. I don't have to be hands-on with it, because the system is already set.

I have the same comfort level with Foge Fazio, now in his second year as our defensive coordinator. Even though we hadn't worked together before I hired him in 1995, Foge brings the same ability, because he came into a system that was established and carried on. Tony Dungy, who's doing a great job in Tampa Bay, put in our defensive system that led the NFL in total defense. When Tony left to become Tampa's head coach, Foge stepped in and continued the defensive philosophy. First, he's always been known as an outstanding defensive coach. When he was at the University of Pittsburgh on Jackie Sherrill's staff, they played some great defense, and he's been a defensive coordinator in the NFL. Second, he worked in a similar system as ours for four years as the New York Jets' linebacker coach. Third, he was a linebacker coach here one season before he was promoted to coordinator.

Steve Wetzel, our strength and conditioning coach, was the strength coach of the Washington Redskins from their power football days. Steve has been one of the elder statesmen in the new phenomenon called strength coaches. Ten years ago, you didn't see many. Now, every team in the NFL has one. I think he's one of the leaders in his profession in seniority as well as in concepts and ideas.

Richard Soloman, our defensive backs coach, is one of the most demanding assistant coaches I've ever been around, yet he can get away with his intensity because he's so close to his players. He and I go way back and were teammates together at Iowa, yet we had never coached together until he joined my staff in 1992. He took my place as an assistant at Iowa when I left to go to Stanford in 1977. When I was head coach at Northwestern, he was defensive coordinator at Illinois. The Illini were outstanding in those years and became the first team in a while to knock off both Michigan and Ohio State in the same year and go on to win the Big Ten championship.

Trent Walters, our outside linebackers coach, is a guy I've known since we were both assistant coaches in the Big Ten more than 20 years ago. He was a player and later a coach at Indiana. He's also spent time in Washington working for Don James. He's established a reputation as one of the better technical, fundamental coaches.

Jon Levra, our defensive line coach, is one guy on our staff who has touched every single base. He's been an assistant high school coach, a head high school coach, an assistant college coach, a head college coach, an assistant coach in the CFL and an assistant now for his fourth NFL team. John totally believes in the art of teaching. He probably does 10 clinics a year; talking to young coaches and helping them understand what the profession is all about.

Carl Hargrave, our running backs coach, is a guy I've known since he was in grade school in Iowa City. He wound up going into the teaching and coaching profession. He was coaching at Upper Iowa when he tracked me down when I was hired at Northwestern. I hired him as a part-time coach, which means making part-time pay for full-time hours. He worked for me for five years at Northwestern and also coached wide receivers at Houston during the Andre Ware era.

Ray Sherman, our quarterbacks coach, is someone I'd always respected from afar. Even though we weren't teammates and never coached on the same staff together, I've always respected him. I've enjoyed his coaching performance throughout his career. When I left the 49ers to become the head coach at Stanford, Ray took my place on George Seifert's staff. He had a lot of experience in the NFL when he came to us and was the New York Jets' offensive coordinator. When I had a chance to hire him, I was pretty excited. He helped bring out the best in Warren Moon and has developed Brad Johnson into an excellent quarterback.

We're proud of Mike Tice, our offensive line coach, because he's one of our former Viking players. He played tight end for us in 1992-93 and returned in 1995 when we needed a versatile tight end. He had a distinguished 10-year playing career with Seattle and also played one season with the Redskins. He coached tight ends for us last season, and we promoted him to offensive line coach this year when Keith Rowen became the Raiders' assistant head coach.

Dave Atkins, our new tight ends coach, has been an NFL offensive coordinator at Arizona and has worked in several NFL assistant jobs in a short period of time. We're hoping this is where he'll stay for a long time, because all that moving is hard on a coach and his family.

Gary Zauner, our special teams coach, has one tough job. I've been a special teams coach once, so I realize how difficult and thankless it is. So I always try to have a special relationship with him and let him know I know how difficult the job is. Football consists of offense, defense and special teams. If special teams are indeed one-third of the game, you have to give them more than 10% of the practice time. He came to us from California, but he's originally from Wisconsin, with his roots in LaCrosse.

Tom Olivadotti, our inside linebackers coach, came to us last year after serving nine seasons as the Miami Dolphins' defensive coordinator. For two years I was on the NFL Competition Committee with Don Shula, and Don will tell you that Tom unfairly became the lightning rod for Miami teams falling short. Naturally, he was interested in a coordinator job, but I told him I thought he needed some time off from that role, and he should come back as a position coach. As expected, he's worked well with the Vikings.

Chip Myers, our receivers coach, has known Bill Walsh for a long time. He played for the Bengals when Bill was a top assistant coach there. In 1979, when I first came to the 49ers, Chip came in as a visiting coach for our training camp. In 1981 he was hired as an assistant coach at Illinois for Mike White, who was a long-time best friend of Bill Walsh. Chip worked with Richard Soloman on those successful Illinois teams. Chip's the best in the business at coaching big receivers, and we have the best in Cris Carter and Jake Reed. Chip is one of the three avid fishing anglers on our staff, joining Trent and myself.

I have a simple working philosophy for my coaching staff. First off, a guy has to like coming to work, and it's my job as head coach to create that atmosphere. When a guy wakes up in the morning, I want him to look forward to coming to the office and the field. It's up to me to create a climate that enables him to do his job, to be really good at it, and to work well with others. That's what a football coaching staff is all about—working together. My title is head coach, but I can't win by myself, and I don't lose by myself, either.

Guys who work for me have to be early risers. My love of early-morning fishing has turned me into an early riser. I don't like to work late at night as a coaching staff. We do like to come to work early so we get a full day's work in. Then we can go home, be with our families and get a good night's sleep.

Our day in training camp might last from 6:30 a.m. until 11:30 p.m. with practices, meetings, weight training and staff meetings. During the season, we usually start at 6:30 a.m., and the days end between 8-9 p.m. We try to take off early Friday nights to have some time with our families.

Coaching football is a long grind. Once training camp starts, you pretty much work every day, except for the bye weeks, when I insist everyone takes off. We give the players Tuesdays off and call that our Community Day. We encourage our players to get out and get involved in some programs. I go out with my wife Marie every Tuesday for part of the day. It reminds me that whether I'm happy we won or disappointed and upset we lost, a lot of people out there in our community are just trying to get through the day or get a hot meal. It gives you great perspective. It keeps you from getting selfish and being totally consumed in your work.

What should make 1997 interesting is the fact there may be as much parity in the NFL as there has ever been. Unrestricted free agency strips a team of some of its best players. The Dallas Cowboys were unable to keep intact their defense that was so dominant three or four years ago because they had to spend most of their money retaining and signing Emmitt Smith, Troy Aikman and Deion Sanders. Free agency also has allowed an expansion team like Carolina to become one of the best teams in the NFL.

There are 11 new head coaches in 1997, too, including guys like Mike Ditka in New Orleans and Dick Vermeil in St. Louis. Green Bay, San Francisco, Dallas and Denver look like they'll be in the NFL's first tier. People expect the Super Bowl champion to come from among those four teams, but don't be surprised if some others make a strong run.

We've had our share of bad luck and games where we just didn't get the right bounce. There's no doubt that for the most part, you make your own luck. In an ideal world, that would be the case. But I strongly believe the ball is going to bounce our way in 1997. After four years of injuries and challenges, when we had to respond and play well and were backed into a corner, I'm confident in 1997 we'll be out in front and stay healthy. Then I think you're going to see the true Minnesota Viking football team, and I think you're going to like it.

# 2

# BUS AND ANNA'S BABY BOY

*"Be prepared at all times. You never know when opportunity will come your way. Believe me, the door will open!"*
—Nellie Leadbetter, maternal
grandmother of Dennis Green

Bill Clinton told Americans of a place called Hope. Let me tell you about a place I call Faith, my hometown of Harrisburg. It's where I learned to believe in God, believe in my parents and brothers, believe in opportunity, and most importantly, believe in myself.

My preparation for the challenges I face today began in the city of Harrisburg, the capital of Pennsylvania, county seat of Dauphin County. It sits on the east bank of the Susquehanna River, 90 miles west of Philadelphia. Named for an Englishman, Harrisburg was home to the Paxton Boys, a band of rangers who eradicated the Susquehanna Indians. The city flourished as a regional transportation center. It's down the highway from Gettysburg, the site of one of the great battles of the Civil War. General Lee and the Southern troops came up through Maryland and tried to roll north, but by coincidence they ran into General Buford and the Northern cavalry at Gettysburg. The Northern cavalry held its ground.

The Civil War had great significance in the history of my hometown and home state, and of course for my ancestors as African-Americans. At the end of the Civil War, Pennsylvania grew into the nation's second most populated state. Prior to the Civil War, the demand for slaves in Pennsylvania exceeded the supply. Blacks no longer were shipped exclusively from the West Indies but arrived directly from Africa, as well. Slavery became so important to the region that no stigma was attached to trading Negroes. In fact, Robert Morris, William Plumsted, and Thomas Willing were elected to the Pennsylvania Assembly while active in buying and selling slaves.

Negroes worked in virtually every occupation. They were bakers, tailors, weavers, coopers, tanners, blacksmiths, bolters, millers, masons, goldsmiths, cabinet makers, naval carpenters, shoemakers and brushmakers. Serving as apprentices to doctors, some even became medical practitioners. The heartiness and efficiency of blacks, coupled with their value as economic commodities, caused the ironmasters to seek a reduction of the import duty on slaves. The success of blacks in the iron industry wasn't appreciated by all. Whites protested the government's failure to protect them from black competition. Slave law eventually gave way to Black codes and the Jim Crow tradition. By the 1950s, Harrisburg was surrounded by independent boroughs, townships and suburbs, but poverty was concentrated in the city, and slums were born.

During my childhood in the 1950s, African Americans proudly worked in a variety of jobs—in federal government (including the post office), state government, the railroad, or the steel mill. All were blue-collar jobs.

People often ask what it's like to be the youngest child in a big family—five kids in a working-class neighborhood in the 1950s qualified as a big family. It made it even more interesting when you consider all five were boys. I've always believed my parents set out to have three children. After having Billy, Bobby and Stan, they decided to try to have a fourth child, preferably a daughter. But instead of having a girl, they had my older brother, Greg. With four sons to feed, they debated for one year whether to try again for a girl. On February 17, 1949, I arrived, the youngest of five boys.

My parents grew up in a section of Harrisburg known as Uptown, a working class neighborhood not far from poverty. They aspired to raise a family on the section known as the Hill, an area considered to have better housing and living environment. Because of the nature of how our family grew, the stopoff point for them, and for most African American families of that day, was the Howard Day federally subsidized housing project. In that multi-dimensional atmosphere, where so many people lived in small areas, there was a survival-of-the-fittest mentality. In that environment, you wanted to move out as soon as you could. That was the original intent of the housing projects—a place where you got on your feet so you could move on to your own home. It never was intended to be a permanent solution for families. One year after I was born, my parents made the move out and purchased their first—and only—house. They had accomplished what they had set out to do—use federal housing assistance as a temporary stopping point.

My parents were Penrose William Green II, better known as "Bus," and Anna Leadbetter. Both were born in 1920, on December 25 and December 5, respectively. They were raised uptown and attended the same junior high and high school. They graduated from high school in 1938.

Bus and Anna were special people. If you went to Harrisburg today and talked to any African American over 65, they'd remember Bus and Anna Green. People would tell you that Bus and Anna went to William Penn, and all of their kids were raised in the projects, or on the hill, and went to John Harris. They'd know that the Green's sons Bobby and Greg still live in Harrisburg and are well known. Everyone talked about my parents' kindness. My Mom's greatest asset? She could make the worst hurts disappear.

My mother, Anna, also was one of the most respected beauticians in Harrisburg. Anna's Beauty Shop—located on the first floor of our house—was one of the heartbeats of our community. It was common then as it still is today for the barber shops and the beauty shops to be recognized as important gathering places. That was where the truth was told, where news started and circulated. In 1962 it was the beginning of the Civil Rights movement. Serious discussions were taking place in beauty and barber shops.

Dad had extremely strong convictions, and that strength made me feel secure. When Bus Green wanted something, he usually got it. He was proud of his accomplishment when he purchased his own home, and felt family should be together on special occasions. Dad made sure Santa Claus delivered a few presents and the Easter Bunny brought Easter baskets. He took us to picnics in the state parks and took us swimming on Memorial, Independence, and Labor Days.

My parents met in high school and always saw things the same way, even though they had somewhat different heritages. My father was light skinned and a relatively big man at 6-feet-tall. My mother was much smaller, about 5-2, and was more brown skinned. Mom's family came from Greensboro, North Carolina. My father's grandmother was half Native American and his grandfather was born and raised in Cuba. It's a heritage like so many African Americans who come from the merging of peoples in the wake of slavery.

Bus' father, my grandfather Toots Green, remarried when Bus was young and had eight more sons after my Dad. While I have many memories of Toots, my father didn't get along with my Mother's father, June, so I never really got to know Granddad June, even though he lived so close to us.

The Greens struggled, but we didn't starve. We had three small bedrooms on the second floor. We rented a room on the third floor. When I got too old for the crib, Greg and I slept in the same bed. He slept at one end, I slept at the other, while Stan slept in the upper bunk. Billy and Bobby each had their own beds.

The large city graveyard separated the black community in Harrisburg.  Ironically, only white people could be buried there. We cut through the cemetery grounds to socialize, and to go to school. "Cutting through" was the only way an African American was permitted to use the Harrisburg graveyard.

I also was exposed to racism as a youth when my oldest brothers were in high school. The opportunity for blacks to compete in athletics was limited by a quota system. Whether or not you were good enough to play wasn't the issue. Just eight to 10 black guys were allowed on the football team. Two were allowed on the basketball team. Tradition kept stereotypes vicious and perpetuated this terrible quota system. Fortunately it ended by the time I went to high school in 1963.

I loved my Dad. Although he was an active man, when he did rest he had a favorite chair. I would sit by his feet and play until he got up. "Where are you going, Dad? Can I come?" I asked every time.

Dad loved us. He was always involved.  It seems just like yesterday Dad took the whole family to the district track meet in Lancaster. Billy was a star and hurdles were his specialty. Dad smiled and nodded his approval whenever one of us competed and did our best. I remember how special that made Billy feel when Dad smiled and nodded to him after his event.

Dad also watched me play Little League baseball, but didn't offer much advice. If playing was important to me, it was important to my Dad. We walked together to the ball park, and saw middle-class neighborhoods alongside really poor families. Working people lived beside unemployed folks. Whole neighborhoods where no one worked existed next to neighborhoods where parents worked two and three jobs.

Dad would pass on wisdom as we walked. I couldn't relate to all of his stories, but I usually learned something new.

Stopping off for ice cream was another Green family tradition. My brothers told me to expect it. "If Dad and you walk to the game," my brothers would tell me, "ask him if you can stop for ice cream. He always says yes." They were right, and at a young age I began to appreciate the importance of family traditions.

My parents taught by example. Mom would slice Dad a piece of sweet potato pie, then she would take a slice. After all my brothers were served, the youngest got the smallest piece. Was it fair? Yes. The hardest-working person with the most responsibility got the first piece. We learned that equal treatment does not mean that everyone always gets the same portion, but everybody gets a piece of the pie and nobody goes hungry.

We never took Sunday dinner for granted. Mother set the time and everyone was expected to be at the table promptly or be prepared to explain their conflict. School, sports and work were the only accepted excuses. Fried chicken, mashed potatoes, green beans, and dinner rolls was the meal of choice. My mother and father were excellent cooks. Although my Dad was a better cook, Mom was much more tidy. When I reached age nine, I started sharing kitchen cleanup duty with Greg, so I appreciated working on days when Mom cooked.

Mother's style of cooking could be described as "Southern soul," while Dad's could be called "Northern urban" with a twist. My maternal grandmom, Nellie, was born in Greensboro, North Carolina, and my Mom was born there, too. They moved to Harrisburg when Mom was a young girl. North Carolina was reflected in my mother's cooking, but in hardly anything else. She was in every other way a woman raised in the city. My paternal grandmother, Grandmom Lena, was born and raised in the north. Dad's grandfather on his father's side was from Cuba, and those Caribbean influences shaped Dad's urban version of soul food. He added the greatest seasoning to pork chops and chicken. We loved it.

If Sunday meals were structured, Saturday meals were unstructured. The only thing we could count on was the menu. Saturdays always meant baked beans and hot dogs and unpredictable meal times. Saturday was the busiest day for Mom's beauty shop. It was also the day Billy or Stan played football. Dad was always at the games. Mom was there when she could be. I was allowed to walk to the field with Billy or Stan if it was a home game. I often dreamed of playing on Saturdays in front of my parents, then going home and eating baked beans and hot dogs.

I recall when a kid named Lawrence Williams moved into the neighborhood. I was 10 at the time, but Lawrence was 12 going on 20, if you know what I mean. He was a hellraiser. He and his 11-year-old sister, Sherry, were much more streetwise than most kids in our neighborhood. One day Lawrence suggested we go uptown without our parents. I said, "Let me ask my parents if I can go." Lawrence cracked, "Your Dad won't let you go, so don't even ask him. Let's just go."

I asked anyway, and Lawrence was right. My Dad said, "Absolutely not. A bunch of 10- and 12-year-olds, uptown alone, that's ridiculous. All you will do is get into trouble or get hurt."

Being a dumb kid, I ventured uptown with Lawrence anyway. We were laughing, joking and being kids on a big adventure. Then a car passed by and honked twice, and I realized I was in deep trouble. It was my Mom and Dad, who were on the way to Grandmom's house. They didn't look happy. "Get in," Dad said. Shaking, I got in the back. I had deliberately disobeyed my Dad.

It was only another mile to Grandmom's. I knew from looking at Dad how much trouble I was in. Mom scolded me. "Baby, you're too young to be going off on your own way up here. Your Dad and I are disappointed and surprised you would deliberately defy our wishes." I started crying.

The whole time we were at Grandmom's, I campaigned for relief. I was in search of sympathy and mercy, but got none. In fact, Dad gave me a more detailed picture of what I was going to get when we got home. "Pleading would not have been necessary, if you had done what was right." There was nothing worse in a childhood than delayed punishment. I worried about it every moment until it happened. Dad gave me a good old-fashioned belt on my butt. I still think about it.

Most of my family memories are happy ones, though. When I was selected to play in the grade school all-city band, Dad was fired up. The best sixth-grade musicians in Harrisburg were chosen, and his baby boy was one of them. My snare drum, like so many other things I used, was a hand-me-down; Bobby used it at least eight years earlier. I looked at that outdated, brown snare drum and considered that everyone else's drums were new and white. When I told my Dad, he said, "So what? Greens don't envy what others have. Do the best with what you have. Don't give a damn what someone else has. Winners use what they have to get the job done. What are the rules? Does every drum need to be white?"

Many of the other drummers hassled me about my old drum. By the third band practice, I got up my nerve to ask the band leader about my drums, only to hear bad news. The drums needed to be white. So I thought, "Great. I'll get a new drum." Dad had other ideas. Dad made me help him paint my drum. When it was done, Dad looked at it and saw a new white drum. I looked at it and saw a brown drum painted white. Today, I have learned to see the positive side in situations like that, and remember that drum fondly.

Our City Concert was held in Uptown, where Mom and Dad grew up and went to school at Camp Curtain Junior High. Our band sounded OK, although Dad and Mom, showing their pride, called our performance "great." It was a triumphant return to Uptown.

I think the moral of that experience is that it's not what happens to you in life, but how you deal with it. Thanks, Dad and Mom. That day became more special later when I realized that would be my only winning trip to Uptown with Dad and Mom.

With few exceptions, Thanksgiving dinner was served at Grandmom Lena's. Thanksgiving Day always meant the big high-school football showdown between John Harris, my brothers' and my future school, and William Penn, my parents' alma mater. My parents rooted for their new school all the way. Grandmom Lena still lived uptown, so after the game Dad would get hassled by Grandmom's neighbors if we lost. Billy's John Harris team rarely beat William Penn, but Stan's team beat them effortlessly in 1958. Dad would have really loved the games in the 1960s. Greg's teams were 2-0 in the Thanksgiving battle, and my teams won all three. Dad said the blessings before our annual Thanksgiving holiday feast. He would break into an enormous smile whenever his sons' teams won.

The reality of how cruel life could be struck me when my father became seriously ill. It was the summer following our successful trip Uptown. I was 11 and I recall Dad looking very sick. It was very surprising, because he usually was a picture of health, seemingly in better condition than TV exercise guru Jack La Lanne. He went to the hospital, but he never came home. His condition was misdiagnosed and he died of a ruptured appendix.

I went to see him at the hospital a couple of times, but each time he looked worse. His spirits lifted when he saw Greg and me. Smiling, he fought the pain. It was frustrating, though, and there wasn't much we could do. Unfortunately, there wasn't much they did about his appendix. Finally, the poison took over his body.

I'll never forget that night, one of the two saddest days of my life. I was home with Greg on a Saturday, while Mom and my three older brothers were at the hospital. The phone rang. It was around 8 p.m., and Grandmom and I each picked up a receiver (she was downstairs, I was upstairs). I heard the Doctor say the unthinkable. "I'm sorry, but Bus Green just passed away." I hung the phone up, ran upstairs to the third floor, and jumped into bed. By then the attic space had been converted into a bedroom for me and Greg. I was crying violently. In shock, I went to sleep with my clothes on. My mother looked badly shaken. It was unbelievable. How could such a strong, vibrant 39-year-old man die so suddenly? Our whole house was immersed in pain. A couple of people came upstairs to see me, but I never talked to them. I just wouldn't.

Soon my other Grandmother and many other family and friends came to our house. I stayed upstairs, feeling confused, sad and angry. Even as my family went through Dad's funeral plans, I still wouldn't talk.

Funerals in our neighborhood were very elaborate. They sent four limousines to our house. We went to the viewing, which seemed to last forever. Everybody was worried about my mother. My oldest brother, Billy, was doing a great job taking care of her, but it was tough. Billy, just 21, still needed Dad's steady hand, too. My brother Bobby and my grandfather Toots tried to comfort my grandmother Lena. My father was her only child, and they were very close.

The atmosphere at the funeral home was emotionally charged. Grandma Lena fainted at least twice. "You are not supposed to bury your children," she said. "It's not supposed to be that way. We should all go before our children go." She just screamed, "Not my baby." I'm not sure what's worse—losing a child or losing a parent. I was thinking, "Not my Dad." I was an 11-year-old "baby."

The next day, the funeral cars came again. Limousines and cars stretched over four blocks. We rode in a procession to the church. After the services we proceeded to the neighboring town of Steelton for Dad's burial. African Americans could not be buried in the Harrisburg Cemetery, even if they were a veteran like my Dad. Everyone came out. We made a left turn and I saw the neighborhood drunk. He was on a corner, his back against the wall. When I looked at him and realized that he was still alive, and my father was gone, it made me furious. Sometimes life just isn't fair. It certainly wasn't fair in 1960. It's hard to understand why Barnie the Bum will probably still be alive in the year 2000, while my Dad was gone forever.

Burying my Dad in another town added insult to our tragedy. If he was buried in Harrisburg, I could have stopped each day on the way to school, or in the evening before or after a party to spend time at Dad's grave, talking to him. I've been cutting through places like the Harrisburg Cemetery ever since.

Mom developed cancer less than two years after Dad's death. Mother already had a very difficult time dealing with life after my father passed away. They had been together since their teenage years. They had a lot of plans and spent a lot of time talking about their future. My parents were a team. It was about a year after my father passed away when my mother first got sick. I was in eighth grade at the time. She went into the hospital but was released a while later. She did a little bit better for a time, but she was diagnosed with breast cancer.

I'll always remember that next fall when she watched one of my football games at Edison Junior High School. Sick or not, my mother decided she was going to see me play at least one game. We were playing Carlisle, a town southwest of Harrisburg. It was the site of a fort during the French Indian Wars and a munitions supply center during the American Revolution. It was also home to the Carlisle Indian Industrial School made famous by Jim Thorpe.

We were ahead by three touchdowns. Our quarterback threw me a pass, but a Carlisle defensive back intercepted the ball. I started chasing him, but it was futile, as he seemed too fast. After 30 yards, I eased up and stopped. I gave up. That evening over my favorite meal, Mom laid it on the line in her own sweet way. "It did not matter if you were going to catch the Carlisle player or not," she said. "Never give up. Never lose faith. Chase that player to the end. Never, ever let anyone see you give up. Not your family, friends, teammates and certainly not your opponents."

Mom watched me play baseball, basketball and run track when I was younger. "Athletics will get you a college education," she would say. This she said even though none of my three older brothers, all very smart and athletic, would get such a chance. Opportunity passed them by, so they followed Dad's lead and joined the military.

As my mother's cancer spread, she developed pneumonia and never recovered. I spent a lot of time in the final weeks with my mother, Grandma Nellie and Grandma Lena. When my mother finally passed away, it almost destroyed me. To compensate, I grew closer to my grandmothers.

The following year, we were playing Carlisle again. I was playing quarterback. My helmet got knocked off just as I threw the ball. You guessed it, the pass was intercepted. This time I chased the enemy down and tackled him. His cleats hit me in the bridge of the nose.

"Mom, I never gave up!" The doctor said the scar between my eyes would be with me forever.

Desire, dedication and determination became the three Ds of my life philosophy. Desire asks, "How badly do you want something?" Dedication asks, "What price are you willing to pay?" Determination asks, "If at first you don't succeed, will you keep on until you do?" Thanks, Mom.

Just when I thought I had hit rock bottom, my best friend Penny died. We were the same age, but I was getting faster and she was getting slower. Arthritis crippled her so badly, she couldn't get around anymore. Blind in one eye with bladder problems, her tail would wag when it was clear I was going somewhere. Part German Shepherd and Collie, she never had a litter. I was the baby of the family, so she mothered me. I recall two times when Penny disappeared—the first was when Dad died, the other when Mom died. After everything was over, we found her hiding in the basement. Loyal Penny knew pain and understood loss. The toughest decision my brothers and I made was to put her to sleep. None of us could look into her pleading eyes anymore and say "No, Girl, you can't go this time." We would have carried her, but she was in too much pain.

The Green family structure had been forever changed. We still did some things as brothers and remained close, but it was never quite the same. We were missing our conduits. The connection between generations no longer seemed the same, either. I still remained close to Grandmom Nellie and Grandmom Lena, who both died in their late 70s, but not seeing our parents on hand to share life with them was sad.

Over time, the heartbreak of my parents' deaths and the bitterness that ensued would ease. My brothers would provide great support and my school and neighborhood helped motivate me to take control of my life. I decided that instead of looking for excuses, I would go out in life and make an impression. Just as we defiantly cut through Harrisburg Cemetery, I decided to cut through unchartered paths and overcome any obstacles in my way.

# 3

# PICKING UP THE PIECES

*"I remember when Dennis was playing football at Reservoir Park, he was about 12 years old, and he snapped his right arm in a pileup. Boom, boom! He broke it in two places, but he didn't cry. He told Mom he might have broken his arm, but she just laughed because he acted fine.*

*"Later, my brother Billy drove him to the hospital and got a cast put on it. Midge—that's what we called Dennis because he was the youngest—learned to write left-handed. He still can.*

*"People don't believe this, but I never had any problems with (Greg and Dennis) after our parents died. I told them to be in on time, do their homework, wash the dishes. It was rough, especially after I got married and had my first daughter in 1964 and a son in '65, but they helped out with the kids.*

*"Midge was always so mature. I'd go to parent-teacher conferences, and the teachers only had good things to say about him. He probably could have been anything he wanted."*

—Bobby Green, on his younger
brother Dennis' high-school years

I sensed that my parents were still with me long after their deaths. Not a day went by when I didn't think about Bus and Anna Green. I wanted them to always be proud of me, and I was in a hurry to make them proud.

As a teenager, I never expected to live past 40, knowing my father and mother died at age 39 and 41. I asked, what right did I have to live to 50 or 60 or 70? I set out to accomplish a lot in a short period of time, just like they did. In fact, I felt it would be a betrayal to live beyond the age of my parents. If my father got all he needed in 39 years, surely I could do it in 40.

After my mother's death, Billy and my middle brother, Stanley, were out on their own, so Bobby took early leave from the Air Force and, at 22, returned to Harrisburg to play Mr. Dad for his two teenage brothers, Greg and Dennis. Dad must have sensed his fate because he often said, "Your brothers are your best friends." I guess we all understand that more than ever.

My four older brothers had a tremendous effect on my childhood. They helped lay the foundation for and inspired me to seek the opportunities that started me on the road to where I am today. My philosophy of life has always been about opportunity. I know the opportunity that was there for me starting high school in 1964 wasn't there for my oldest brothers in 1954, 1956 or 1957. The opportunities were just starting to come, but they really didn't arrive until the time when my brother Greg (two years older than me) and I started to think about going to college. The opportunity for Greg and me to attend college was an important milestone for our family. That's what our parents would have wanted us to do.

All my brothers have really done well. So much of what I've tried to accomplish in football and coaching, through tenacity and opportunity, they've accomplished in their careers the same way. In fact, if you rank a lot of traits like intelligence, book smarts and instincts, I'd probably rank at or near the bottom of the five-brother pecking order.

My oldest brother, Billy, has been very successful in his career. After high school, he served in the Air Force for four years. He came back to Harrisburg in 1962, but realized opportunities just weren't there for him. So he moved to Washington, D.C., and worked for a short period of time in the construction business. Then he got into the computer industry when it was just ready to emerge as a giant industry—back when the computers were as big as refrigerators. He did that for 10 years, then landed a fulfilling job with the federal government, where he worked until he retired at age 58. Now he's living his dream of pursuing his passion for fishing—deep sea, river fishing, so forth. He's always fishing in the Chesapeake Bay and Potomac River. He's a captain, so he can charter boats and fish in tournaments, too.

Bobby, the second oldest, unfortunately has battled some health problems. He had a stroke about 15 years ago at age 43, recovered from that, but had another one in 1996. So he's back in the rehabilitation process now, is doing well, and is retired, living on disability. He was really Mr. Consistency from 1962-1995. He worked 11:00 at night until 7:00 in the morning for the U.S. Postal Service. That is very much reflective of the kind of opportunity that was available for black Americans when he started his career. If you were fortunate you could get a job with the city, state or federal government. Otherwise you tried to get a job at a steel mill or other factory.

Stan, the third son, like me, always had the music bug. He was in a musical group, The Thundering Senturies, and during their heydey of 1961-62-63, I played drums with them in the summer of 1963. It was so gratifying for me in 1994 when we started a record company, Savannah Street Music and put out the Sunset Celebration album. Stan sang the final cut, a ballad called "Better Days." He has an unusual voice that makes an impression, and there were people in New York who said, "Who is this undiscovered talent?" The undiscovered talent was my 54-year-old brother. He did a good job, and it's a project he and I both enjoyed. Anytime you can do something significant to help your brothers, I don't think there's any better feeling.

Stan works for Paul Allen Chevrolet in the Pittsburgh area as an auto detail specialist. He can take a car and make it shine like it is brand new. Stan and I had a lot of different jobs together in the old days. When I was in high school we tried to make some money in the janitorial business. Stan has always been a hard worker and he got together with his buddies to pursue their dream of making it big in the janitorial business. When it was going good, it was good for them, but they just missed on reaching the kind of customer base they needed. It didn't quite happen for them, but I admire their guts and effort in trying.

Greg is the brother closest to me in age. When I was in seventh grade, I was playing football for Coach George Hoenscheldt. But Greg was a little bit too smart to do the coach's notorious nutcracker drills and suicide drills in practice. Even though Greg was a very talented athlete, he didn't go out for junior high football but we played on the varsity together in high school. I still remember the first time we were on the field in the huddle together, and how it was nice to have him as a buffer. I didn't quite do my assignment the way the older players thought I should. They didn't say anything to me, but one guy just looked at Greg and said, "Tell your brother to get his act together, and I mean now." I thought they were going to throw me out of the huddle. It helped motivate me, though, because I wasn't going to let my brother take heat for me. It just underscored that our team had an expectation to win every game. I had to realize this wasn't junior high anymore—there were, figuratively speaking, live bullets flying out there.

Greg went on and had the most clear-cut education. He went to Shippensburg State College, about 45 miles from Harrisburg. He played a little football but mostly focused on academics. He had virtually all his education paid for, since our father was a military veteran, and he qualified for some academic grants with his excellent grades. Greg considered going into teaching but eventually went into business. He now works as a personnel director in one of the Pennsylvania state agencies.

All my brothers have always pulled for me and taken pride in my accomplishments, just as I've felt pride in their successes. You can never rise to the top of your profession by yourself. You need a real strong support mechanism. Sometimes I'm particularly sorry if I lose a big game or go through tough times, because I don't want my brothers to be disappointed. We've remained very close.

As a 14-year-old in the inner city of Harrisburg, I still had not gotten over my parents' deaths. When I see friends who lose their parents and are hurting, I understand. Losing your parents is one of the biggest hurts that anyone can suffer in life—I thought so at 14, and I think so now. The difference is that time has helped me learn to live and deal with it now with some semblance of acceptance.

At 14, I was doing my own thing. I wasn't a hellraiser, and I wasn't involved in anything illegal. It's just that my three older brothers, then in their early 20s, and their wives could not and should not have been expected to ride herd on me, like teenagers sometimes need.

My passion became sports and all the juice that came with it. Like all American kids, I loved to play the games. Football, basketball, baseball and track kept me busy, and socializing with teenage girls kept me off the streets. The Boys Club and the YMCA provided great sports venues and competition. What more could a boy want, short of his parents' reassuring smiles?

My goal was clear as a ninth-grader in 1963—play football well enough to earn a full scholarship, and get good enough grades to pick the university that I wanted to attend. This was a tall order for a 14-year-old to take on, but this was the era of equal rights and opportunity. If I did my part, I really believed that the right university would offer a full scholarship. I was fortunate in my teen years to have teachers who pushed me. Just because you are black, live in the inner city, and most of your teachers are white, that still should not prevent everyone from being on the same page. I always was expected to do well.

Most people in my neighborhood were not surprised that Greg and I were still doing the right things after our parents died. They expected us to stay on the right course and weren't afraid to step in and do their part. The saying today, "It takes a village to raise a child," was the rule in my neighborhood 35 years ago. "Community Privilege" was a loose law that meant that if an adult saw misbehavior that was bad for the neighborhood, they were supposed to do something about it —tell you to stop, stop it themselves, or call their husband to get you to stop. Then the next step was to call your parents even after you stopped. Many times if you did something wrong, your parents knew before you even got home, and you faced the disadvantage of not having enough time to get your story straight.

My involvement in sports provided me a ton of recognition and the neighborhood a feeling of pride. It started in 1963 in ninth grade when we would sling our football shoes over our shoulders as we walked to school. Of course, everybody in my neighborhood knew we played, but I had to walk through about four different neighborhoods to get to school. The socioeconomic make-up of these areas was as different as night and day. If you were a black kid coming up Walnut Street, then you had to be coming from my "hood." Yet when you walked down the fancy street with football shoes and your team was as successful as ours was, there was big-time pride that made you feel equal with anyone. The word was out—the Walnut Street Hill area had some cats who played dynamite football.

When I was growing up, Harrisburg was considered a small city, with a population of 80,000. It was better than many cities then and especially today for African Americans. With numerous government jobs available as a state capital city, there's less discrimination in those fields because your rights are protected a little more. There were a lot of industrial jobs, too, like in the steel mills. My dad and one of my brothers worked in the post offices.

So much of the city revolved around sports. The community has received a lot of its identity over the years from the teams and athletes that represented Harrisburg well. I was only six years old and watched my older brothers play when I knew that that was the thing I wanted to do—play sports. It was a way to get appreciation and help build a good self esteem.

My junior-high football experience was extremely valuable. George Hoensheldt said he always wanted to coach and teach in junior high school. His way in 1961 was as old fashioned as it could be. It also worked for him for more than 40 years. First, there was only one team for grades seven through nine in a school with 1,500 students, in a football-loving city and area. Coach felt when you were good enough, or big enough, or mature enough, you would make the team. This also required a lot of desire, dedication and determination on every player's part. He put you through a daily test to discover how badly you wanted to play for Edison Junior High School.

It was a typical inner-city situation, with no grass fields around the school. To get to practice we had to run to the high school field. That's right, run. We would get dressed, Coach would blow the whistle, and out the door we would go to start the 3/4 mile run to practice. John Harris High School sat alongside the most expensive housing area in Harrisburg. This was also the only expensive area that fed into the school, though. We ran right through the elite neighborhood everyday to practice. The idea was to keep everyone in shape. If you walked and were caught, you got hit on the behind twice with a big paddle, by the coach, in front of the entire team at the end of practice. If you didn't want to suffer this fate, you had three choices. Either run all the way, all the time, take the paddling like a man, or quit the team. This rule really made you show your commitment to football. Coach would ride around in his big General Motors car, and if he caught you walking, he'd just write down numbers. He didn't bother calling you by name until you made the team.

The second big challenge came at tryout week. There would be about 150 players competing for the 70 or so spots available. Even if you were on the team before, you still had to try out. Coach divided his hopefuls up as either halfbacks or tacklers. One drill was the dreaded nutcracker, with two lines of tacklers and one line of ball carriers. When the ball was punted, the two tacklers took off down the field. The ballcarrier who caught the punt had to maneuver between the two tacklers without getting crushed. It was one of the most physical football drills that I have ever experienced, but it did uncover the most skilled and athletic players. Coach would just write "good" or "bad" beside your number. There was no in-between with Coach Hoensheldt —he only wanted tough players who loved football and would do anything to play. If a player was not tough or did not love football, the nutcracker drill would reveal that quickly.

In pro football today, sometimes guys are playing strictly for the money. They have lost that great desire to do whatever it takes to play and win. In those cases it's the head coach's job to keep only players who will pay that required price. A lot of my success as a coach is tied to being able to identify and solve those problems.

My teenage years were interesting times. It's always challenging when you're growing up and trying to make those difficult decisions, and it's compounded when your parents are gone. There always was a lot going on in the housing projects for a young teenager. It was a real congested area, with a lot of people hanging out, a lot of sports pick-up games and other activities, and a chance to socialize with girls. They weren't as grim of a place as many of them have become today. Everyone had lived in the projects at some time it seemed. We lived there one year right after I was born before we moved up into what was called the Hill, one step up the social scale.

At that time, gangs were starting to become an issue. There was a group called the Harrisburg Dragons who became visible on the streets. One night when I was about 14 as I was coming back from the projects and taking the shortcut through the cemetery, these five Dragons jumped out and were ready to do what gang guys do—try to rob you, beat you and take your money. As I was trying to decide which way to run and how quickly I could do it, one of the guys says "Is that you, Greenie?" I stopped and I noticed that it was a guy named Tank who I went to grade school with. Tank was a very talented, powerful athlete, but he didn't have a clue about what was the right thing to do. He was consistently in trouble all his life. He told his guys, "This is my guy, he's cool. He's an athlete." I wasn't just some guy cutting through their graveyard, their turf. I was an athlete, somebody doing something positive.

That was a lesson for me at an early age; how athletics could give you respect and status. It also showed even then, and it's still true today, that the status and encouragement you get in athletics can keep you from joining a gang. Kids get into gangs looking for recognition, fellowship and a sense of purpose. Those are all things athletics can provide, but athletics also provide hope and a positive direction.

My parents certainly wanted me to have other positive choices than those a lot of inner-city kids face—stay in school or quit; join a gang or don't. They wanted us to have other outlets that would help us make the right decisions. That's really what sports did in my life—helped me make the right decisions.

I played all sports growing up. I really enjoyed baseball but phased it out when I was about 14. The game was starting to lose its popularity by then in the inner city. Baseball had gained popularity in inner cities when Jackie Robinson came into the game, but people of my age started thinking about college athletics as a new opportunity. I started thinking about earning a college athletic scholarship when I was in eighth grade. Mickey Minnich was a substitute teacher who had just gotten out of the military. He wanted to get into coaching in our school district, and the first thing he did was try to learn who the athletes were and check into their grades and the classes they were taking. At that time, Harrisburg teams were terrific, but most of the guys didn't understand the discipline and study skills you need to be successful in college. I remember guys who went away to play sports at college but were back home in a month.

That's why I've always tried to talk to kids in the seventh and eighth grades like Mickey did for me. You're preparing to be successful, or you're preparing to fail. Those are the cold, hard facts that many people won't tell you. The decisions you make as a 14-year-old are decisions that will affect you the rest of your life. Maybe not if you live in the upper suburbs of Colonial Park in Harrisburg, but if you're living in the inner city, you're going to be forced to pick. I'm not saying this applies to everybody, but if you're a guy who's in what I call the "lane" —who likes to go to parties, likes to be real social, wants to make a name for himself—that lane can lead you one or two ways. It can lead you to trouble, or it can lead you to a positive activity like sports. As a young teenager who had lost both his parents, I was on that road. Fortunately, I chose sports, but others I knew made bad choices. By the time I entered high school, I knew three guys who had committed murder and were incarcerated.

I had been a successful junior high student-athlete and I went into high school with determination. We had one of the best football teams in the entire nation. I was elected student council vice president, junior class president and senior class president, and was chosen as an American Legion Boys' State delegate. My goal was to earn a football scholarship, go off to college and do everything I could in life. I wanted my parents to be proud of what I would become.

I was a sprinter in track and field and also competed in the long jump, triple jump and high jump. My best track memory came in my junior year when we were taking some athletes to the Penn Relays at Philadelphia's Franklin Field. The Penn Relays have always been one of the big four track meets in America, along with the Texas, Kansas and Drake Relays. It has always attracted several world-class athletes, primarily top college teams, and also provides Pennsylvania high school athletes with some events. With its crowds of more than 25,000, it's quite a thrill for a young man to compete in the Penn Relays.

By this time, Mickey was our track coach, and he'd be reading a book on track and field technique practically as he was coaching you. I was junior-class president and we had our prom set for the same weekend as the Penn Relays. Our team was focusing on the mile relay in the high-school division, but I was more of a 100-yard and 220-yard dash man, and I didn't think I'd be needed. I told Mickey that as class president, I had to go to the prom. I knew we'd be staying up most of the night and wouldn't get much sleep, and I wouldn't be able to run very well after that. Coach said he wanted me as the alternate, just for insurance. I agreed to drive over the day of the race—about three hours for the trip—with the understanding they probably wouldn't need me.

Sure enough, we had a great time at prom and I got about three hours of sleep. I drove to the Penn Relays hoping I could watch and rest. It turned out that one of our quartermilers pulled a hamstring muscle, and I would have to run after all. They switched the relay order a bit and made me the leadoff guy, hoping I could keep it close and the other guys would be able to recover. There were 10 teams and a double stagger start—meaning two waves of five runners sprinting the first 100-plus yards then making a mass merger on the opposite side of the track. Everyone was telling me to make sure I went out hard and didn't get caught in the back or too far outside. I wasn't crazy about the 440-yard dash anyway. If you've ever run that event you know that "440 yards" and "dash" are a contradiction in terms.

It was cold and raining in the middle of April, but as much as I was tired and didn't want to race, I started getting excited. I had been at Franklin Field once before when I was 13 for a Junior Olympic meet and won the high jump with a leap of 6-feet. But there wasn't the crowd and atmosphere that day that there was for the Penn Relays. Once the race started, I decided not to risk going out too hard. I was in eighth place when the runners merged and brought us back to sixth at the handoff. Our second and third runners put us in the lead, and we had the amazing Jan White running our anchor.

Jan was 6-3, 210—unheard of for a wide receiver in those days—and would later play tight end on a football scholarship at Ohio State. Jan didn't like running the quarter mile, but he had won the Pennsylvania state championship in the 180 hurdles as a sophomore, an event he would win three times, and he also would later become a two-time state champ in the 220-yard dash. We were trying to hold off our big rival, William Penn, and they turned this into a two-team race with their anchor, Snake Wright. Snake had placed second in the open quarter at state the year before and was a big-time guy who could really roll. Jan was running in the lead but Snake was moving up, and everyone thought Snake would eat him up on the backstretch. Jan held him off, but right when they hit dead man's stretch—that point in the final 100 yards when you really tighten up—Snake closed on him. But in the end, Jan held him off at the tape by a nose. Man, that was exciting. People still talk about that race.

William Penn and John Harris were the big-city rivals in Harrisburg. The William Penn Tigers and the John Harris Pioneers always played a Thanksgiving day football game, and it was always the highlight of the season. At one point, all the African Americans in town were in the William Penn school district. Although I grew loyal to John Harris to the core, the rivalry was a bit awkward for me because both my parents had attended William Penn, both my grandparents had lived up there, and my father had eight brothers, and they all lived up there. Everyone in the projects went to John Harris. Over time, more African Americans, like my family did, moved out of the public housing into the Hill neighborhood, and still attended John Harris.

In football we didn't have the playoff system we have today, but we were unbeaten and won the mythical state championship designation when I was a junior and senior. In my era, we were far superior to rival William Penn simply because kept our best athletes on the field and they didn't.

At that time in Harrisburg, race wasn't a big deal. We had black housing projects and white housing projects. There were poor people, working-class people and middle-class people in the same schools. Growing up in junior high and senior high, race didn't matter. We had a good mix. My neighborhood was segregated, but as it extended out, the area that made up my junior high and senior high was integrated. I've always had teachers and coaches who were both black and white.

I became the first African American elected senior class president, partly because I was so well known as an athlete, but also because I was a leader. I was proud my classmates elected me and took that job seriously. The theme of the class of 1967 was that we felt that this was our time. We were going to have the chances for college that our older brothers and sisters never had.

As a high school senior in the fall of 1966, my three D's of desire, dedication and determination were tested. I rushed for over 500 yards in the first two games of the season. In the third game, while running down the sideline en route to a touchdown, I tore my hamstring muscle. It sounded like a gunshot. The doctor said I would miss the remaining eight games, a tough break for someone counting on a productive senior season to earn a big-time college scholarship. I never gave up. Slower, but more determined, I came back after missing just four games. Our team finished undefeated, and I came back and led the conference in scoring and rushing yards.

Sports brought me a ton of recognition. My head coach, George Chaump, summed up my football skills for the *Harrisburg Evening*

*News*:"Denny is not the fastest back, but he has quickness and a great natural running style."

My dream came true when the college recruiters called. Football was my ticket.

# 4

# "WE ARE PLAYING, WE ARE STAYING"

*"The black player revolt at the University of Iowa in the spring of 1969 was unfortunate, but it was the by-product of some combative times in our society. My class was among the first large wave of blacks to earn scholarships to play college football. There were just five black players on Iowa's roster the year before I came to campus, but there were 15 black players in my freshmen class alone. After two seasons, there were a lot of issues, and the bottom line was we felt the school wasn't ready for us.*

*"It was a conflict born out of the times. The black players wanted more individual attention and respect. At the same time, we wanted to prove our manhood and boldness, and stand up and be counted.*

*"A lot of communication got lost in the wash, but the bottom line is, as a young man from Harrisburg, Pennsylvania, I wasn't letting anybody back me down."*

> —Dennis Green, explaining the origins of the decision he made to join 15 other black players at the University of Iowa in a boycott of all spring practices in 1969.

I've always felt I was born at the right time. There is no doubt that my parents felt some disappointment they didn't get a "Denise" after Mom's fifth pregnancy, but they made "Dennis" feel just as welcome. Being born fifth instead of first in my family would have its rewards in my teenage years in terms of more opportunities in society.

When I hit ninth grade, my teammates and I began concentrating on sports as our ticket to a better future. I don't mean pro sports, which in 1963 were not even close to what they are in 1997 in number of teams, number of jobs, salaries or exposure. There were only 12 teams in the NFL back then, and it was common for many pro players to work off-season jobs to supplement their playing incomes. There were far less opportunities for black players, too, with less than 120 in the NFL. Black coaches? Don't even ask. (Speed ahead 17 years to the NFL in 1980 and you still would only find a total of 14 black assistant coaches. The first black NFL head coach didn't come on board until 1991.)

So it was logical to set our sights on major-college sports. It seemed like utopia. Get a full scholarship of tuition, room and board and books—three hots and a cot—and get to continue playing a game you loved. Football, basketball, baseball or track and field, no matter. Take your pick and go for it. We were convinced that everything about college life was going to suit us Harrisburg, Pennsylvania, guys just fine. We made a vow at this early age to "Make it, and make a difference."

Unfortunately, we couldn't turn back history and erase the mistakes that denied our fathers and older brothers their chances. Numerous great Harrisburg athletes from the 1940s and '50s never got their shot for various societal reasons:

- participation limits—a fancy term for quotas—were imposed. High schools limited the number of blacks to 10 in varsity football and two in varsity basketball;
- a lack of confidence to leave the comfort level of the 'hood;
- a lack of academic preparation and study skills;
- girlfriend or family choices.

Until my era, most guys with major-college athletic ability wound up in the military, working at factories, or getting married and starting families. But by the mid-1960s, the window of opportunity had improved for the inner-city student. In my junior and senior seasons at John Harris High School in 1965 and 1966, we never lost a football game. We were the best, in part because we were the hungriest. We didn't have a chip on our shoulders, just a fire in our bellies. Our motto was, "If you're afraid to say it, than you're surely not tough enough to do it." The senior players from these two unbeaten John Harris teams were going places and were determined to become trailblazers for their the families, school and city.

Not only was I living my dream, I also was part of the beginning of a revolution in college athletics in that fall of 1967, as black players were being recruited widespread. Things would never be the same for my race and for college sports. It was 50 years ago that Jackie Robinson made his debut as the first black American to play major-league baseball. Not only was he a pioneer in major-league baseball, Jackie was the greatest all-around athlete of his time. A four-sport star athlete at UCLA, Jackie stared blatant discrimination in the eyes and never blinked. He helped plant the seeds of opportunity for many and must be smiling down on society today when he sees the number of black athletes competing from high school to professional levels. One look at the Green Bay Packers, the New York Yankees, the NCAA champion University of Florida football team and NCAA champion University of Arizona basketball team tells you that things have changed. The trailblazers had to fight the original fight. In 1967, we understood this and we would not forget their sacrifices. Our window of opportunity had opened, and we were poised to charge through.

My senior year at John Harris was productive, even though I missed five games with the torn hamstring. I was starting to seriously consider which school I would attend. Iowa sold itself as a football program ready to take off and contend for a Big Ten championship. Ray Nagel, the Hawkeyes' head coach, was smooth, committed and knew how to recruit a young African American student-athlete from the inner-city. I always felt that Ray's progressive approach to equality in his treatment of student athletes came from his attending UCLA, where Jackie Robinson starred in football, basketball, baseball and track during the 1940s.

I considered Iowa, Michigan State and Kansas during my college football recruiting experience. Penn State was closer to home, but I think that was Joe Paterno's first year as coach, they weren't quite as established yet, and they didn't have a lot of African Americans on the team at that time. I was one of the first African American guys to get recruiting letters from schools like Tennessee and Kentucky, where all-white teams were the rule throughout their history. Just a decade earlier, an African American whose team played at southern cities like Lexington and Knoxville couldn't stay at the same hotel as his teammates.

Iowa had previously recruited numerous black players. Frank Gilliam, who recruited me and now is the Vikings' vice president for player personnel, played for the Hawks in the 1950s. Calvin Jones won the Outland Trophy in 1955 as the best lineman in the nation. Wilburn Hollis played quarterback on the 1960 team that almost won the national championship, finishing second in the final coaches' poll to Minnesota. (That Gopher team was quarterbacked by Sandy Stephens, another standout black player, who I watched play in a Pennsylvania all-star game). I was quite familiar with the Big Ten, and it made my decision easier. The first time I ever flew on an airplane was on my recruiting visit to Iowa City. The Iowa trip was great, and I knew that weekend I wanted to play for the Hawkeyes.

I was already married and a father when I went to college. I met my first wife, Margie, in high school in Harrisburg. We were married when I was 18. I went to college and lived in the dormitory as a freshman, and Margie and Patti joined me in Iowa City my sophomore year. We lived three years in married-student housing. Our marriage lasted until 1993, when we split up and got divorced.

Our daughter Patti got to know Iowa City well. She was the apple of my eye then and still is. I called her Rose, and I loved her dearly. I would take Patti to the day-care center in the morning before class. She was a good girl—always well behaved. I tried to do the best I could as a young, married father who was going to college at the same time. Most people say you're a man when you turn 21, but I became a man after Rose was born and I had to make sacrifices to provide for her. I was man enough to work a job—sometimes two or three jobs—all while playing college football and pursuing my degree.

Iowa Hawkeye football was outstanding in the 1950s and caught fire again under Hayden Fry in the 1980s and 90s. The Hawks played in the Rose Bowl in 1957 and 1959 after winning the Big Ten championships in the 1956 and 1958 seasons. Among the top players on those teams was lineman Alex Karras, who won the Outland Trophy in 1957. But in the early 1960s, a difficult stretch began. In 1965, with Jerry Burns as head coach, Iowa was picked No. 1 in the national preseason poll by *Playboy* magazine—one of the few publications that published rankings in those days. The Hawks lost their last eight games of that season, however, and finished 1-9. Everyone said that team was loaded with talent. One theory was the ranking went to their heads, and another was they all got caught up in wanting to play pro football and played a little passively to avoid injuries. I think as many as 10 Hawkeyes were drafted at the end of that season.

There was a lot of politics behind the scenes, though. The former successful coach Forest Evashevski became the athletic director and created an atmosphere that made it hard for any coach to be successful. It wasn't until Bump Elliott was hired as athletic director that things started to change. The first head coaches Bump hired couldn't get it done, either, but Bump finally got it right when he hired Hayden Fry in 1979.

In my era, NCAA rules prevented freshmen from playing with the varsity. We had two freshmen games—we went to Northwestern and had a home game against Iowa State—and otherwise just practiced, practiced, practiced. We won both those games, and we were projected to be a tremendous team when it was our chance to lead the varsity. We expected to challenge for the Big Ten championship in our career, even though recent history was not on our side. In my freshman season, the Iowa varsity won its opening game but was 0-8-1 thereafter. The Hawks went into 1968 just 1-25 in their last 26 Big Ten games since mid-1964.

We had some exceptional recruits coming onto the varsity, and we were sure we would start a new winning tradition. I was one of 15 African American recruits who arrived in 1967. That was about five times the number in previous recruiting seasons. Our class also included Larry Lawrence, a tremendous competitor at quarterback. With his curly blond hair and flair for athletics, he was destined to be the state's golden boy. As a high schooler in Cedar Rapids, he was the type of guy who led his football team to the state championship and hit the winning basket to win the state basketball title. His father joined the Iowa football staff as freshman coach—that's probably why Iowa was able to get Larry.

Man, did I like being a college student. My freshmen class brought to Iowa the pride from each of our cities. Guys shared their stories of how things were so rough back home, or how everyone was poor back in the 'hood, or how everyone back home was counting on them to make it. And believe me, they meant it. Suddenly, there was little difference between Harrisburg, Chicago, New Orleans, Memphis, Houston or any of the other cities where young athletes were seeking an opportunity to use their sports ability to receive a free education. When our 15 black student athletes came to Iowa, 15 others went to Ohio State, and 15 went to Michigan, and 15 went to Arizona State, and 15 went to Wyoming. Yes, this was the dawn of a new generation of sports activity, participation and spectatorship.

What created this newfound fortune? Was it equal rights battles that were fought and won, television, or numerous other reasons? We didn't know it at the time, but we were birthing this new generation that we live in today. Iowa's varsity football roster went from five black players in 1967 to 20 in 1968 and 30 in 1969. All came with dreams—their own and everyone else's. Most of us were the first in our families to go to college. Some were the first to graduate from high school. Our motto was, "We are playing and we are staying." This became the rallying cry around the country. It was about playing. (Ironically, two years later, that very concept was challenged with the revolt of the black athlete.)

I remember being a wide-eyed sophomore coming to Kinnick Stadium the day of my first college varsity football game. We were riding the team bus to the stadium when I noticed that right next to Kinnick there were some tennis courts. I was amazed to see people playing tennis on the day of a football game. I was insulted. I was coming off a promising freshman season and a spring practice where I won the starting tailback job. We were playing Oregon State, the No. 7 team in the country, in our home opener. I expected the whole town to be glued to our game.

My career started off with a bang. Our first opponent, Oregon State, had a running game that featured All-American center Jim Didion and 255-pound fullback Bill "Earthquake" Enyart. In those days, 255 pounds was rare. We upset Oregon State, 21-20, and I scored the winning touchdown in the fourth quarter to rally us from a 20-14 deficit.

For our second game we traveled to Texas Christian, and I took the second airplane flight of my life. I had my best game of my career. Unfortunately, Texas Christian rallied for two fourth-quarter touchdowns to post a 28-17 victory. I rushed for 175 yards—which at the time was the third highest single-game rushing output in school history. I had touchdown runs of 65 and 23 yards. I felt like I was in the groove again, just like in my glory days at John Harris High School.

In our third game, we played Notre Dame at home. Under coach Ara Parseghian, Notre Dame was ranked in the nation's top 10 (and would finish the season No. 8). The Fighting Irish had All-American Terry Hanratty at quarterback (backed up by Joe Theismann), and two other offensive All-Americans—tackle George Kunz and end Jim Seymour. Their defense was led by end Bob Kuechenberg, who would go on to a distinguished NFL career with the Miami Dolphins. I caught a 38-yard scoring pass early in the game, then had a nine-yard touchdown run to tie the score at 14-14. I ended up with two touchdowns in the game, but we lost, 51-28. It was gratifying after the game to read Coach Nagel's comments: "We knew last year that Dennis Green was going to be something special. He just does some things that most athletes can't do, and he's really a competitor. We're delighted to have him at Iowa."

We closed our non-conference season with a 1-2 record but were encouraged by our potential. We were ready to roll into the seven-game Big Ten season. But in our next game, the conference opener vs. Indiana, I tore ligaments in my ankle. Certain ankle injuries can be even more severe than knee injuries. Coming into the game, I was focused, I was on my game, and I felt like I could help the Hawks win. You can imagine my disappointment in this, our Homecoming game, as I stood on crutches and watched us lose, 38-34, and drop to 1-3.

It took a couple of days to confirm it, but I learned I'd be out for at least a month—and maybe for the rest of the season. So Coach Nagel had to make some offensive changes. Eddie Podalak had been the starting quarterback in those first games. Eddie, who went on to a great NFL career with the Kansas City Chiefs, was one heck of a runner but just a so-so passer. The golden boy, Larry Lawrence, was cooling his heels and waiting to play quarterback anyway. So they switched Podalak to running back and put Larry in at quarterback. I didn't play again that season and ended up with 279 yards rushing and an average of 6.0 yards a carry.

Our team finished 5-5 for the best Iowa record in several seasons. Five of our opponents finished in the top 18 of the national rankings. We lost 33-27 to eventual national champion Ohio State, and beat Minnesota, 35-28, in Minneapolis for a rare Big Ten road win. It was hard for me to sit on the sidelines and watch. Even though I was scheduled to start again at running back as a junior, this was a difficult time for me in my football career. The disappointment of having such a good season ended so abruptly by an injury didn't help my attitude heading into the winter of 1969, when some issues for black players boiled over.

The revolt of the black athlete exploded on the major-college football scene in 1969. Sixteen of Iowa's 19 black football players voted to boycott spring practice. This action splintered the team and caused friction that never healed between the team's black and white players. The key issues were the same throughout the land in football. We came to the school feeling that we had earned our football scholarships. That scholarship entitled us to an opportunity to get an education, and play big-time football, in that order. Yet there were some coaches who felt football should come first. The coaches' message seemed to be, "Don't complain, don't think for yourself, don't rock the boat. You should be happy to be here on a free ride." We decided to show our black manhood because we felt that the coaches and the system were wrong.

The window of opportunity for blacks was opened in 1967 because college football was starting to lose out to pro football in popularity. The reason was simple—the college game was falling behind the times. In 1966, there were probably less than 100 black players in the Big Ten Conference. In fact, most major conferences were in total denial. The game was not as fast paced, as exciting, or as well viewed as it was in previous decades. There was a definite, deliberate attempt to keep the numbers of blacks down. How else can you explain it? In 1966, there were five black players on the entire 100-plus Iowa roster. Yet in my freshmen class of 1967 alone, 15 of the 30 recruits were black. This was the scene throughout the land in big-time football.

We knew we were there because the door had been forced open. Now we were demanding the respect that comes with the territory. Harry Edwards, the prominent sports psychologist, said in 1968, "White coaches in America can't win without the black athlete, and are catching hell with him." I had first met Harry Edwards in 1969, when he was an organizing force of the boycott by the black U.S. Olympians in Mexico City. He always has been a visionary. He knew where society was going, and he knew in 1969 we were headed for trouble, particularly in college football. He was among those who spoke out on the need to improve conditions for the black athlete. There had always been African American players but never in this amount. Previously there were some suburban blacks, now all of the sudden, there were blacks from the inner cities. Harry wasn't actively involved in our Iowa players' boycott—he went out to the real hot spots—but we felt he was with us.

As newly emerging black men, we were more than willing to challenge the football establishment. What did we want? Let guys pick their own classes without eligibility considerations. We also wanted more black coaches. We felt it was the natural next step. Of the Big Ten's 80 assistant coaches in 1969, only Iowa's Frank Gilliam and Ohio State's Rudy Hubbard were black.

We knew there would be consequences to our boycott, although nobody expected it to fully play out like it did. We were called boycotters or troublemakers, words that have negative connotations. We subsequently were suspended from the team, and faced the prospect of having our scholarships revoked.

I usually went home to Harrisburg over school breaks because my brothers still lived there. On my trip back that summer after the 1969 boycott, I had a lot of explaining to do. The most difficult thing was facing all the people who were trying to understand what I'd gotten myself into. At that time I wasn't an official member of the Iowa Hawkeye football team, and I didn't have a clue whether I still had my scholarship or would ever be allowed to play football again. We were basically cut adrift. There was a pretty big article in the Harrisburg newspaper when I went home that said, "Green is one of the guys who was kicked off the Iowa team because he took part in the boycott of spring practice..."

But some things in life are more important than football. That was the only time in that period where I put politics ahead of football.

I haven't done it since then. For that one, brief period of time, I didn't love football. I look back on it now and realize that other things were more important to me than football.

A lot of it related to the social climate in the 1960s. My college era from 1967-71 was a constant time of change. In 1969 there were boycotts taking place all over the country. It was a very combative time, not only at the University of Iowa, but everywhere. There was so much stuff going on with people being challenged to take stands. Children would come home for college break and their parents wouldn't recognize them. Guys would have hair down to their shoulders, and women would have different clothing and hairstyles. There was the Civil Rights movement, the hippies, and just huge commotion. We were a generation that had lost faith. The assassinations of President Kennedy, Bobby Kennedy and Martin Luther King were devastating, especially to African Americans. Dr. King was our greatest fighter for civil rights, and the Kennedys were identified with equal opportunity. It seemed like all the good guys who wanted to help couldn't survive in America.

There also was the Viet Nam war, which was going hot and heavy and dividing the country into factions. In 1967, there were basically two choices for a high school graduate—go to college or go to Viet Nam. (In the inner city, in cases of people in trouble with the law, the choice was go to Nam or go to jail.) Most of my friends and I were lucky—we went off to college to play sports and got a free education. For others, life was not nearly so simple or safe. Some made the ultimate sacrifice, giving their lives for their country. Many others served bravely in the military. There were those who supported the war but stayed in college and left the actual combat to others (Have you ever heard the saying, "Action walks, but B.S. talks?") Finally, there were the war protesters—people old and young who saw through the whole scene and spoke up against it or even just flat out said no. People may forget that the most famous of the latter group was Muhammed Ali, the "greatest" himself.

I had brothers who had been in the Air Force, and my dad was in the Merchant Marines and the Army Reserves. I wouldn't have hesitated to serve in Viet Nam if the situation had arisen. When they initiated a draft lottery in 1970, my birthday was drawn No. 189, meaning that I might be on the bubble of being called up when my college exemption was completed. They went as high as 220 in the first year. But in 1971, when I was graduating and eligible to be drafted, President Nixon had reduced the number of troops sent over to Viet Nam, and they only went as high as the 160s. A lot of guys enlisted in the Navy because they didn't want to get drafted into the Army or Marines and face a higher risk of ground combat.

The climate in Iowa City fed into the nation's unrest. This was not, as some might think, some sleepy town in the middle of farm country. The university had a lot of professors and students from large cities like Chicago, and had a very liberal, active feeling. People in western Iowa talked about Iowa City like it was a modern day Sodom and Gomorrah. A lot of people sent their children to Iowa State University in Ames because it was considered more conservative. In 1970 the university had to close down the Iowa campus because of riots. School closed early for the spring semester, and the grades you had at the time were your final grades. There were speeches and rallies. The Students for Democratic Society (SDS), applied enough pressure that the university moved the ROTC program off campus. There were boycotts, sit-ins and building takeovers.

Most athletes didn't get caught up in the political scene. Maybe some of that was because football resembles the military with its need for discipline, a chain of command, structure, pride and teamwork. You were caught in between sometimes, though, if you had a coach who wouldn't let you wear long hair, for instance. Those were the days of the big afro hairstyles.

You also had the 1968 Olympic Games in Mexico City and the black power protests that fueled the 1969 player boycott. We knew guys over there fighting in Viet Nam, and we said, "They're fighting for us, now we can't be afraid to be men. They've got to be men, we've got to be men. They're over there standing up, we've got to be here standing up." All those things began to boil. As African American players, we felt it was necessary to take a stand.

That's what I was trying to explain to people that summer in Harrisburg. Football was not everything. I expected to be back playing again. If not, I knew I'd still get my degree. At the time, I was clearly not someone who loved the game of football. People probably wouldn't have been surprised if things had not worked out for me. Many times we get trained to think that if you're a football player, that's all you are. But that was the attitude we were rebelling against—that we were just guys recruited to help the university win football games.

What did I learn from it? I think I had some balance in my life before, but you always have to have balance.

I've been asked what would have happened to me if I wasn't reinstated or had lost my scholarship. Would I have transferred or even quit school? Some guys never did recover from that experience and to this day have bad feelings about it. But I knew I was going to graduate.

I wasn't the greatest student, but I knew my degree was more important than football.

In August, after the boycott, Coach Ray Nagel asked the players who didn't participate to vote on which of the protesters would be allowed to return the next fall. I was one of 11 brought back.

If we had stuck together from start to finish, ready to sit out the year and give back our scholarships, we could have put all 16 protesters back on the team. I learned two valuable lessons. Every time I start a job, I must be ready to see it through to the end. The second lesson is I must always do what I say I will.

After I was voted back on the team for the 1969 season, I shared the starting tailback job with Levi Mitchell. I rushed for 396 yards and led the team with seven touchdowns and we finished 5-5 again.

More controversy hit our team in my senior season. Evashevski fired Coach Nagel and then quit himself as athletic director. Bump Elliott took over as athletic director and hired Nagel back. But in the meantime, Larry Lawrence decided to transfer to Miami. I thought Larry was the best quarterback in the Big Ten, even better than Ohio State's Rex Kern, who was an outstanding all-around athlete himself. You can imagine the blow to the team when a quarterback of his ability, a state icon, transfers out. I don't think he ever played at Miami, but he did eventually play professionally in the Canadian Football League. All that turmoil didn't help our team, and we finished 3-6-1. They moved me to wingback because they said they could get more of our top players on the field at the same time. As a player, you line up wherever the coach asks you to if it will help your team win.

In our second game, we played Southern Cal at home and I got to play against my high school teammate and friend Jimmy Jones, who was the starting quarterback for the Trojans. Jimmy and I were quarterbacks together at Edison Junior High—I was in ninth grade when he was in eighth. I started our first game and we lost by one point. He started the next game at quarterback—they moved me to running back —and he never lost a game until midway through his college days at USC.

Even though we didn't have a winning season or go to the Rose Bowl, I had a great college experience at Iowa. I appreciated the great Iowa football fans. Despite all the things that happened to me with injuries and being part of the player boycott, I really liked the community. I especially liked coming back to be an assistant coach under head coach Bob Cummings during the 1970s. The people there really care about their Hawkeyes. All of us who wore the black and gold are loyal, die-hard Hawkeyes.

I graduated in 1971 with a degree in recreation education. The NFL didn't draft me, so I signed with the CFL's British Columbia Lions. That turned out to be a big disappointment. For the first time since I was in grade school, I wasn't involved in football.

# 5
# LEARNING THE COACHING BUSINESS

*"In my first season as head coach at Dayton, I hired Denny as an assistant coach. We lived together for three months as the only tenants of a 47-room campus monastery. We were guests of the university until our families could join us.*

*"We talked football morning, noon and night. Every night for three months we ate at the same Bob's Big Boy. We didn't have much money, and Denny would always say to the waitress 'I want (the food) to look just like in the picture on the menu.'*

*"Iowa coach Frank Lauterbur had recommended Denny to me and he called the next year to ask how he was doing. When Frank asked what I thought of Denny, I told him he was everything I expected, and more. Plus he coached the kicking game. I told him that even as we were speaking, Denny was out recruiting, and doing a great job in that area, too. Frank said he was glad, because he wanted to hire him back at Iowa."*

—Ron Marciniak
former Dayton coach and
Dallas Cowboy chief scout

When I finished my playing career at Iowa in 1970, fewer playing opportunities existed in pro football than today. Just 20 teams made up the National Football League at the time, which meant far fewer players were needed than in today's 30-team structure. The NFL in those years was going through changes of its own. It had recently merged the old 14-team NFL with the ten teams from the American

Football League (AFL)—the Kansas City Chiefs, Oakland Raiders, Denver Broncos, New York Jets, Boston Patriots, San Diego Chargers, Houston Oilers, Miami Dolphins, Buffalo Bills and Cincinnati Bengals.

I wasn't drafted by an NFL team and had no NFL free-agent tryout prospects in 1971. My college injuries certainly held me back. Realistically, I didn't have great size and speed to play running back in pro football. I was versatile enough, though, having played both running back and receiver at Iowa, to market myself to pro scouts as a defensive back. Whatever interest I might have received from NFL scouts was killed by my participation in the Iowa boycott. Although nobody in the NFL would acknowledge it, all of us players were, in effect, blackballed from getting an NFL opportunity. Boycotts are a threat to structure. That was a sign of the times in the 1960s.

With my personality and background, I was better suited to play in the old AFL than the ultraconservative NFL of 1971. When the AFL was gobbled up in the NFL merger, also lost for good was the upstart league's wide-open flavor and its ability to showcase new talent. The AFL was wilder and woollier, with a more wide-open style. You didn't have to be from Michigan or Notre Dame, or be an All-American or someone without controversy to play in the AFL. It was where guys who everyone said couldn't play in the NFL found a home, like linebacker Willie Lanier, big Buck Buchanan, little Lance Alworth and the controversial Fred "The Hammer" Williamson. All were stars in the AFL who were virtually ignored by NFL scouts when they came out of college. Our Iowa black player boycott, a situation that offended the conservative NFL, wouldn't have been a big deal to the old AFL teams. The AFL's demise meant that the Canadian Football League (CFL) was the only legitimate option to the NFL.

I signed with British Columbia in the CFL, still reeling from my Iowa football career. My ankle ligaments never really healed after my sophomore year injury. I also had lost that great love of football, probably back in the spring of 1969 during that boycott and the tumultuous aftermath. I think I was still a little rebellious at the time, too. The confusing and political times we endured in college probably made us better people, but didn't necessarily make us better football players. So I wasn't really surprised when football didn't work out—it just didn't happen for me. It was ironic that my incoming college class of 1967— born at the right time of expanded opportunity—didn't carry that wave into pro football in 1971. We graduated and started new chapters in our lives, not without some growing pains. I took my college degree and went to work.

My son, Jeremy, was born that summer, July of 1971. He came into the world with an even temperament and he still has that magical smile.

The next two years were restless ones for me. I was not involved in football for the first time since my childhood. It also was the first time I didn't have a clear direction or single focus for my career. I interviewed for jobs in recreation management and social work in the state prison system. I flew to Dayton, Ohio to interview for a position as a college recruiter at Wilberforce College. All of the opportunities were intriguing, but they did not grab my soul.

I returned to Iowa City and called Tom Neriem, the president and owner of Universal Climate Control, a heating and air conditioning contractor for commercial projects. I had worked for him as my summer job during two of my years in college. Tom had told me he would always have a job for me, but I think he was surprised to see me walk into his office. True to his word, he hired me to drive one of his trucks and deliver sheet metal to construction sites. I was loyal to Tom, and Tom was loyal to me. After a few months with his company, when I had a chance to sit back and sort out my feelings, I realized how much I missed football. It was February of 1972, and I was behind the wheel of a tractor clearing the parking lot at Universal Climate Controls. The temperature had fallen to 20 degrees below zero, but my spirits were even lower. My mind kept drifting back to my playing days, replaying the highs and lows, the rewards and regrets:

*...Maybe my NFL chances would have been better if we had found another forum to vent our frustration as black players in 1969?*

*...Maybe I allowed myself to become preoccupied with other aspects of campus life during the 1960s?*

*...Maybe my concentration level and commitment to football were not what they should have been after the ankle injury?*

Of course, all the second-guessing in the world can't undo the past. The competitor in me was ready to seek an NFL tryout at one of the 1972 training camps. The realist in me was willing to accept that the boat had passed me by as a player. The problem solver in me worked on a plan to fill the void I was feeling.

That spring, Tom Neriem offered me the general manager position of a new company he planned to create, servicing and selling residential heating and air conditioning. I really appreciated Tom's confidence in me. But I had a plan that might get me back into football.

I went to see Frank Lauterbur, who had replaced Ray Nagel as head coach of the Hawkeyes just after my eligibility ended. Lauterbur had arrived in a blaze of glory from the University of Toledo. At the time, he was busy preparing for his second year after a disappointing 1-10 debut season. I asked Lauterbur if I could work on his coaching staff as a graduate assistant for the upcoming football season. He told me he already had eight coaches in this capacity and had no additional funds. As we continued to talk, I convinced Lauterbur that my goal was experience, not the $1,000 stipend.

He let me work as an unpaid volunteer on his staff, and a coaching career was born. I knew I had a lot to learn, but I felt confident that I had a lot to offer. I was determined to earn a reputation as a good coach. I quickly learned that three of the best traits a coach can possess are patience, understanding and an ability to be demanding.

So much for the glamour of the coaching profession. With a wife and two young children to support, I had to keep my job at Universal Climate Controls to make my football dream a reality. To free up my afternoons, evenings and weekends for coaching, I worked a 5 a.m. to 1 p.m. shift. I awoke at 4:30 a.m. to get to work by 5 a.m. sharp. My responsibilities included preparing the shop for the metal cutters; emptying scrap barrels with the tractor; and loading the delivery trucks. I started my deliveries by 8 a.m., and got in three or four big runs a day. By 1 p.m., my eight-hour shift was over and I was out the door headed home. I'd shower and grab a quick lunch on the fly before driving to the football facility.

Working in the shadows of Kinnick Stadium again reminded me how much I loved this game. As thrilled as I was to come to Iowa City as a college freshman in 1967, I felt even luckier to get the opportunity to return in 1972. My passion for football was back, and I promised myself I would treasure every play and every day as a coach.

That first year of coaching was challenging, difficult, rewarding, and disappointing all at once. Nobody was pleased with Iowa's 3-7-1 finish, but we weren't far from being a decent team. We held eight of the 10 opponents under 25 points but couldn't score enough ourselves. We dropped three road games by a combined 14 points (at Penn State, Wisconsin and Indiana). If we could have pulled those games out, we would have had a winning season.

Another disheartening development occurred in 1972 when the National Collegiate Athletic Association (NCAA) lowered academic standards for athletic scholarships to a cumulative high school grade-point average of 2.00. That sent a terrible and devastating message to the student athlete, particularly in inner-city schools. Hard-fought gains in the 1960s to pursue equal access to scholarships were being denigrated. The effects of these low expectations were seen immediately. Today every major city in the country has trouble with its public high school football programs. When I was in Cincinnati this August, there was a story in the newspaper that one of that city's public high schools only had 28 boys playing football. The same is true for many of the Minneapolis and St. Paul public high schools. With a high dropout rate in schools and a lack of funding for equipment and top coaches, it's no wonder the interest in participation has dropped. If you have no opportunities, no goals and no hope, it's hard to be motivated.

In February of 1973, I was hired by the University of Dayton for my first paid assistant's job—I earned a $6,000 salary to coach quarterbacks, running backs, receivers and special teams. I learned that there's more to teaching football than just coaching on the field. A coach has to earn the confidence of his players. At Dayton, we had a five-man coaching staff, even though our opponents had staffs of nine or more assistants. But it was good for my development as a young coach, because every one of our coaches was forced to make major contributions.

It was important to create an atmosphere in which the player feels he can succeed. My high school coach, George Chaump, was one of the most successful coaches in the entire country. Under Coach Chaump, John Harris had a winning streak of 46 games (one of his classes never lost a game). By the time I entered high school, we were on another winning streak. The lessons I learned as a young player were carried into my coaching philosophy.

Likewise, the lessons I learned from my junior high school coach, George Hoensheldt, came back to me. How bad does the player want to play? How was he going to prove it to himself, to his teammates and to his coaches?

Athletes had to answer certain questions in order to succeed:

- Why are they playing? The only good reason to play is for their own personal satisfaction. It is my job to discover if there are any other reasons. The team needs to know that everyone on the team has a responsibility to give his all and never quit.
- Do they understand the team concept? A football team is a large group that stands together with a purpose. Gangs rarely impact young people who play sports. The football player already has a feeling of belonging. The team is unified because it knows it could play without regard to race, religion or financial standing.
- Do they possess and display the three Ds—Desire, Dedication and Determination? Desire is the essence of life. It measures how badly you want to achieve something. Dedication is the price

you are willing to pay to get what you wanted. Determination measures how many times you are willing to get up after being knocked down.

- Are they having fun? It's only a game, and there are no life or death consequences. If a player doesn't know the difference, he either hasn't grown up or is deceiving himself.

I worked at Dayton just one year before I was given the chance to return to Iowa, this time as the Hawkeyes' receivers and tight end coach. I jumped at it. Over the next three years we made progress but never reached a bowl game. I learned a lot about fighting with your back against the wall.

In 1977, I received a phone call from Bill Walsh, who had just been hired as Stanford's head coach. I accepted his job offer and within two days started working in California.

Walsh and I hit it off immediately. He would hire me three separate times during my career. The Stanford job was the only assistant job I would have left Iowa for. I loved working in Iowa City. There was something unique about working where you attended school. You knew everything and everybody. All was forgiven from the black boycott days. Instead of being labeled an S.O.B, now I was considered a son of the university. New Iowa coach Bob Cummings hired me as a 24-four-year-old coach, which was rare. After three seasons, I left Iowa in 1977 with a heavy heart, but Stanford is one of the finest universities in the entire world, one with a love of sports.

If I hadn't taken the Minnesota Vikings head coaching job in 1992, I probably would have stayed a long time as Stanford head coach. It was one of the few college head football jobs—the University of Iowa was another—that I might have considered leaving the San Francisco 49ers for in the late 1980s. The appeal of Stanford for me was obvious. The university's reputation for excellence, its proximity to my job with the 49ers, and my two previous stints there as an assistant coach made it a no-brainer. As for Iowa, everyone dreams of coming back and being the head coach of their alma mater. It took Iowa a while to get its football program on the right track, but since 1979, Hayden Fry has done a fabulous job. The situations weren't exactly the same, but the things we tried to do at Northwestern in 1981 were like many of the things Hayden had to change at Iowa. People forget that Iowa had not had a winning season since 1961 before Hayden came in.

One of the best lessons in coaching is to be a teacher and a learner. Some of the most challenging aspects of coaching come when players don't execute the way you want them to, or when players don't seem to be able to pick up things you're saying to them. In those situations, we can never let frustration kick in. What I used to do as an assistant coach, whenever I'd start to feel frustrated, I would force myself to play racquetball lefthanded. It's a great teaching tool because your mind knows what it wants to do, but the coordination and reaction of my left arm and hand just doesn't work as well as my right side. It looks pretty awkward, but you get a little better as you keep playing. It makes you more humble and makes you realize that when you try things yourself that don't come easily, you'll be better prepared to relate to what your player sometimes goes through. It's always easier to teach than to learn.

Any time you're teaching, you need to do new things and face new challenges. I think many of our teachers in our schools get a little stale because they never take on anything new. They don't understand what it's like to go waterskiing for the first time and not be able to do it well, or go fly fishing or rollerblading. I think you constantly have to try new things—both mental tasks, like learning a new language or taking a computer class, and  physical tasks, like swinging a golf club.

It's important for every teacher or coach to remember that the student really does want to get it, but many times you have to be able to frame it differently. You shouldn't get frustrated with that fact. When you go out and try to learn something new yourself, like trying to speak French, you can relate to feeling insecure and questioning whether you're smart enough to learn. We can't afford to be just teachers, we have to be learners as well and become students ourselves.

Often when a player does something wrong on the field, you ask them to reconstruct the play and explain their specific task. They usually know what they're supposed to be doing but are unable to transfer it onto the football field. In these cases you're only one step away. When you get a player to combine the preparation (what to do) with proper technique (how to do it), you build confidence. It's hard to be confident as a player if you don't understand what you're trying to do or don't have proper technique.

In the NFL, all players are good. Everyone has first- or second- or third-round draft picks, so teams are much more evenly matched. The level of play is much more competitive than in college. Look at the numbers alone to see what percentage of guys can make it. There are approximately 1,500 guys in the NFL today, with maybe 250 jobs opening up every year. There are 10,000 guys in Division I-A programs, not counting several thousand more in I-AA Division II or III and NAIA. The things a guy can do in college when he's so much faster than anyone else won't work the same in the NFL because the linebackers are just as fast as the running backs. Plus the NFL intensity level is a lot higher because guys are playing for their paychecks and their livelihood. You can either play, make the team and get paid, or be forced to go out and do something else in life and miss out on this exceptional salary and opportunity.

There is certainly more teaching that goes on in college football because you have so many players, but the best NFL teams still teach. That's often what separates the successful teams from the teams that don't play up to their level of talent. As an assistant coach, I've been associated with two of the greatest players the NFL has ever seen—Joe Montana and Jerry Rice. They accepted coaching and teaching extremely well. They understood their coaches were trying to make them better players, and they were willing to accept that. Yet I've seen many players who weren't nearly as talented who seemed to resent being taught or coached. They felt that because they were already on a pro football team, they had all the answers. I just started my 26th year in coaching, and I know the learning never stops.

My experience as a player helps me relate as a coach. One specific area where I empathize with players involves injuries. It's always tough to miss a game because of an injury. One of our best Viking players, running back Robert Smith, had been very unlucky in the injury department. When he's healthy, he's one of the best players in the NFL. Unfortunately, he hasn't played a full season for us in his four-year pro career. This did not deter us from signing Robert as a free agent this year. I'm confident a healthy Robert Smith would make a big difference for us in the playoffs.

I learned the hard way, as a high school and college player how important it is to be patient and not try to come back too soon. My senior-year hamstring injury threatened my team's No. 1 state ranking and my chance to earn a football scholarship. Although the doctors said my hamstring in the third game would put me out for the remainder of the year, I made up my mind that I would be back in two weeks. My backfield coach, Mickey Minnich, was doing all he could do to help me rehabilitate. After missing the first game, I made up my mind that I could play against our next opponent.

We played neighborhood Steelton, who always played us tougher than anyone on our schedule, a small school in a tough, hard-nosed town. Their playing style was as blunt as the town name. They were proud of the town heritage in the steel industry. Their fans loved football or any sport that gave you a chance to be challenged physically. Steelton had a special place in my heart, because it was the city where my Mom and Dad and so many African Americans from Harrisburg were laid to rest when they were denied space at the Harrisburg Cemetery.

Even though my John Harris teams were usually among the state's highest scoring teams, when we played Steelton it regularly turned into a defensive struggle. That year was no different. We were both undefeated when we took the field at their home stadium. I wanted a piece of the action, and my guts and heart said I was well enough to play. Coach Chaump disagreed and said I could suit up but wouldn't get to play in the game.

True to the pre-game billing, it was 0-0 at halftime. Time after time, our talented, high-potency offense moved the ball well, but someone from Steelton would make a big defensive stop or force a turnover.

By halftime I grew frustrated standing and watching, knowing I could make a difference. But my pleas to Coach Minnich and Coach Chaump were denied. I was ticked off. I did my best to cheerlead for the team, but I definitely thought they were making a mistake by not playing me. We used a defensive touchdown for the only score of the game and escaped with a victory. After we got back to school, I told Coach Chaump he should have played me. He marched me outside, past the locker room and onto the stadium field. "Your leg isn't ready. You can't even beat me in a 40-yard race. I am going to prove it to you." We raced, and I lost. Coach Chaump and Mickey were right. If I had tried to play, I would have torn the hamstring even more and been out the remainder of the season.

Coach said, "We are 6-0, we have five games left, and we miss you. If you stay patient, you can be healthy enough to play in two weeks." I did and I was. The goals I had set for myself and we had set for the team were met. Whenever I try to help an injured player, I reflect back to that time. The player wants to play worse than anyone. But it's my job as a coach to let him know that while he's valuable and missed, he has to show patience. If we use a player who's not 100 percent, both the individual and the team could suffer.

# 6

# WAKING UP THE WILDCATS

*"The losing streak was so embarrassing to the students, because it was the only thing outside people knew about (Northwestern University). Tell someone you went to NU and they'd say, 'Oh, that's the place with the bad football team.' We were grateful to Green for changing that."*

—Dennis Manoloff,
sportswriter at NU student newspaper

*"That's all right, that's OK, you're going to work for us someday!"*

—Brainy students in the Northwestern
student section, chanting to opposing
players during the Wildcats' football
woes

When Bill Walsh left Stanford to become the 49ers head coach in 1979, he took me along as an assistant. Stanford replaced Walsh with another one of his assistants, Rod Dowhower, but he lasted just one year. So Stanford was looking for another head coach in 1980, and contacted me about interviewing for the opening.

Even though I had a great NFL job in an up-and-coming organization, my No. 1 objective was to become a college head coach. I loved Stanford, but realistically I knew they wouldn't take a chance on a young coach—particularly a young black coach—whether that individual was ready or not. Just as I expected, they hired Paul Wiggin, a Stanford alumnus who had never been a head coach but had plenty of professional coaching experience.

Like in Walsh's case in 1977, Wiggin had to make a swift transition from pro football—where most of his contacts were—to the college game. He didn't have the luxury of bringing an assembled staff from a previous college program. He followed others' recommendations and invited me to work as his offensive coordinator. My college coaching background and familiarity with Stanford and the PAC 10 made me a logical choice to be a coordinator.

Because I wanted the head coaching job, I admit feeling a bit like a vice presidential nominee. At first I felt insulted, but in time it made sense. Once I got the pride and ego factors out of the way, I realized the best place for me at age 31 would be up sitting in the press box as Stanford's offensive coordinator.

Despite having its third head coach in as many seasons, this Stanford team had tremendous talent and high hopes. On offense alone we had four future NFL stars—John Elway was our quarterback, going into his sophomore year; senior Kenny Margerum was at wide receiver; junior Darrin Nelson was at running back; and senior Brian Holloway was at left tackle.

Rod Dowhower was the quarterbacks coach in 1978 when we were recruiting Elway. I went down with Rod to scout a couple of Elway's games in southern California. He was the best-looking high school quarterback I'd ever seen. His arm, his ability to run, his instincts on the field all were superb. He was an ideal fit for Stanford, too, because he was a good student, and the university already had prepared All-American quarterbacks like John Brodie and Jim Plunkett for strong NFL careers. It helped our chances of landing Elway when the guy who had recruited him the most, Dowhower, was selected in 1979 to replace Walsh as head coach.

Unfortunately, as great a career as John Elway had, he never played with a Stanford team in a bowl game during his record-setting four years. His last game was the famous one with Cal when Stanford's band came on the field prematurely in the closing seconds, and Cal used a Three Stooges-like rugby-style play to win the game. As you can imagine, that game is still highly disputed and controversial for Stanford fans and pleasing to Cal fans.

The 1980 season was my first and only one as Stanford's offensive coordinator. With Elway in command, our offense broke several PAC 10 records, but we didn't have the outstanding season we expected.

Having Elway as our offensive focal point for two more seasons made it easier to go out in the winter of 1980-81 and recruit. Then another twist of fate changed my plans. Opportunity called, and for the fourth time in five years, I was moving to take a better job. That is if you consider becoming the head coach of the 1981 Northwestern University football team a better job. Many people didn't.

The wheels were put in motion when my friend, Doug Single, Stanford's assistant athletic director, was approached and offered the job of Northwestern athletic director. Single was a former coaching mate of mine when we were assistants on Bill Walsh's first Stanford team. Just two years removed from coaching, Doug was getting his shot to be an athletic director at a Big Ten school. Northwestern had a lot of problems, not the least of which was a football losing streak that stood at 20 and was fast approaching the NCAA Division I record of 28. Single's football background and ties to Stanford impressed Northwestern officials, and from day one, the job was his for the taking.

When Single decided to accept the job, he called me and told me he wanted me to become his head football coach. I was surprised, thrilled, flattered and proud. I believed I was ready to run my own program, but I thought it might take a few years for the chance to present itself. After all, no African American had ever been head coach of an NCAA Division I football team. Single knew the football job would take someone with broad shoulders who was tough enough to take some hits as he put his program in place.

We were assured that the official search process that would follow for both jobs was a formality. Northwestern would turn to a couple of Stanford guys. The hope was that we could bring along some California gold dust to get the Northwestern athletic program off life support. The jobs called for positive thinkers who were familiar with the problems. If Stanford could win in football with its excellent academic reputation, we believed that Northwestern could as well. We set out to incorporate some Stanford pride and can-do attitude.

Although Northwestern regularly fielded competitive teams in women's sports and many of its men's sports, it had just two winning football seasons since 1963. A lot of people thought a private school like Northwestern, with its tougher academic standards, could never win in football. Some people even said they should be like neighbor schools DePaul or Loyola and drop football, turning their emphasis to basketball. Some felt the time had come to get out of the Big Ten and join a less challenging conference. No thanks to the losing streak, football attendance was low and few games were competitive for even one quarter. There was a definite group that wanted to give up. Fortunately, there was an even stronger group that wanted to keep on trying.

A factor that probably helped save Northwestern football from the chopping block when I took over as coach was a desperate need for new campus athletic and recreation facilities for all students. The school knew if it dropped football, it would never be able to raise the kind of money it needed for facilities. Many of the best donors have strong feelings for the tradition and visibility football brings to a major university. So Northwestern needed to jump-start football to give a fundraising campaign a realistic chance at succeeding.

That wasn't all that was at stake. Outsiders worried that if I failed at Northwestern, like so many others before me had, it wouldn't help the cause for another African American to be hired anytime soon at another NCAA Division I-A school.

My family had mixed feelings about leaving California. My former wife knew she would miss her friends and the weather. My daughter, Patti, then 14 and going into high school, was extremely excited. She never has been a big fan of California, and was hoping the diversity of the Evanston, Illinois, community would be to her liking. We were only in Evanston one week when she told me, "Dad, you have to stay here at least four years until I finish high school, because I love it." She still is close today with some of her high school friends. Jeremy was going into the fifth grade and was in love with the basketball opportunities Evanston presented. Our house was 10 minutes from the Northwestern campus, 10 minutes from Evanston Senior High School and one minute from Central Park playground—a popular place for sports activities. We had a constant flow of teenage visitors in those years.

I knew a lot about the Big Ten and its recruiting area through my various experiences at the University of Iowa. I was a recruited athlete, I played football, I was a volunteer coach and I was later a full-time position coach with the Hawkeyes. Things hadn't changed much in the four years since I last worked in the Big Ten. I understand the awesome challenge of trying to break through against the likes of Michigan, Ohio State, Michigan State, Purdue, Iowa and Illinois.

The bottom line was this—Northwestern had not made the commitment in finances and facilities to really build a successful program. It was up to Single and me to try to teach them what it would take to really be successful.

I said many times the only difference between the "N" on the Northwestern players' helmets and the "N" on Nebraska players' helmets could be defined by expectations and commitment. If you're unsure, you won't win. If your players and your entire organization aren't pulling together and doing all the things it takes, you won't win. The key to Stanford's success was to want to do it all. Win in the classroom and win in the sports arena—again, expectations and commitment.

One of the things I tried to get the administration, alumni and fans to understand was that if you did a comparative analysis of facilities and budgets of all Northwestern sports, the women's sports were in the top four or five consistently in the Big Ten. The same for basketball and most sports. Northwestern compared well in all sports but football. If you measure all those things where you can show your commitment levels—like facilities, budget and personnel—football was ranked last.

Northwestern simply had a hard time believing in football. There were some definite whispers that you can't win without the black student-athlete. The question in some minds was whether or not there would be enough black student-athletes who could qualify for admission. If not, would the university be forced to compromise its high academic admissions standards in order to win? You could see how a coach might lobby for special admissions consideration for his sport, but I told Northwestern over and over again such action was unnecessary. In fact, we felt the better the student, the better the chance we had of recruiting them.

The thought of not winning a game was never part of my plans. I was wrong. We had our best chance to win in the first game of the season against Indiana University. Trailing 21-0 in the second half, we scored two touchdowns to make it 21-14, then were in position to score again. At that point, a victory was in reach, and we knew what we had to do. Once we scored, we would go for two points—foregoing the tie that could have broken the losing streak—and win the game. The two-point attempt was a swing pass to the fullback to the right flat. He was expected to catch the pass, shield the ball from any defenders and quickly get into the end zone. For at least two weeks in training camp, I had been trying to get our starting running back to catch the ball and carry it in his outside arm. We could not seem to break him of his habit of carrying the ball in his left or inside arm. We tried patience and we tried screaming, but to no avail.

After our third TD of the game pulled us within 21-20 in the waning minutes, we had no option but to seek the win with a two-point conversion try. We called time out and talked about what to expect from the defense. "We have run this play many times," I said. "Let's execute and win. A few key points to remember: 1) Tight end—look for the linebacker covering the fullback and get in his way. 2)

Quarterback—expect the blitz from the strong safety. Make a solid throw to the fullback who will be the hot receiver. 3) Fullback—be alert for the blitz, watch for the ball early, catch the ball and carry it in your outside (right) arm into the end zone."

Every thing went according to plans, except the fullback kept the ball in his inside arm (left arm), he was therefore off balance and stumbled and he was stopped short of the end zone. If he had done what he was coached to do, he would have scored the winning points.

We lost the game and went on to lose the last 10, too. We were never close again in 1981. I never blame a loss on someone, because a team never really wins or loses a game because of one play. But I had to shoulder the blame for this loss. It was not the player's fault that he did not do what he was told to do. It was not the running backs coach's fault. It was my fault. I was the one who had him in the game because I mistakenly thought that being the best player was enough. However, he consistently carried the ball in his wrong arm in practice, so why did I expect him to carry it in the proper arm in the game? I learned a valuable and costly lesson in that first game as a head coach. Since then, I know what to expect from any player who goes on the field. Players play like they practice. If a player didn't think he needed coaching, he was playing for the wrong coach.

As the losses continued, we all tried to stay upbeat. I worked my players hard and they all gave 100 percent. Every week with each new game and opportunity to win I'd say, "This could be the week." But with each game we lost, we fell further and further back. Besides the 21-20 defeat vs. Indiana, the only game we stayed close at 60 minutes came against Minnesota and resulted in a 35-23 loss. We went 0-11 and finished in last place.

I think my lowest point as a college coach came when we lost to Wisconsin that first year in Madison, 52-0, to drop to 0-8. That tied the NCAA Division I record for consecutive losses at 28 held by Virginia (1958-61) and Kansas State (1945-48). I think it was October 31, and the Badger fans are well known for their antics on Halloween weekend. You might say we were like Charlie Brown in the classic Peanuts story about the Great Pumpkin—we got rocked. A 61-14 home loss the next Saturday against Michigan State put us alone in the record book, and a 70-6 loss at Ohio State the next week took the losing streak to 30. We finished 0-11, but the next season we improved to 3-8.

My most difficult time in all my years of recruiting came in the winter of 1981-82. The big thing I asked my staff to do was to go out and recruit with confidence, not in shame. We had to go out, look a recruit in the eye, shake his hand, be up front about what we were trying to accomplish, and convince him we can reach our goals if we could get them to join our team. You hoped they knew your record and wouldn't bother bringing it up. But many players or parents who weren't following the records closely would ask that dreaded question —"What was your record last season?" You just had to say, "We didn't win a game, we were 0-11, but we're going to be better next year, and if we get you, we'll be a lot better." That was tough, but we never backed down or tried to make excuses.

I didn't feel discouraged. I knew I was being tested. My grandfather, Toots, went to work before 5 o'clock in the morning at the same job for 45 years. Now that's a hard job. I was just in a situation that required a lot of guts and determination, and that's what I was going to give. No excuses. My father worked two jobs most of his life.

We lost our first three games of 1981 before scoring a 31-6 win at home over Northern Illinois. That probably was my highest moment, at the time as a college coach. We played well and beat them soundly. Our band members were able to put their hats on backwards. There was jubilation throughout the town—the streak had ended! We were OK. Lost in the all the hoopla was the fact it was my first win as a head coach.

The locker room was finally a happy place on a Saturday. The emotion was great. As a coach you try to bring a certain uniqueness whenever the situation presents. You had to try a lot of motivational tools at Northwestern, because we were outmanned and outgunned most of the time. So after this victory, I called the team together, climbed up on a table and congratulated them. Everyone was fired up. Then we did our postgame prayer. When that was over, I stared out into that happy group of players, and did an impromptu swan dive off the table. Fortunately, my players caught me. We had a lot of fun with the swan dive, and whenever we won, I would give my team another one.

When the losing streak ended, the media attention was amazing. I was flown to New York and appeared on both "Good Morning America" and the "Today" show on the same day. It has to be a hot or inspirational topic when these shows agree to share a guest. They are in such fierce competition they almost never interview the same person. But I sat in with David Hartman at "Good Morning America," then was driven by limousine to the "Today" show where I was interviewed by Bryant Gumbel. The losing streak obviously was a hot topic, although it was also a negative story. I had to keep the focus on how we were going to rebuild the program. It was up to me to put as positive a spin on the situation as I could. But it's something you have to face often when you're trying to turn a lagging program into a consistent winner.

When we ended the losing streak and started gaining some momentum, Northwestern announced a $20 million fundraiser to improve the overall campus athletic facilities. Things got better around campus, although I never felt they made a strong enough commitment to improving the football facilities.

We didn't have a lot of great players, but we received a lot of great effort. Some of the guys who helped us turn it around were quarterbacks Sandy Schwab and later Mike Greenfield; Steve Tasker, a talented receiver and running back from Dodge City Community College who was Mr. Versatility for us on our special teams and still is playing in his 14th NFL season; John Kidd, who's still punting in the NFL; and lineman Chris Hinton, one of the most talented players at Northwestern in years.

When I arrived at Northwestern in late December of 1980, Hinton had just finished his sophomore season as a tight end. He was a very affable guy who went by the nickname "Yogi Bear." The only problem was that this wasn't a very good football program, and here was its best player who from all reports wasn't playing up to his potential. Before training camp in 1981, I called him into my office and told him I was very disappointed. I gave him John Robinson's telephone number and told him he ought to transfer to USC. Then he could be around some real players and might live up to his potential. I gave him about a week and a half, and he called me twice, but I wouldn't let him come back. I was starting to get nervous he wouldn't call back again. But he kept up his appeals, and I eventually gave him a chance to prove himself. In the 0-11 season, Hinton played OK, but I liked to remind him he didn't get a single vote for all-conference. He had pretty much established to everyone that boy, Northwestern was a bad place for him to be because he never developed. So when he became a senior and had no options of transferring within Division I or II, I turned up the heat. I moved him from tight end to left tackle. He grew up even more as a senior, and helped us break the streak and finish 3-8. He received some All-American mention, was the No. 4 pick in the 1983 NFL draft, and became a perennial Pro Bowl pick during a 10-plus year NFL career.

The guys we recruited all graduated and left college with the right attitudes about life and about sports. I think they felt positive, even though it was tough in the beginning. They could look in the mirror and say they paid the price and know they did the best they could. They developed a special pride in Northwestern. Jeff Robinson is a former Wildcat who works for us now with the Vikings in personnel. We recruited him to Northwestern out of Minneapolis. He still keeps in contact with a lot of those guys from our teams. When Northwestern got it going under Gary Barnett a couple of years ago, these guys all went to the games and most of them even went to watch Northwestern play in the Rose Bowl. The guys from my era at Northwestern know they laid the foundation for this later success. They were the ones who saved the program from being eliminated. Those guys held it together. We showed that Northwestern could compete in football in the Big Ten.

Francis Peay, my replacement as head coach, continued to battle and kept the program from sliding backwards, then it took Barnett three years to put it all together. Northwestern didn't win more than four games in his first three years, then in 1995 the Wildcats hit it big. Getting a player like running back Darnell Autry was huge, as was their ability to put together a physical defense. They are there now. They persevered, worked hard and they believed.

My experience at Northwestern reaffirmed something I learned long ago—you have to leave your ego out of the picture when you coach. You have to believe in yourself and understand that if you work hard and don't win a game, that doesn't mean you can't coach.

After five years at Northwestern, we were never able to get over the hump. We won 10 games over the last four seasons, and we only finished in last place in the conference once. I felt I had done all I could do as one coach. If you stay in that situation too long, you really forget what it's all about.

I had an opportunity to go back to the 49ers in a prominent role. Bill Walsh wouldn't name an offensive coordinator, but I had the responsibility. I know Bill feels he saved me by bringing me back to the 49ers in 1986, but Bill needed me, too. By 1988, I was Walsh's trusted chief of staff. I was in charge when Bill was absent. During games, I was the guy on the headset up in the booth talking to Walsh.

Going back to the NFL and working in an organization run by Walsh meant a chance to get back into a winning situation. That was a terrific coaching staff—Mike Holmgren and I worked up in the press box alongside defensive coordinator George Seifert. We had guys like Ray Rhodes and Sherman Lewis on the sidelines. We really had it going on, and we won a lot of games. It was good for me to get back into that situation.

There's nothing like winning. Later when I went into Stanford as head coach, that's the message I tried to bring. They had fallen on some hard times but I brought the mindset that we could win. It was the same message that helped guys like Bill McCartney turn around Colorado and Bill Snyder jump start Kansas State. The lesson is that you don't have to compromise—just do your thing. If you really believe in your approach and stick with it and get administrative and fan support, you'll get the players and eventually you will win.

# GHOST CHASING

*"When you give up your dream, a little part of you dies."*

—Unknown

*"I always dreamed of being a head coach
in the National Footall League."*
—Dennis Green

In 1988, I was nearly 40 years old, and I'd reached a point of frustration in one aspect of the coaching profession. I'd had too many experiences in what I call "ghost chasing," where you chase something that realistically doesn't exist. Teams would call you and interview you for a head coaching job, but in the end it was clear the interest was more out of courtesy than seriousness. The media would put your name in the running for every prominent head coaching opening, even though the reality of your chances didn't match the hype.

I took some of it as a compliment, but being high on the list of qualified black coaches doesn't mean much if the list never turns over. It was our version of "Reality Bites" in the dog-eat-dog world of coaching opportunity. Like Cheers regular Norm Peterson, African American coaches were wearing milk-bone coaching shorts.

The process has been called institutional racism, where the established network of white administrators and coaches perpetuate the status quo. They hire their friends or people recommended by friends. Things have slowly started to improve in the 1990s, although there's still a long, long way to go. But in the 1980s and earlier, prominent coaches in football—college and professional—were almost exclusively white. Not enough blacks were in the right circles, and not enough administrators had the guts to take chances and be bold in hiring. It makes it hard when schools are afraid to go outside the box. Pro and college basketball had a better track record of hiring black head coaches, but like football, major league baseball in the 1980s still had an embarrassing lack of African Americans in managing and executive jobs.

My frustration started back with the San Jose State job opening in 1978 and happened at Stanford with its openings in 1979 and '80. My opportunity to be head coach at Northwestern was an exception, of course. While I was qualified and proved my ability in my five seasons there, I realize that without my friendship with Doug Single, I probably wouldn't have been hired there, either. A lot of people even said the symbolism of my hiring at Northwestern was diminished because it suggested that the only place where a black man could get an opportunity was in a place where he was destined to struggle.

There I was in the late 1980s, with a better coaching resume and the full maturity of having been a major college player, assistant coach, head coach, recruiter and an NFL assistant. I had proven I could juggle the myriad of head coaching tasks from working with players, a coaching staff, administrators, media, alumni and fans. With no disrespect to my brethren in high schools and smaller colleges, who do some of the best teaching in the game, I also had worked at the highest levels, whether in the Big Ten and PAC 10 or under Bill Walsh's guidance with the 49ers.

But my ghost chasing continued. In 1988, I was courted but not hired for head coaching jobs by the Los Angeles Raiders and the University of Illinois. One of the problems in our profession is that there's no criteria for hiring head coaches. I pursued the Stanford job in 1980, but came in second to Paul Wiggin. Paul is a Stanford alumnus, a nice guy and has a good professional football resume, but he had never coached one down of a college football game before he came back to Stanford. Just as it's difficult for a college coach to jump into the NFL, it's also hard for a lifelong pro coach to become a college head coach. Sure enough, the Stanford program that Bill Walsh had revitalized and led to a 9-3 record with a No. 15 national ranking in 1977 had fallen on hard times by 1983.

The best of my ghost-chasing episodes came in January of 1988. I was in Mobile, Alabama, scouting at the Senior Bowl all-star football game. Most all-star games are like conventions, a chance for guys to get some important work done by day and hang out, socialize, shoot the breeze, tell war stories, and reminisce about old times at night. It was kind of like a big indoor fishing trip without the mosquitos. We scouted players and wrote reports during the day. Then we hung out in the lobby, hung out in the restaurants, got in late and got up early. On one Wednesday night I got back to my room around midnight. I had about five phone messages slipped underneath my door, and the light was blinking on the phone. It was obviously something serious, because the messages were from home and from some of my closest friends. I picked up the phone to check those messages, and there were more than a dozen.

I feared something bad had happened to one of my children or to another family member. It just scared the hell out of me, and my heart raced as I dialed my home telephone number. My son Jeremy answered.

"Where are you calling from?" he asked.

"I am in Mobile. What do you mean, where am I?"

"We keep getting calls from people saying you're in Los Angeles. Have you been watching television?"

I clicked on the TV and right then Erik Clements from ESPN showed a picture of me and said, "Dennis Green is expected to be named the head coach of the Los Angeles Raiders tomorrow at a press conference." The report went on to say I was reportedly at a Los Angeles hotel registered under my own name, and I was the logical choice. Al Davis was going to make the announcement tomorrow.

I assured my son that while I'm not the smartest guy around, I could tell the difference between L.A.—Lower Alabama, and L.A.—Los Angeles, and I was very much in Sweet Home Mobile, Alabama. There was probably some paper-clip salesman on a business trip in Los Angeles named Dennis Green who was in for a long night of phone calls at his hotel room, though.

I hung up, searched the messages and returned a call from my friend Willie Brown, who was working with the Raiders as an assistant coach. He asked me where I was, and I started to wonder if I was doing the old Abbott and Costello bit, "Who's on First?" I assured him I was in Mobile. I thought it was odd that none of the Raider coaches came down to the Senior Bowl, and I asked him what was up. He said the word in Los Angeles was that Tom Flores had just quit as Raider head coach, and everyone said I was going to get the job.

I assured Willie I hadn't talked to Al Davis, period. His name wasn't among my pile of messages, so obviously either someone else was getting the job or Al was not going to have the kind of press conference that everyone expected.

I had messages from Ted Koppel's "Nightline" office, Bryant Gumbel's "Today" show office and "Good Morning America." When I talked to one of the "Nightline" producers the next morning, I told him I wasn't in Los Angeles, I was still in Mobile, and I didn't know what Al Davis was going to do. He pressed on: "All of my sources tell me you are the man picked to be the first African American head coach in the NFL. When you get the Los Angeles Raiders job will you commit to come on "Nightline"?"

"Nightline"? I don't watch that show unless there's some really big issue, and now they wanted me as a guest. This was getting pretty unbelievable. I almost was waiting for a film crew from Dick Clark's Bloopers and Practical Jokes show to storm in and say "Gotcha," or Allen Funt to walk in and say, "Smile, You're on Candid Camera."

Apparently Al Davis, in his marketing flair, had announced a Thursday press conference of monumental and historical importance. The reporters, in their infinite wisdom, began analyzing it. There's no doubt that Flores was under the gun. Even though he'd won a Super Bowl championship, the Raiders had just completed a disappointing season. People were talking about changes.

The whole Los Angeles scene had not gone well for the Raiders since they abruptly moved from Oakland. The crowds were not what they should have been, and the word was that people who made promises to Al Davis broke virtually all of them. It seemed logical that Al was trying to stop the bleeding and make a change. The Raiders had always hired from within the organization, though, and it was a big part of their tradition. Whether in Oakland or Los Angeles, Al strived to make the Raiders a team to be reckoned with. Davis didn't seek a pure image for his team, and seemed to relish the Raiders' take-no-prisoners image. What Lombardi said (or didn't actually say) about winning in eight words, Davis said in only three: "Just Win, Baby."

I knew I was not in Los Angeles, and I knew I wasn't getting the job, at least right then. But I was hopeful that at that afternoon's L.A. press conference, Davis would say the search was on and that I was in fact a top candidate. I fell back into the trap of ghost chasing.

We were on the practice field that Thursday morning at the Senior Bowl when Wayne Fontes, who went on to become head coach of the Detroit Lions, related a funny story to me. He had just had a guy walk up to him and whisper, "I got a hot tip. Denny Green's in L.A. right now to get the Raider job, and there's going to be announcement today." Wayne looked over at me across the way and waved. He pointed to me and suggested to the tipster, "Why don't you go tell Denny Green that?"

I learned later that Al Davis and Tom Flores indeed sat at the main table at the Thursday press conference. Al Davis wanted a great turn-out, and he wasn't disappointed. There were more people assembled on that day than at the press conference when the Raiders moved to Los Angeles. The social and historical significance of an African American being hired head coach, possibly during this press conference, turned it into an even bigger national story. Everyone was anticipating Tom Flores stepping down, but when Dennis Green or someone else wasn't there with Davis, it added to the mystery of the day.

Al Davis took the podium and talked about the great Raider tradition, all the memorable victories, the Super Bowls, the influence that the Raiders had when the National Football League and the American Football League merged. Then he announced that Tom Flores, one of the greatest Raiders of all time in his roles as an assistant coach and head coach was stepping down after many great years of service.

Everyone waited for the other big announcement, but it never came.

"Al, are you going to name a successor today?" a reporter asked.

Al responded, "I will not."

It was like a balloon had just burst. The questions continued. "Is Dennis Green a leading candidate for the job?"

Al reportedly responded, "I have a lot of respect for Dennis Green. He is one of the candidates for the job."

"Are you going to hire from within the Raider organization as you've done in the past, or are you going to hire somebody from the outside?"

Al said it didn't matter, and hinted that there was a distinct possibility he might select somebody outside of the Raider organization as head football coach.

I was excited when I heard how the press conference played out. I had always had respect for Al Davis, and to this day consider him, along with Bill Walsh, among the smartest and toughest football executives in the history of the NFL. Even though I heard the horror stories —"Al is such a dominating and domineering personality that his head football coach has little authority... the coach can't make a decision... everything has to be Al Davis' way..."—the opportunity to work as Al Davis' head coach was a dream. I looked forward to talking with him and judging for myself whether I could work well with him.

I learned later that Al expressed interest in me because of my long-time association with Bill Walsh. I received a call  from Raider executive George Karras, who spoke of Al's interest in me, and we started the process of talking philosophy. Eventually I would get two face-to-face visits with Al Davis. The first was brief in Indianapolis in early February, where we quickly covered a variety of subjects.

Nearly three weeks passed and nothing had happened. Normally in the NFL, when a job opens up after the season, it is filled within two weeks. If it takes three weeks, you've got a president or general manager who procrastinates. If it takes more than that, you've got a guy who doesn't know how to make decisions. The exception to that rule would be Al Davis, who knows how to make decisions but has his own ideas on why something should take as long as it does.

Bill Walsh, who knows Al well, was among several people who kept telling me that I was going to get the job. Assistant coaches, media people, friends—everyone kept saying I was going to get the job. I kept seeing in the papers that this job was going to come down to Dan Henning and Dennis Green, then Joe Bugel and Dennis Green, then somebody else and Dennis Green, and then finally Mike Shanahan and Dennis Green. Mike had been an assistant coach with the Denver Broncos.

After maybe six or seven weeks, it came down to Mike Shanahan and me. I flew to Los Angeles to meet with Al Davis. I remember that meeting distinctly. George Karras picked me up at the airport and took me to the Raiders' facility, which was clearly unimpressive. I thought it was a bad idea that they renovated a closed-down grade school as their headquarters. It was just too big, and everything was too spread out. People were housed in two different buildings, which could have a negative effect on team unity and chemistry. There's nothing wrong with tight quarters. In small offices, people work side by side very effectively as long as they're focused on their jobs.

The meetings with Al went well. We talked a lot about personnel. I think some of our biggest disagreements came in organization. I felt that the old style of practicing offense on Wednesday, and defense on Thursday and special teams on Friday was outdated and really wouldn't work in modern times. I suggested:

- getting your game plan ready for both offense and defense on Wednesday
- incorporating your base defense and offense on Wednesday, as well as your nickel pass defense.
- covering long passing situations and your nickel defense on Thursday, along with short yardage, goal line, red zones and the two-minute drill.

- reviewing and polishing what you've already introduced on Friday. I also advocated practicing special teams every day for 30 minutes prior to practice, but Al scoffed at that idea.

Al had a more methodical approach to game planning. My approach was fast and explosive. I felt we should spend a lot of time looking at film in the off season. When it came to a game plan during the season—you have to be decisive. I hated seeing coaches who were too fatigued to get on the field, ruining a crisp practice. My opinion has been that practice is what it's all about. If you work hard and concentrate during practice, you're preparing yourself to succeed in the game.

Al and I disagreed over scheduling. I gave him a specific, daily schedule from February until the first game. I went through in detail, and explained how we assembled our coaching staff. The first thing Al objected to was vacations. He couldn't understand how taking a job in February you're going to get a vacation three weeks later—a vacation for one week then in the last part of February, a week vacation in the last part of March, and then the NFL draft in April. You would do mini-camps in May, take another week of vacation in May, take two weeks vacation in June and one week in July. Al added it up. Six weeks vacation in a six-month period of time.

I recognized Al's concern, but I also knew that if you were working hard, coming in the office at 7 a.m. and working 10-12 hour days, some extra time off was good for the mind and soul. I also liked to give guys Fridays off to spend with their families or get out of town for a weekend. Al thought I was soft, but I assured him that I was not. I just liked to work hard and then play hard. I wanted my staff to get away from football, think about other things and then come back and dig in full speed.

We looked at a lot of film. I thought Al was picking my brain for what we did with the 49ers. We also talked about defensive philosophy, how we liked to play nickel defense, and the combination coverages. I tried to get Al to understand that being a guy who worked for Bill Walsh, I understood the Raider foundation. I was tough enough to handle the challenge. I was tenacious enough to make sure things were going to happen. I told him for the Raiders to be successful from then on, it would require changes. Al wasn't sure about wholesale change, and thought the head football coach was the only problem. I disagreed.

I countered, "You need to find new road map. If you are going somewhere and you want to get to L.A. and you are leaving from Chicago you are going to have to use a road map. If you rely on an outdated road map, using the same techniques you're probably going to end up in Seattle. A new driver, a new map, from Chicago to L.A., you get there as soon as you can be there."

At the end of the day, Al and I said our goodbyes. He told me to stay in touch. George Karras drove me to the airport for my flight back to San Francisco. As George and I were en route to the airport, the car telephone rang with a call from Al Davis.

George answered, and Al told him to bring me back. George smiled at me. I thought maybe I was one of his favorites for the job. We headed back to the facility. I was excited. I felt, this was it, this was the end of the ghost chasing, this was opportunity, I was the best man for the job. I was going into an organization that loved to win. The kind of organization that tells a head coach, "Whatever it takes, I'll give you the money you need. Whatever it takes for you to be successful." I thought I had the job.

But when we got back to the facility, I learned that Al was just playing head games. Al said, "Denny, I have one more question on that nickel defense..." Even though I was let down, I didn't let it show. At age 39, I had too much pride to let Al see how disappointed I really was. We talked about the nickel defense, and how to go to combination coverages. The San Francisco 49er defense under defensive coordinator George Seifert was great. We had shutouts, and teams sometimes would go zero-for-12 on third-down conversions. George was a brilliant and magnificent defensive coach. He had techniques that were complex and unique. It appeared that Al Davis had me brought back to pick my brain some more.

In the end, I didn't get the job—it went instead to Mike Shanahan. Al Davis decided to hire someone from the AFC West. In this case, Al was getting a good assistant from his chief rival opponent, the Denver Broncos. I thought the Kansas City Chiefs were his biggest opponents. But Denver had been to a few Super Bowls. Unfortunately, Al Davis and Mike Shanahan were at each other's throats from the beginning. I could have become the first African American coach in the National Football League, but the circumstances were not right.

The timing was absolutely terrible for me. After a year and a half, Shanahan was fired and Art Shell got the job as the Raider coach. Art had been a great Raider player, and a pro football Hall-of-Famer. He was in the organization as an assistant coach before he was elevated by Al Davis to become head coach. He became the first NFL African American football coach in modern times.

After the Oakland ghost chase, I started questioning whether I would ever have equal access to the better head coaching jobs in football. I was happy with my present duties with the 49ers, but I didn't expect the opportunity to be a head coach there any time soon. There was some speculation that if Bill Walsh won one more Super Bowl—which he did that next season—he would retire and go out on top. Even though I was in effect his offensive coordinator, I expected Seifert, who had been there longer, to be picked to replace Bill, which turned out to be the case. So later in 1988, having been in coaching for 18 years, I decided to explore the possibility of leaving the coaching profession.

I interviewed with Golin/Harris Communications in Chicago. It's regarded as one of the top advertising and marketing companies in the country and has an impressive office on Michigan Avenue in downtown Chicago. I interviewed with Al Golin, the president and CEO—I knew Al from my time at Northwestern a few years earlier. I telephoned Al and talked about my frustration in the coaching profession. My perception in 1988 was at that time, there were no African American head coaches in the NFL, and I wasn't sure when there ever would be. I told him the business world seemed more fair and progressive for equality. My perception was in business, if you did good work, you got the promotion. Golin/Harris is a large company that worked on major accounts like McDonald's and Coca-Cola. It was considered one of the best places to work for someone with ambition.

Al was surprised at my interest, but was very receptive to it. He told me my organizational and leadership skills, combined with my instincts and my willingness to work hard would make me an excellent manager. I knew I'd have a lot to learn, but managing people is what I've always done. I felt it would have been a good match. A business with the reputation of Golin/Harris was a place that definitely would have provided the excitement level I was accustomed to. Many times the jobs coaches take after leaving the profession don't offer the same satisfaction and recognition. I felt the intensity of the big-time advertising and marketing industry would provide the pressure, rewards, challenges and the recognition that I thrived on while in college and professional coaching. I was offered a chance to work in their New York office, with the understanding I'd eventually be assigned to work near my hometown in Philadelphia.

I was seriously thinking about leaving coaching at the end of the 1988 season to join Golin/Harris. I wasn't afraid of taking a chance. I knew I could be happy and fulfilled for a long time with the 49ers, but I wanted a higher challenge. I wasn't a guy who wanted to get comfortable in just one job, anyway. I had never stayed in a job longer than five years until my present job with the Minnesota Vikings. And I don't expect to be in my present job in six years. I'm 48 now and when I'm 54, I'd like to be in a better job making more money and have all the things that come with it. That's the American way—it's called ambition.

In the end, the only reason I didn't take the Golin/Harris job was that I finally got the kind of quality football opportunity that had eluded me. Late in 1988, the Stanford job opened again and I was chosen to be the university's new head coach. I think I would have been an ideal guy for Stanford before in 1979, and I knew I was still the right guy in 1989.

# 8

# THAT SUPER SEASON

*"Denny was a young man when he joined our staff at Stanford, and he dived in and learned everything. He has been as well trained as any coach in our passing game. He is tough, strong, aggressive, organized and creative. He can judge talent. He is a solid, solid coach.*

*"He's been with me since he was 25. I feel about him as I would a younger brother. I was sensitive (to his development) because I didn't have anybody looking out for me when I was an assistant with the Bengals. (Cincinnati coach) Paul Brown was no mentor. He was selfish. I wasn't about to let the same thing happen to anybody under me. I wanted Denny to get what was due him.*

*"He's damn smart. I've had Paul Hackett, Sam Wyche and Mike Holmgren. Dennis Green is as bright—and probably brighter—than all of them.*

*"He'd call (when coaching Northwestern) and only talk about the positive, the positive, but I knew he was dying. He did an excellent job at Northwestern, but it was hopeless. I felt I was saving him when I brought him back (to the 49ers) in 1986."*

—Former 49er head coach Bill Walsh, in 1992, reflecting on his mentoring of Dennis Green

The San Francisco 49ers organization of the 1980s, headed up by president and head coach Bill Walsh, will always be regarded among the best teams in the history of the National Football League. Leaving that organization wasn't easy, but twice I encountered unique opportunities that I felt justified such moves.

Bill was always supportive and felt that career ambition was good. He tried to build a foundation in which the team was bigger than the individual, one that encouraged his coaches to pursue opportunity and growth if they were presented. It's like being in the workplace when you interview for another job—you appreciate a boss who will support you and give a strong reference and not try to hold you back for selfish reasons. You could still be loyal to Bill and really concentrate on winning, yet still try to broaden your career and expand your horizons.

As a football coach, you always try to put your players in the right place at the right time. Even though I was an assistant coach for only one of the 49ers' five Super Bowl championships, I was in the right place at the right time years ago, and feel fortunate and proud to have played a role in one of the franchise's best decisions.

There have been various versions of this story, but here's the real one. In 1979, I had just come over from Stanford with Bill when he was hired as the 49ers' head coach. It was my first NFL opportunity, and it was an exciting time. I felt particularly honored because Bill decided he could only take two guys with him from his Stanford staff to the 49ers. It's a very difficult situation when you leave a college head coaching job for the pros, because you aren't always able to bring along all the people who helped you be successful.

I was given coaching responsibilities for receivers and special teams. The 49ers had gone downhill in recent seasons, and one of our needs was at quarterback. Bill was also intrigued by a running back named James Owens of UCLA. Owens had competed in the Olympics in the hurdles and played one year of football at UCLA. He was considered one of the fastest guys anywhere. Bill sent me down to California to work him out.

"See if this guy can be a receiver," Bill told me.

So I called James Owens at UCLA, told him we wanted to work him out, and he said that would be fine. I asked if there was a decent quarterback who could throw to him for his drills. He said the UCLA guys wouldn't be available, but he mentioned a guy who had just played at Notre Dame. He now was living near Los Angeles in Manhattan Beach, and came up to work out at UCLA every once in a while. Owens figured this quarterback would be eager to participate, because he was hoping to get drafted himself.

I called Sam Wyche, who was coaching our quarterbacks at the time, and he agreed to come down with me. I'd work out James Owens, and he'd check out the quarterback. We had already made up our mind that we would draft Steve Dils to become the 49ers quarterback of the future. It was a no-brainer for Bill Walsh because Dils was an All-American for us at Stanford and already knew Bill's system. We knew what we were getting. Bill was very high on Dils—he was going to be our guy.

We told Bill that along with James Owens, we were going to work out this Notre Dame guy at quarterback, too. Bill was a little ambivalent about it, but Sam Wyche called the prospect, who was very excited to get a workout.

Everything went according to plan. The only hitch was that James Owens had problems catching the ball. And you couldn't blame the quarterback because every pass was right on the money. Yet Owens wasn't catching very many. We came away so impressed with the quarterback, we couldn't believe it. The guy had had some problems with his college coach and had only started one year, but he sure looked like a winner in these workouts.

We got back to 49er headquarters and broke the news to Bill that James Owens doesn't catch very well. Bill said, "That's no problem, you've developed other guys." And I said, "No, he *really* doesn't catch very well." I told him that despite the quarterback throwing picture-perfect passes, Owens wasn't catching them.

In fact, this quarterback was so impressive we felt obligated to tell Bill. "He looked great," I said, and it was seconded by Sam Wyche.

Bill answered, "Really? Better than Dils?"

And we said, "Yes."

So Bill decided to go down to UCLA to work out this quarterback himself. He came away agreeing with the recommendation that Sam Wyche and I offered. So instead of taking the talented Steve Dils, a player we were very familiar with, the San Francisco 49ers wound up drafting this Notre Dame grad who was living in California and seemed like an ordinary Joe to many football fans.

Dils was drafted in the fourth round by the Minnesota Vikings and enjoyed a successful NFL career as a backup. Remember James Owens, the speedy hurdler trying to become a receiver? We drafted him in the second round, and he lasted two years in the NFL. Then there's the quarterback we picked in the third round—you know all about Joe Montana. Tell me something he hasn't done.

The other part of that story was that Bill also went out to Clemson that spring to work out the Tigers' quarterback, Steve Fuller. And that's how we found Dwight Clark, our terrific wide receiver. Dwight was Fuller's favorite target. People used to think Dwight was too slow, just a big, white guy who couldn't run well. In fact Dwight could really run, so Bill worked him out, liked what he saw, and we drafted him (in the 12th round). Joe Montana and Dwight Clark obviously became the hit of the 49er rookie class of 1979 and went on to greatness.

It was 10 years later, I was in my third season back with the 49ers after the challenging five seasons as Northwestern's head coach. It was January 1989 and I had just taken the Stanford head coaching job. I thought I should have gotten the Stanford job earlier in 1979 as a 28-year-old, but Rod Dowhower got it.

I was at Northwestern in 1984 when Stanford called again. They had just fired Paul Wiggin and they were looking for a head coach. They called and asked me to interview for the job, but I told them I wasn't interested. They couldn't believe I would balk at the chance, but I told them that I knew they weren't going to hire me. I expected them to hire Jack Elway, John's father, who was head coach at San Jose State. It's amazing that 90% of the guys he recruited at San Jose State were junior college players, and only 5% of Stanford's players went to junior colleges. It didn't make a lot of sense to me, yet they were going to give the job to Jack Elway anyway. I refused to ghost chase.

Five years later, during the 1988 season, I was an NFL assistant with the 49ers when the Stanford head coaching job opened up again. They called to check my interest and convinced me I had a decent shot to be hired. Another prime candidate appeared to be George Seifert, my colleague on the 49ers staff.

Our 49ers team had made the playoffs and was hoping to reach the Super Bowl. George decided to pull out of consideration at Stanford, figuring that when the San Francisco head coaching job opened up after Walsh left, he'd get hired. (He was right).

So on January 3, 1989, I accepted the offer to become Stanford's head coach. The timing was odd for me. I was torn between the loyalty to the 49ers in finishing a job I'd started and my desire to get an immediate start at Stanford, as the prime college recruiting season had about six weeks to go. I was determined to work both jobs as long as the 49ers stayed alive in the playoffs—hopefully for four weeks until the Super Bowl game.

Usually, the logistics would make this kind of job share impossible, but because the 49ers' offices and the Stanford campus were only 20 minutes apart, I could shuttle back and forth. Stanford gave me the OK, but Bill Walsh wasn't so sure it would work. Bill recommended me for the job, and I think he was worried it would make a bad first impression. But I told him he'd have to fire me to keep me from finishing my job with the 49ers. I was doing both jobs until the 49ers' season was over.

In fact, it probably helped my Stanford recruiting because of all the 49ers' publicity and their playoff games being aired on national television. They regularly mentioned that I was the new Stanford coach, and I think that exposure helped us sign a big offensive lineman, Bob Whitfield, our top recruit.

You don't like to cause a distraction, but the 49er players were very supportive of my decision. I had never missed practice in my career, so the day I was introduced as a morning press conference as Stanford's coach, I rushed back to the 49ers for practice. The players already were warming up, and Charles Haley, who was a big practical joker, watched me hurry onto the field. Haley stands up and says, "Hey, man, what did they do, fire you already?" He said it loud enough so the whole team got a really big chuckle. The players were congratulating me, shaking my hand and saying they were excited for me. That probably said something, too, about the respect Stanford carries, especially in California.

With the 49ers, I was one of three guys who had coordinator-like duties—even though we kiddingly called ourselves head clerks or head organizers. Bill Walsh didn't give away job titles very easily. My official title was receivers coach, but I worked with Bill on the weekly game plan, did scripting for practice, directed the practices, and also had other miscellaneous tasks.

I felt lucky to be surrounded by so many bright, talented coaches and players. It was a dream coaching Jerry Rice, who many feel is the best receiver in the history of the game. He's broken virtually every receiving record. Many of those records will be hard to break when you consider Rice's longevity and work ethic. Since he's been in the league in 1985, he's never missed a football game. John Taylor was the other receiver we developed. He was starting to have a big impact playing opposite Jerry Rice.

The 49er roster in our 1988 season could be divided into three waves—a few guys like Joe Montana were still around from the 1981 Super Bowl championship squad; a larger group of guys were still there who were part of the 1984 Super Bowl victory, like Roger Craig; plus the new breed who had come in about 1985-86—guys like Haley, Rice and Steve Wallace.

Bill always believed that everyone was part of the success or part of the failure. You set goals as an individual and a team and if you met those goals, you'd all benefit together. As we say in the profession, one guy's departure is another guy's opportunity. If a team reaches its goals, a player might get a better contract or an assistant coach might get a chance to run his own program. That would open up the opportunity for a new coach to come in as an assistant to keep the fire stoked. That new guy wants his own piece of the rock. It's the same thing with the players. They will come into an organization like the 49ers and recognize the tradition of success and immediately want to establish their own success. It's a team thing, driven by individuals, just like any company. General Motors is the biggest corporation in the world. Its workers don't worry so much what their father accomplished on the job as they do how they're going to make their contribution and get their piece of the rock.

I always considered myself a leader. I was captain of most of the teams I played on and foreman on the jobs I worked when I was younger. I have a take-charge personality, and with that there's an upside and a downside. You get tremendous gratification when things go well, but the downside can be criticism and failure when you don't accomplish your goals. Of course, many people don't like that feeling of not being able to succeed. They'd rather sit back and let someone else take the heat.

I was 27 years old in 1977 when I first went to work for Bill Walsh when he was hired as Stanford head coach. He was coming off a big disappointment of not getting the Cincinnati job and felt maybe he'd be eternally passed over. He came into Stanford to prove he was the man. Even though he had not been a head coach since high school, he had all the makings to be a terrific head coach. He had not worked the college game in years and was not familiar with a lot of the coaches. So he was scrambling around a little bit to put his Stanford staff together.

I was an assistant coach at Iowa at the time and had talked to the Philadelphia Eagles the year before. Their coach, Dick Vermeil, was contacted by Bill, and he was one of the guys who recommended me. One of my former college coaches, Lynn Stiles, who was working then at San Jose State, also recommended me to Bill.

We had never met before Bill called me on the phone to discuss my interest and qualifications. At that time, I didn't think I would ever leave the University of Iowa for any job. You always have a special feeling working at your alma mater. But I really had a lot of respect for Stanford and the caliber of players they tried to get. That first discussion was a good one, and he invited me out for a visit. I went out and interviewed for the job, and I asked him about his search process. He said he'd be talking to three or four other people and he'd get back to me in a couple of weeks. But by the time the day was over he had offered me the job.

In my two years at Stanford I recruited and helped develop some outstanding players. As expected, Bill turned around the sagging Stanford football program in his two years there before his opportunity came to be the president and head coach of the 49ers. I was the first guy Bill invited to join his 49ers staff—the same day he got the job. He told his Stanford staff he'd like to bring everybody but didn't know how many guys he could bring right away. I was one of the two guys who moved with him, along with Norb Hecker. Rod Dowhower moved up to replace Bill as head coach, and George Seifert stayed to become Rod Dowhower's defensive coordinator.

I worked for the 49ers for one season until I took the opportunity to become offensive coordinator at Stanford in 1980. That job helped me land my first head coaching job at Northwestern in 1981. Bill's first two years called for rebuilding, but by Bill's third season he won the Super Bowl. Then in 1986, he hired me back to the 49ers and I stayed three seasons until my opportunity to coach Stanford came up.

People talk so much about Bill's offensive prowess, and he is an excellent Xs and Os coach. I still say his overriding strengths were: 1) he knew how to put a football team together from the organizational aspect, and 2) his willingness to deal with the tough personnel decisions you have to make when putting together an NFL roster. I think that skill explains how under his watch the 49ers got a Joe Montana in the third round of the draft; a Dwight Clark in the 12th round; a Jerry Rice as the 16th player taken in the draft; and how Ronnie Lott, who everyone expected to play cornerback, became a future Hall of Famer at safety. The list goes on and on. Those are some of the things that influenced me a lot when I went to Northwestern for my first head coaching job in 1981. I was able to take some of the things I learned from Bill with me.

Bill's 49ers coaching staff overflowed with talented and bright minds. George Seifert is one of the most amazing assistant coaches I've ever been around. During the years he was our defensive coordinator, he would sit down at his chair at 7 a.m. and he literally wouldn't get up until noon, when he might take a 30-minute lunch. Then he would come back and not move from his desk until 5 o'clock. He was almost like a mad scientist and just stay and stay and focus, focus, focus. I never saw a guy who could stay put like that, and he did that every Monday and Tuesday in preparation for that week's game. Most guys would take a walk, get some air or take a racquetball break. George had that ability to stay focused, and the results were phenomenal. He was one of the best defensive coordinators I was ever around.

We had some games in the 1987 season, when we didn't go to the Super Bowl, and in 1988, when we did, the nickel defense George designed was brilliant. It was so effective it would appear we had 13 guys on defense instead of only 11. Our players were so well drilled and had that aggressiveness to get to areas so quickly, that the opposing offense was totally inept. In fact in 1988, when I interviewed for the Oakland Raiders head coaching job, all Al Davis wanted to talk about was George's phenomenal nickel defense.

Another of our great young coaches was Ray Rhodes, who now is the head coach of the Philadelphia Eagles. He's probably one of the toughest assistant coaches I've worked with. Sometimes a personality can be strong enough to will success, will a team to victory. When you watch Ray's teams at Philadelphia—they're not one of the heavy-duty spenders and have not had exceptional talent—he's taken them to the playoffs the last two years. Literally by willing his team to win, facing down his detractors, facing down teams that had better talent, facing down games where it looked like he couldn't win yet he had to win and was able to win.

The 49ers' 1988 journey to the January 1989 Super Bowl championship began on a sour note the previous season. It was a bitter disappointment to miss the Super Bowl after 1987. We had the best record in the league and played very good football at the end of the season. But we had a disastrous playoff game vs. Minnesota where everything that could go wrong did, and we lost, 36-24. The Vikings went on to the NFC championship game but lost to Washington, 17-10—it was the closest the Vikings have been to the Super Bowl in the post-Bud Grant era.

We came back in 1988 still reeling a little bit from the year before. We had some injuries, and after a 5-1 start we hit a slump. It seems like every season has a defining moment and for this team it came in a national television game vs. the Washington Redskins. We were stuck in a four-game losing streak and were 5-5 on the season. The Redskins also were 5-5. It was Bill Walsh coaching against Joe Gibbs. Both teams had very high expectations at the start of the season, and this was a pivotal game. It was a well-played game, and we were fortunate to have the game on our home field. We won and eventually finished the regular season 10-6, even after losing the final game after we had the playoffs clinched.

After a first-round bye in the playoffs, we faced the Minnesota Vikings, who had embarrassed us the year before in the playoffs. We already had beaten them during the 1988 regular season, though, and came back and beat them handily in this playoff game.

Next we were on to Chicago for the NFC Championship game. The forecasts were warning of "Bear weather," with sub-zero temperatures at game time. It was clear that mental toughness would be the order of the day. Everyone was ruling the 49ers out, saying the brutal conditions would be too much for a pass-happy California team to overcome. What people forget is that a pro team is made up of players who grew up all over the country. The 49ers could very well have more guys who played high school or college in a northern climate than the Bears did. Take one of our stars, Roger Craig—he grew up in Davenport, Iowa, and played college football at Nebraska. Or consider Jerry Rice—he would let nothing affect the way he would perform. Maybe the Bears fans would love the atmosphere, but they don't play the game. It wasn't relevant to the game itself.

The biggest factor wasn't the weather, but the fact the 49ers were on a mission. It actually felt good to be considered the underdog. We weren't going to let anything stand in our way. It might have been the coldest playoff game in history—it had to rank up there with some of the those famous Lambeau Field ice bowls that Green Bay has hosted. But the 49ers won handily and it was on to the Super Bowl.

Those two weeks leading up to the Super Bowl became an even more hectic time for me as I juggled crucial transition tasks at Stanford with my 49ers coaching responsibilities. Because of my full plate, Mike Holmgren and I switched roles—I just concentrated on being receivers coach and Mike became the primary organizer of the offense, reporting to Bill. This foreshadowed 1989 when Bill Walsh quit and was replaced by George Seifert, who promptly made Holmgren his offensive coordinator.

That Super Bowl pitted Bill Walsh against the Cincinnati Bengals and a chance to gain another small measure of payback. Bill had spoken many times of his disappointment in 1976 after being an eight-year Bengals assistant coach on Paul Brown's staff only to be passed over as the next head coach in favor of Tiger Johnson. It was a big surprise to everyone, and Bill left Cincinnati feeling embarrassed, tremendously disappointed and let down. He then regrouped as the San Diego Chargers offensive coordinator for one year, then came to Stanford as head coach in 1977, where he spent two years. He landed his NFL head coaching job with San Francisco in 1979, and in his third season beat Cincinnati in the Super Bowl. Tiger Johnson was gone by then and replaced by Forrest Gregg. Bill finally got his revenge on Cincinnati in

that one and was hoping to do it again in the 1989 Super Bowl. Sam
Wyche, who was on our staff with the 49ers, was now the Bengals
coach. He was recommended for the job by Bill.

So it was off to Miami for Super Bowl XXIII. One thing about the
49ers during Super Bowl week—nobody moons photographers or does
TV commercials or makes music videos while dancing the Super Bowl
Shuffle. Bill was always very good about getting his players to understand it was a one-game playoff, a winner-take-all. You have to play your
best game. The pomp and pageantry are all peripheral. No matter how
many interviews you're asked to do, no matter what all the talk is about,
no matter how many corporate tents are set up, you have to play one
game. You have one chance at winning a world championship. You
have one chance to be the best team in the world. If you don't play
your best game, you'll always remember it.

One of the reasons the 49ers have been so successful in the playoffs is that while Bill stressed focus on the ultimate goal, he struck a
balance by injecting some humor at the right times. He was a master at
keeping players relaxed. He knew when to poke fun at a particular
player or coach—one he's been kidding all year—and it would bring
some laughs and some light moments to a tense time. In the 49ers' first
Super Bowl in Detroit following the 1981 season, the players came in
wide-eyed. Bill arrived early and dressed up as a bell hop. When the
49ers bus arrived at the hotel, he tried to take Joe Montana's bags.
Players always carry their own bags, and Joe didn't give in to him. It
took a minute until the players realized it was Bill, and it set a relaxed
mood.

But in meetings and in practices, it was difficult to find anything
with the 49ers that would detract from this game. This team wouldn't
allow curfew breakers, nor would it allow a guy to use the Super Bowl
as his stage to launch another phase in his career—whether it be a
comedian or anything else. There was a distinct lack of headline-mak-
ing quotes in the days leading up to the game. I know the media gets
bored easily during the two-week buildup to a Super Bowl. They always look for something to add spice to the actual game. But the 49ers
did everything they could to make sure that would not happen. We all
understood we were on a mission. The 49ers' 5-0 record in Super Bowls
reflects the fact they know how to play a single game with everything
at stake.

For me, I figured it could be the only chance I had to get a Super
Bowl champion ring and contribute to a Super Bowl team. For all I
knew it could be my final NFL game—you don't go into a job like I was
as head coach of a PAC 10 Conference school like Stanford thinking
you'll ever get a better job. I'd been around the 49ers before and had

paid my dues, and I knew this was going to be my chance. I knew I could have stayed and been a part of the 49ers' previous two championships, but I had the guts to leave the security of Bill Walsh's circle for a coordinator job at Stanford. That led to a risky move to Northwestern, where I took my lumps. I also shared the disappointment when I returned to the 49ers coaching staff and our team fell short in the 1987 playoffs. This was my chance to see if my guys—the receivers—could play their best game.

Of course it turned out to be one of the classic finishes in Super Bowl history. We scored in the final two minutes for a 24-20 victory. The Bengals had gone ahead 20-17 late in the game. There was a penalty on our kickoff return, and we started our drive on the six-yard-line. Joe Montana started his memorable 94-yard drive with 2:00 to go. Sometimes late in a game you score too early, and you leave a Joe Montana, John Elway or a Dan Marino too much time on the clock. Certainly this game proved again the least amount of time you leave Montana the better. He's done that many, many times, but this game became one of his defining moments.

This was the kind of Super Bowl victory a team feels most excited about because it was all on the line. You're on center stage with the whole world watching, and you have to display the poise and pride of a champion. With the clock ticking away, you know that one mistake —a bad pass, a bad snap, a penalty, a wrong play call, a wrong audible, a poor receiver's route or a bobbled handoff—could mean the difference between Super Bowl victory and defeat.

When we got into Cincinnati territory, still trailing by three, we had to decide whether to get somewhat conservative and be prepared to settle for a tying field-goal attempt, then play for overtime, or whether to go for the touchdown and the win, and not worry about a sack, a fumble or an interception. We got in field-goal range and knew we couldn't afford to make a mistake. But Joe Montana doesn't think that way—at times like that he just thinks, "What can I do to win the game?"

Jerry Rice made two big catches to keep the drive alive, and the winning touchdown came on a third-down play. Obviously, it was a situation meant for Jerry Rice, but sometimes he has to be the decoy. We used a play where Jerry goes in motion and breaks to the outside. We thought they would be in a two-deep zone, and they were. When Jerry Rice went in motion, that pulled the safety with him, and Roger Craig went out the opposite direction. John Taylor lined up closer to the quarterback, then broke to the middle of the field and caught a picture-perfect pass from Montana for the touchdown.

I didn't get to celebrate for very long. The next morning we flew back to California. The 49ers were busy making plans for a parade through the city. But I was on my way to Stanford to hit the job, full-steam ahead. That Super Bowl victory did provide me and my new team some momentum. It was nice to see the pride Stanford felt. I was considered a local guy, pretty well known, and popular with the media. Everyone was very excited for me. There's nothing like success to reaffirm the ideas and principles you preach.

The great memories and friendships of my 49er days weren't limited to coaching colleagues and players. Prominent sports psychologist Harry Edwards, who had just joined the 49er organization as a consultant, sat next to me on every road trip during those three years. As a west coast team, our trips were often long, and we regularly covered topics like the role of the athlete, not just the black athlete; poverty in America, not just black poverty; the education system in America. We had many discussions about key social issues that are going to have to be addressed in the 21st Century. We didn't come up with many solutions, but we always tried to take the high road.

I don't think about that Super Bowl season very often. I'm very proud of that ring, although I haven't worn it since I came to Minnesota. It's tucked away in a safe-deposit box. I figure I'm not going to wear one regularly again until, God willing, I get one with the Minnesota Vikings.

# 9

# STANFORD MAN

*"The first time I met Denny Green, I thought he was crazy. I was sick and at home from school with the flu. He had gone to my high school to see me, and when I wasn't there, he came to the house. So there's this knock on the door and I get out of bed, and there he is.*

*"He was really sure of himself. It was almost like he was turbo-charged. He started opening windows and the blinds, and then he sat down and talked to me for a long time. He convinced me to take a visit to Stanford, and I'm glad he did."*
— Darrin Nelson, telling a reporter about a recruiting visit from Dennis Green

When I was hired as head coach at Stanford in 1989, I saw more potential than I did eight years earlier when I started as Northwestern's head coach. But Stanford was still a football program in a funk. The school had a special heritage in college football history. Among the men to wear the big "S" on their coaching caps were:

- Walter Camp, a Yale graduate who helped turn a campus recreational game into a game that's become so prominent in American culture;
- Pop Warner, a giant in coaching circles;
- Clark Shaughnessy, a pioneer with the T-formation;

- Fielding Yost, a guy whose name just sounds like one a legendary coach would have;
- John Ralston, who led Stanford to back-to-back Rose Bowl berths in 1970-71;
- Bill Walsh, who's earned his place among the best to ever coach the game in the NFL.

But in 1989, the Stanford football program had lost track of what it takes to win big. The school had lost its proper commitment level.

I did some unconventional things when I took over at Stanford to try to create a winning environment. One of my first rules was to require that everyone would graduate in four years. Most college football teams require players to stretch out their school over five years to ease the time demands and gain a redshirt season for physical maturity. The major programs pay for summer school so they can keep tabs on the players and make sure they're going to class and working out. Stanford's Dean of Admissions didn't like my four-year rule. She feared it would backfire and put too much pressure on the student-athletes. But I felt the players were spoiled.

Stanford is a campus full of hard-working student-athletes with tremendous national success up and down the men's and women's sports lists. When I came back to campus in 1989, there were at least 20 Stanford athletes still competing collegiately after taking part in the 1988 Summer Olympic Games. (Stanford has won the Sears Directors Cup, a national Division I all-sport competition, the last two years for having the best overall and men's and women's NCAA team finishes. In 1996-97, Stanford set an NCAA record by winning six team championships.)

But the high level of intensity that Stanford athletes are known for wasn't displayed by the football team before I arrived. Football had just lost confidence that they could compete at the highest level. It didn't help that prior to my arrival, the university had five different head coaches in the 13 seasons from 1976-88. My goal was to take a football team regarded around campus as passive and unmotivated and make it Stanford's hardest-working team.

I came in to find a country-club atmosphere in the program. So I told the players that if they wanted to go to summer school, they would pay for it themselves. We expected our players to get a meaningful summer job. When you're young, you need to wake up early and go to work. So the guys landed summer jobs—many of them physical, outdoor jobs. In just two years we snapped the team out of cruise control and began to establish a program based on physical and mental toughness.

Much of our Stanford success was a result of an aggressive recruiting philosophy. Many people think schools like Northwestern and Stanford are at a disadvantage because of their higher admissions standards. I look at it and say there are still plenty of recruits who are top-notch students. You can't look to make excuses, and we didn't.

It's true that many elite high school players rank marginal to average academically. These are often the inner-city, skill position athletes who can have a tremendous impact on your team's success or failure. One example is what Troy Davis did for Iowa State the last three seasons.

But instead of softening the admission standards at Northwestern or Stanford to widen your recruiting pool, I believed in turning a potential negative into a positive. Why apologize for having high academic standards? We went after the very best student-athletes we could find. The competition was always intense to sign a blue-chip player who could qualify academically. If Michigan or Notre Dame was interested in a top lineman who was a B-student, why would he come to Stanford? So we had to find the very best students who also were excellent players and convince them they couldn't make any other choice than to come to our campus.

We talked up our students in other sports, our Olympians and other prominent people in the Stanford family—we called it the Stanford talk. Today, Stanford head coach Ty Willingham can talk to kids about Tiger Woods or even Chelsea Clinton picking Stanford. The kids who really took pride in their academics appreciated the fact that at Stanford they'd be seen first as a guy with a 3.30 GPA and secondly as a good football player. At other more traditional football powers, their first identity would come as a player and then, maybe, as a student.

The idea, of course, is to find players who want to win on the field as badly as they want to win in the classroom. Smart players deserve a chance to succeed and play in bowl games, too. In 1991, when we went 8-4 at Stanford, 25 of our 85 scholarship players were either in pre-med studies, computer science or some form of engineering—mechanical, electrical or civil. That's 30% of our football team. The academic loads were heavy, but we used that as a motivator. They came to college for academics and they controlled their destiny. We provided academic support when needed, but they would make themselves scholars. As coaches, we sold the concept that we could make them tough football players.

Recruiting, like the military, is one of the hardest jobs you'll ever love. The travel and the hours are hard and there are no guarantees. Finishing second on a player, like in poker, can be worse than folding early. But it reminds us why we love our profession—it's a chance to get to know so many people, an opportunity to sell your school, and to guide young men through one of the most important decisions of their lives.

The three things I was looking for as a high school senior in 1967 are the exact three things young student-athletes should be looking for now:

- You want an opportunity to get a good education. Anyone who's not interested in getting a good education is foolish.
- You want a chance to play during your career. You don't want to be an upperclassman satisfied with sitting on the bench and never making a travel squad. If the level you're at is too high for you, go to Division II, or if that's too high, go to Division III.
- You want to win. Whatever the sport you compete in, when you go out and put the time and energy as a member of a team, you want your reward, and winning is the ultimate reward.

Education. Playing. Winning. That's my recruiting philosophy in a nutshell, what I call the real deal.

In recruiting I always try to sell the school first and foremost. I believe in being honest with the players and selling the school and everything it has to offer. I wasn't selling Dennis Green, instead I was selling the young man on his own potential. Students need to understand that high school is over, and mom and dad won't be there to do things for them. They have to be willing to do things for themselves if they hope to reach their potential in college and later in life.

Too often we see the tragic cases where a young man comes into a school and it's not a real deal—he doesn't get a good education, he plays little if at all and he doesn't win. What could be worse than not getting any of the three things you went into college to achieve? So it's up to the player to set these goals and have the determination to reach them: get an education; play as early as he can in his career; do everything he can to contribute to a winning program. If he does that, it's a real deal.

At Northwestern, we tried to redshirt as many players as we could so they could get bigger, stronger and faster. At Stanford, we didn't redshirt much at all. We expected our players to come in and play at a pace where they would successfully handle academics and football. I really believe in challenging young people.

I remember recruiting Darrin Nelson—I was supposed to go see him in Los Angeles then fly out to see a recruit in Detroit. I went to Darrin's school and they said he was sick at home in bed. I didn't want to miss this appointment, because Darrin was the kind of player and student who was especially attractive to us. I got his address and figured I'd drive to his house and say hello. I knocked on the door, woke him from sleep, got him up and moving, and opened the blinds to let the sun in. He wasn't that sick. We talked about what Stanford could do for him and more importantly what he could do for himself. He could expect me to make him a better football player, but the quality of his education and college experience would be determined by how he applied himself and took advantage of what Stanford offered academically and socially.

I never like to talk too much about our football program or my philosophies until a player commits to us. I don't want to be seen as somebody just blowing smoke. But once I had them signed to a letter of intent, I would expand the message and tell them how great it will be. I had so many success stories at Stanford—guys graduated, won a lot of football games, and several went on to the NFL. On the 1997 Vikings team alone there are three guys who have achieved a lot in football and also have a Stanford degree in their pocket. Chris Walsh has been an underdog all his career, now he's standing on the threshold of being a starting receiver for us and catching a lot of passes. Ron George was a walk-on, non-scholarship player when he came to Stanford and is now playing linebacker for us. Jason Fisk is playing defensive tackle and is an important guy for our defense.

As if my first season of rebuilding wasn't tough enough, I had to deal with something few coaches do—earthquakes. When you see things shaking and see the ground give way, that will send fear through you. People on the Florida coast survive hurricanes, and in the Midwest, tornadoes and hailstorms are a way of life. But in those cases you usually can seek shelter and get "Hurricane Warnings" or "Tornado Warnings" from the U.S. Weather Service. But there are no "Earthquake Sightings" or "Earthquake Warnings." They erupt so suddenly and can't be predicted, and that's why they invoke so much fear.

I was in the two biggest earthquakes to hit northern California in the last 20 years, and by coincidence I was on the football field each time. In July of 1979, I was an assistant coach with the 49ers and we were at training camp in Santa Clara when—BOOM—it just happened. It felt like a train or a truck had roared right under the ground you were standing on. Some of the players instinctively dove to the ground. I tried to balance myself. Being in California just three years, I had felt some mild tremors before, but that was my first experience in a major earthquake.

The biggest earthquake in many years hit in October of 1989. The San Francisco bay area was all wrapped up in the World Series between the San Francisco Giants and the Oakland A's, and all eyes were on California. Fortunately, a lot of people got off work early to get home to watch the World Series, so when that earthquake kicked into gear, the major freeways and bridges weren't as crowded as usual.

We were in the middle of practice when I felt the ground moving. I was standing right beside this temporary tower we built for our video cameras. I looked up to the guy holding the camera and said "Hold on." He said, "What?" And I said, "Hold on—earthquake!" A lot of guys hit the ground. When something like this erupts, it seems like it lasts forever, yet it may only last 30-45 seconds. But once you feel this big, explosive roar and you feel like the earth is going to split, it's a pretty scary experience. Once it died down and we got our wits about ourselves, we resumed practice. Out on the field, we didn't have a radio or TV and we didn't know at that time how serious this earthquake was. We immediately heard fire alarms going off around campus, and it wasn't long until we heard the sounds of police, fire and ambulance sirens filling the air. So we ended practice early.

When we came inside and saw the TV reports, we were stunned to learn the extent of damage in the area. I also found out that the epicenter was just 10 miles from my home in Santa Cruz. Fortunately there were no deaths in Santa Cruz. Many houses in Santa Cruz had serious structural damage, and some were even knocked off their foundations. We had some broken glass on our largest windows, but no structural damage to our home.

Getting to Santa Cruz was another problem. My home was 50 miles from Stanford, about one mile off the coast. The only way to get there was to drive through a very treacherous mountain on Highway 17. If the weather is good, it's a beautiful drive, but if the weather is stormy or something unusual happens, it's a monster. This earthquake caused major earthslides and shut down Highway 17. That left only two routes to get to my house. One involved a lot of winding side roads, and the other added about 50 miles to the trip by driving north to Half Moon Bay, the city that Alfred Hitchcock made famous in the filming of the movie "The Birds."

It obviously was hard for the players and coaches to focus on school and football for a couple of days. We took off the next day from practice but practiced again Thursday and Friday. Our stadium was checked out pretty thoroughly and deemed safe to use, which saved us some headaches, because we were scheduled to play Utah that Saturday at home (we lost 27-24). A lot of stadiums in the area had too much damage and were ruled unplayable.

In 1990, my second season at Stanford, we traveled to South Bend to play Lou Holtz's Notre Dame team. I had played against the Irish in Iowa City in 1968, in the third game of my playing career, and even though we lost to the nationally ranked Irish, I was fortunate enough to score two touchdowns. I didn't play or coach against Notre Dame again until 1989 when my Stanford team lost, 27-17 at home. But this was my first trip to the sidelines of South Bend, Indiana, and the Notre Dame campus.

Like every major college power, Notre Dame likes to fill its home schedule with prominent universities, preferably ones who are mediocre at football. Most of the 1980's Stanford football teams fit that role. We were coming off a 3-8 finish in 1989 that included the 10-point home defeat to Notre Dame and four losses by eight or less points. We came in with a 1-3 record for 1990, including a 21-17 loss at Colorado and a 32-31 loss at UCLA in our first two games. The Fighting Irish, who held the No. 1 national ranking, stood 3-0, including close wins over Michigan and Michigan State. Holtz's team had won the national championship in 1988, was second in the final poll of 1989, and later this season would go on to lose 10-9 to Colorado for the national title in 1990. When ranked No. 1 in the nation, Notre Dame hadn't lost a home game since 1951.

As you can imagine, few people expected us to give Notre Dame much of a game. We had lost 29-23 the previous week to San Jose State, not known as a national power. In 1989 we resumed playing a home-and-home series with Notre Dame, and a glass trophy was kept by the winning school. The Irish were so sure they would win again that they didn't even bother to bring the trophy out to the sideline. We learned later it was locked in some trophy case, and nobody was sure who had the key.

When I walked the sidelines before the game, I reflected on our school's great traditions. I thought of the legendary coaches who once represented these two schools—legends like our Pop Warner and Notre Dame's Knute Rockne. But on this day it would be Dennis Green vs. Lou Holtz. Prior to our 1989 meeting at Stanford, we had coached against each other twice before in the Big Ten, when Lou was at Minnesota and I was at Northwestern, and we split those two games.

Playing a team of this caliber in the unique atmosphere of South Bend required an extra dose of that mental toughness I was trying to develop in my players. It was a situation where Notre Dame invited you into its lion's den, treated you nice with a lot of kind words, then led you to the slaughter. For all of the aura and national respect that

Notre Dame football invokes, the stadium itself, in the pre-renovation days of 1990, wasn't as impressive as you might expect. It's not even close to the beauty of Iowa's Kinnick Stadium, where I was fortunate enough to play and coach for several years.

Many times players walk into Notre Dame's tradition-rich environment, and start worrying about the ghosts of guys who played there before. But I didn't bring the team in and get on a step ladder and measure the goal posts, like a wise basketball coach did with the nets in the film *Hoosiers*. In fact, we didn't want to see the stadium until game day. We just wanted to go into South Bend and play some dynamite football.

We stayed at a motel in Michigan City, Indiana, about 45 minutes away. After we loaded up to come to the stadium, we had a police escort. The sirens were blaring, the excitement was building. Cars were getting out of the way. As we were flying down the highway to South Bend, I felt a run of emotion come over me. I felt like getting up and yelling, "Get the hell out of the way, here come the Stanford Cardinal, and we're going to take care of Notre Dame." I really felt that way going in. But it was time for our players to step up and make the noise. After a slow start, that's just what they did. It turned into a sad day for loyal Irish like Rudy's dad and all the subway alumni, and a great day to wear Cardinal.

Notre Dame took an early lead and had its crowd revved up, but then it seemed like the Fighting Irish got a little complacent. It's easy for a team ranked No. 1 in the nation to relax, especially at home against a school that had only played in one bowl game in 11 years. Right before halftime, Notre Dame led, 21-7, and had the ball near midfield. The Fighting Irish gained eight yards on first down, but we held them to one yard on the next two downs. Instead of punting, they decided to go for the first down on 4th-and-1 but we stuffed them again and took possession at midfield. It took us just five plays and about 35 seconds to get a touchdown. Ed McCaffrey, our All-American wide receiver who now plays for the Denver Broncos—the same guy who caught the tipped pass in the end zone in the Metrodome in 1996 with seconds to play to deny us a victory—caught a scoring pass, and we went back to him for a two-point pass play. Suddenly it was 21-15, and the momentum had totally swung.

Our explosive fullback, Tommy Vardell, scored three more touchdowns for us in the second half. How many visiting players can say they ever scored three touchdowns in one half in South Bend? That's when I gave Vardell the nickname "Touchdown Tommy." He's a 235-plus pounder who later was drafted in the NFL's first round by Cleveland. We relied on Vardell's physical running to grind out a 36-31 upset.

That stunning upset helped our players see that they could play with the best in college football.

Unfortunately, as often is the case in a program trying to learn how to win consistently, we let that success go to our heads. The players stopped listening and forgot the positive things that had taken us to that point. We lost three in a row—37-22 to USC, 52-16 to Washington and 31-0 at Oregon. The Oregon loss was the low point because we fell to 2-6 and couldn't have a winning season. We roared back to win our final three games of the season, then went 8-3 in the 1991 regular season.

To conclude the 1990 season, we upset Cal, our rivals from Berkeley, in the biggest and wildest game of the year by scoring the winning points with no time left on the clock. It may sound strange to an outsider, but as great as the Notre Dame upset was, there's nothing a Stanford player savors more than a victory over Cal. It's one of the best, friendliest rivalries I've ever seen. The game was always a sellout with either 75,000 or 80,000 fans. I was fortunate to win all three games I played against Cal.

I remember during our first season, one of my players suggested we change uniforms for the season-ending Cal game. I told him we would think about it. We warmed up in our usual red jerseys and white pants and when the players came back into the locker room, I had them change into red pants, which is something we never wore. I think it gave our guys an extra edge and we scored a 24-14 win to end 1989 on a positive note.

The 1990 game, at Berkeley, was wild. We trailed 25-18 and scored with 12 seconds left in the game to pull within 25-24. We went for two points and the victory, but they stopped us. Their fans stormed the field, and it was chaos. I went to the official and said, there's still 12 seconds to play, and we're not leaving until you clear the field. I don't care if it takes three hours, we're staying to finish. The announcer had to say, "Please leave the field, there are still 12 seconds left to play." They eventually moved everyone back at least to the backs of the end zones and sidelines. It took at least 15 miutes to clear the field.

That turned out to be the longest 12 seconds in Cal history. Cal got a 15-yard penalty for the unsportsmanlike celebration, so we kicked off from the Cal 45. Of course we had to try an on-side kick, and we recovered, with one second coming off the clock. We were looking at about a 50-yard field goal, so we tried one pass play. It went incomplete, but they were flagged for a late hit on the quarterback. We got the ball at the 21 and kicked a 38-yard field goal as time expired. You never give up until the game is over—as a coach you always say it, but your players don't always believe it.

I tried to have fun with nicknames for my Stanford players. Besides "Touchdown Tommy" Vardell, I gave nicknames to our offensive linemen ("The Road Warriors"), and when our 1991 team went to a bowl game, I called them "The Now Boys." That was a takeoff on the Stanford 1920's "Vow Boys," whose freshmen players vowed never to lose to USC in their three varsity seasons, and the Stanford 1940's "Wow Boys" coached by Clark Shaughnessy and included the great athlete Chuck Taylor of Converse sneakers fame and All-American quarterback Frankie Albert.

In 1991 we won eight games, missing a ninth victory in the Aloha Bowl on a TD surrendered to Georgia Tech in the final seconds. The foundation was laid and the process of believing and achieving was in full gear. Had I not taken the Vikings job in 1992, I believe we eventually would have won a PAC 10 championship and played in the Rose Bowl. There were 19 players on my 1991 Stanford team—sophomores, juniors and seniors—who now are playing in the NFL.

But a series of events over the holidays in 1991 caused me to leave a job and a school I loved. It was the kind of opportunity that every football coach dreams of, but few experience. For a football coach, the NFL offers a chance for you to compete at the top of your profession. I had received plenty of calls from NFL owners before, but I didn't think they were serious. Pittsburgh called, but I told them I thought they would hire Bill Cowher. They disagreed, but I was right. I spoke with John Shaw of the Los Angeles Rams, but I told him he would hire Chuck Knox. He disagreed, but I was right. The coaches have a pretty strong grapevine on these kinds of matters. I also didn't want to be in that ghost-chasing mode, where you get your hopes up, then are disappointed. But when I answered a telephone call from the Twin Cities, the wheels were set in motion on a legitimate adventure.

# 10
# COMING TO MINNESOTA

*"When I put together lists of things I was looking for in a head coach, Denny's name was on nine of the 10 lists. But what most impressed me was the amount of homework he had done in preparation for meeting with me, the things he prepared about himself, about the Vikings, about coaching in the NFC Central.*

*"I talked with a lot of prominent coaches. Dick Vermeil told me that Denny ran a practice as well as any coach he'd ever seen.*

*"A coach just can't be a coach anymore. They have to know the workings of the entire organization, and (know) that players represent 64 percent of our gross revenue. Jerry Burns didn't want to know that stuff. Denny does."*

—Vikings president Roger Headrick
on his hiring of Dennis Green

On December 27, 1991, I was catching my breath from an exciting Stanford football season and thinking about my 1992 New Year's resolutions. Our Stanford football team had just posted an 8-3 regular season and earned just the school's fourth bowl trip in 20 seasons. We had just gotten home from the Aloha Bowl in Hawaii where we lost 18-17 on a last-minute touchdown to the Georgia Tech Yellow Jackets in an exciting, hard-fought game.

Fortunately, my children, both in their 20s at the time, made the trip, and we shared some good family time. I still can see myself body surfing and loving every second of it. Other than the loss, the trip was great.

The telephone rang. Normally, I wasn't home in the middle of the day. I walked to the phone expecting it to be one of my brothers from out east, asking about our trip and holiday.

The voice on the other end was unfamiliar: "Dennis, I'm Roger Headrick, the president of the Minnesota Vikings. Do you have an interest in being the head football coach of the Minnesota Vikings?"

Initially, I thought to myself that the Vikings job was one I'd never contemplated, and this probably wouldn't be a serious inquiry. I was happy at Stanford, and our best seasons were yet to come. Living close to the ocean in the beautiful city of Santa Cruz, I had become a sun-worshipping, ocean-loving Californian. But I listened to what Roger had to say. The man did call unsolicited. I had received a lot of calls about jobs through the years and was getting pretty good at quickly ascertaining which were the serious inquiries, and which were token conversations.

Roger started our chat by telling me about his background. He grew up in Lancaster, Pennsylvania, 30 miles down the road from my hometown of Harrisburg. Roger told me about being in high school in the 1950s. When he mentioned the McKaskey High School district track meets, I knew we had some things in common.

I asked Roger about his NFL background. I assumed that he had been a general manager or an assistant general manager, or in personnel somewhere. If not in the pro sports then maybe in college administration, like an athletic director. I found it interesting that Roger hadn't worked in professional sports before. But he didn't have an inferiority complex about his resume. He spoke with confidence about his successful business career—he was a long-time executive for the Exxon Corporation, and prior to coming on board to run the Vikings, Roger worked as the chief financial officer of the Pillsbury Corporation in Minneapolis until his job was eliminated in the lucrative sale of the company. He told me he was one of the members of the Vikings Board of Directors and ran the franchise's operations as president. He is one of 10 people who own 9% shares in the team.

It was certainly an interesting conversation. I knew a little about the Vikings from my years with the 49ers in 1986-88. I always associated Mike Lynn, the general manager who traded for Herschel Walker, with all the team's major decisions. Mike Lynn had a reputation as a showman and self-promoter. Even though he abruptly left as team general manager earlier that year, his mark was all over the Vikings' front office. It was a Mike Lynn coaching staff, and a Mike Lynn administrative staff. It was Mike Lynn's assistant general manager, and it was Mike Lynn's personnel director. It was Mike Lynn's secretaries—everybody in the organization was there because of Mike Lynn. Roger sounded like he was in a challenging situation, like being a Republican governor trying to work alongside a Democratic-controlled House and Senate. Roger made it clear that his style was drastically different than Mike Lynn's, and he assured me the hiring of a head coach would be his call.

The Minnesota Vikings had excellent personnel in the previous five years but never were able to put it all together. Led by Jerry Burns, the 1987 Vikings knocked our 49ers out of the playoffs then played the Redskins down to the wire in a 17-10 loss in the NFC Championship Game. But Minnesota finished 6-10 in 1990 and 8-8 in 1991 under Burns, and his resignation at season's end came as no surprise.

The more I talked to people, it became clear that the Vikings were considered underachievers. Some players worried more about making the Pro Bowl than the Super Bowl. While the Herschel Walker acquisition proved costly in terms of the loss of so many future draft picks, I didn't like the fact that it gave some of the players an excuse for the team to be mediocre.

Roger emphasized that he had been on the job for one year. Unlike most NFL executives, he didn't have the usual network of friends and former team assistant coaches. He was willing—even eager—to go beyond the predictable candidates in his search for the right Minnesota Viking head coach. He wanted a coach loyal to him and one who would bring consistent winning football to the Vikings.

There were only 28 NFL teams in 1992, yet a whopping nine of them would hire new head coaches that winter—Minnesota, Green Bay, Pittsburgh, the Los Angeles Rams, Tampa Bay, Indianapolis, Cincinnati, San Diego and Seattle. Even though 67% of the NFL players are African American, only one team, the Los Angeles Raiders, had an African American (Art Shell) as head coach at that time. No black coaches were serious candidates for any of the other eight NFL openings.

The NFL grapevine said the Vikings would hire Pete Carroll, a former assistant coach. He was a finalist with me three years earlier when I was hired as Stanford head coach. Pete was an assistant coach at the time with the New York Jets but still was considered a Vikings insider. From the tone of the media coverage, it was clear that most people were lobbying for Pete. He had kept in contact with a lot of the media members in the Twin Cities and was seen as a guy who would maintain the status quo. It was assumed that Carroll's hiring would keep intact the Viking organization that Mike Lynn assembled.

Besides Pete Carroll, I asked Roger who were some others being considered. He didn't reveal all the names, but did mention two guys not in the NFL at the time— Bill Parcells, who had won a pair of Super Bowls with the New York Giants but had retired because of some health problems; and Howard Schnellenberger, who led the Miami Hurricanes to a college National Championship in 1983 and also had NFL experience.

When it was my turn to talk about myself and my vision, I assured Roger that my strength was turning around struggling programs. I would come in and make the changes necessary to turn the program around. Done right, it would create fan excitement and player loyalty. Minnesota, which finished 6-10 in 1990 and 8-8 in 1991, needed a turnaround. The Vikings had the NFL's third highest payroll, behind the 49ers and Redskins, but the money didn't produce a winning chemistry. From what I was hearing, some of the Vikings needed an attitude adjustment.

Roger cut to the chase and invited me to come out to the Twin Cities and interview for the job. Sensing that this was a unique situation that called for more investigation on my part, I agreed to an interview. I suggested we forego the Twin Cities, though, and meet instead in Chicago in three days on December 30. I didn't want the story to come out that I was shopping for an NFL job and hurt my Stanford recruiting. We each agreed to make the reservations ourselves so there wouldn't be a leak coming out of the office. I told my athletic director and president at Stanford that we had set up an "exploratory" meeting—to see if each party's goals were similar and our interests were compatible.

As I researched the Minnesota Vikings, it was clear that something was missing. I sensed that part of the team's problem could be traced to the lack of positive atmosphere and chemistry. You can't control the outside atmosphere—the media will write or say what they want, and the fans will see what they want to see. But a coach has to make sure that the inside atmosphere is solid and intact. A head coach who takes the brunt of criticism himself allows his players and coaching staff to relax and concentrate on their play, and hopefully, win.

I flew first class to Chicago and we met at the Airport Hyatt Regency Hotel. I liked having the opportunity for a confidential discussion without worrying about media. The interview went well. I was able to sell myself and make my case, and I could tell that Roger did an excellent job of listening as well as taking notes. We were relaxed. I began to think that Roger wanted to make a bold hire on his own, to establish himself and prevent a Mike Lynn return as the Vikings president. Roger had to be concerned enough to hire the best person for the job, too. As he got to know me and my references, he knew that a Dennis Green hiring would not be an Affirmative Action move.

After my three-hour interview, I thought Roger was in a unique situation—he had to hire the best man for the job, which is all I ever want in a job search. Maybe this was my opportunity to buck the odds and become an NFL head coach. That would be quite a thrill for me when you consider the NFL's poor record of hiring African Americans as head coaches and executives. Unless you can catch or run with a football, shoot a basket, sing or dance, there is an invisible but real glass ceiling on executive opportunities for African Americans in this country.

We started discussing personnel. My philosophy demands that a head coach deal in reality. If a guy can't play anymore, the coach must say, "I don't think he can still play." That's not designed to put a player down but rather to acknowledge that the head coach must be strong enough and empowered enough to make those calls. My saying is, "The best players playing at their best give the team the best chance to win."

There were some Vikings who I thought were living on reputation alone. I went on to discuss what I felt was one of my strengths: How to organize and get a team ready to win. Some of the important tasks are assembling a coaching staff, calling meetings, organizing the practice sessions, and carrying out the game plan. Believe me, when you work for a guy like Bill Walsh, the emphasis is on organization, getting your players on the field, and making sure that they have a clear understanding of what it's going to take to win. In many ways, practices should be more difficult than the game. For the game plan to work, the team must get on the field and practice the plan.

It also was clear that Roger and I related well to each other. I thought our philosophies were in sync. Throughout his career, Roger had made a lot of money and gained a wealth of knowledge of people and business. He understands what it takes to become a success. The Mike Lynn enthusiasts always underestimated Roger and assumed he would take the safe route and bring Pete Carroll back to the Vikings. But they were wrong. Roger didn't want to give control back to Mike Lynn. If Roger brought in his own man as head football coach, he could chip away at Mike Lynn's stranglehold. The battle was on.

At the conclusion of our meeting, I told Roger I enjoyed my opportunity to make my pitch. I stressed that I was still interested, and that I felt it would be a good fit. Roger told me he would be in contact soon, and I hoped he heard enough positive ideas to stay interested. We agreed that Roger would return to Minnesota and give our conversation some thought, and I'd return to California and do the same thing.

One thing I emphasized was that we couldn't continue this dance unless he was seriously thinking about hiring me. I wasn't doing this just for my ego, and I hoped Roger wasn't doing this just so the NFL knew that the Minnesota Vikings interviewed a minority coach. (Interestingly, no other minority coaches were finalists for any of the other eight NFL jobs that were open that winter.)

I received another call from Roger a few days later. He was still very much interested in me as one of the candidates. I told Roger, "If you feel I'm one of your top two or three candidates for the job, then call me back." I went through a lot of soul searching in the meantime. I already was in discussions with Stanford about a new contract. My agent/attorney, Ray Anderson, was visiting with my athletic director, trying to negotiate a raise to reward our progress. Doesn't everybody want a raise, if they do good work?

I thought we had improved the Stanford program a great deal. I was looking for some of the personal rewards that come with success. We were in the process of building a new all-sports complex and a new football building. I was involved in some heavy-duty fundraising, too. We had interest from some very influential Stanford alumni. John Arrillaga, one of the guys they call "The Land Baron of Silicone Valley," led the fundraising along with guys like John Kissick, Brad Freeman, Phil Knight, Tom Ford and Dan Elliot, who since has passed away.

There were a lot of reasons to stay in California, not to mention the excellent weather. But I was intrigued by the opportunity to coach in the NFL, trying to face down a Don Shula or a Marv Levy and prove that I could compete.

Roger called a few days later. Again he expressed that I was one of his best candidates. He said that talks with Parcells never got serious, and I thought Parcells was more interested in Tampa Bay, where the weather was better. I started to think that Pete Carroll might have the inside track. If not Carroll, then one of the assistant coaches on the Vikings' staff at the time. I told Roger I wouldn't come to Minneapolis until it was clear that I had the job. I was going to be in Dallas that week for the NCAA Convention as one of the keynote speakers. As fate would have it, Roger was going to be in Dallas, too. So we decided to sit down again face to face in Dallas.

I told Roger more people were going to have to know of my discussions. I had to update my athletic director and president that I was more than mildly interested. I didn't want things to come as a total shock if I became the head coach.

That weekend before my Dallas trip I really thought a lot about the Vikings job. As head coach, I would need to have the authority to be make the changes I deemed necessary, however unpopular those

My father, Penrose William Green II. Everyone knew him as Bus. A great man with pride who refused to bow to the stereotypes or prejudice of his time. My father was a military veteran, who died at the young age of 39.

My mother, Anna Green. A childhood romance with Bus led to their marriage after high school. She was the best mother the five Green boys could ever have had. She passed away at the tender age of 41.

My family—front row: (left to right) Bobby, Greg, me and Stan. Back row: (left to right) Our dad, mom, and brother Billy. Is it my imagination, or does it look like my mom and I are the only ones smiling.

This is my Dad, Bus, when he played football for the Harrisburg Lions semi-pro team. He was not yet 21 years old. It was 1939 and Billy and Bobby were the only two boys born at this time. My family was living in the Harrisburg housing project.

This is me in the ninth grade at Edison Jr. High School—now you can see where I got my love for football.

Here I am as an Iowa Hawkeye running back, #44, looking to break through some holes and run for daylight.

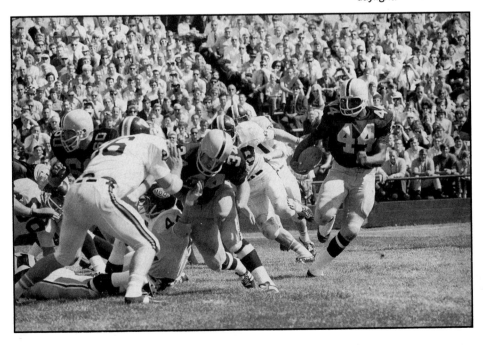

No, it's not the Five Tops, it's the Green Men. (Top row) Stan, Billy and Bobby. (Bottom row) Greg and me. I was 30 at the time of this photo. Too often large families only get together for weddings or funerals. Both of my grandmothers, Lena and Nellie, died around this time. I loved them both very much because they helped me grow up to be a man.

Here I am with a catch during my college days. I have always considered fishing one of my favorite hobbies.

My oldest brother Billy and I posed together in Washington D.C. He is one man that I really look up to and I respect his opinion on all subjects. He's strong, brave and tough as hell. He has handled the pressures of being the oldest son well.

Here I am with my brother Greg and my son Jeremy in a luxury box at an NBA game. I love hanging out with them; a lot of times when we get together, we go fishing.

My brother Stan and I are in a big limousine heading to a "Sunset Celebration" release party. Stan sang the solo, "Better Days" on the album, and did a great job.

This is my son, Jeremy, age 3, with my daughter, Patti, age 7. I laugh at this picture every day in my office; I love it! My kids, however, do not. Sorry, kids.

Jeremy and Patti are both terrific people. Sweet and sensitive, but tough when they need to be.

My daughter Patti's college graduation picture. She went to the University of Maryland and loved it. It was a great experience for her. She worked in the basketball office and athletic department. She is now an Event Coordinator for MCI.

Here is my son, Jeremy, in his high school basketball uniform. He earned a scholarship to Iona College. He is now a Personnel Specialist Coordinator working for Pro-Serve and working with a new venture company specializing in football information called "The War Room."

Hamming it up on a Harley-Davidson motorcycle with Marie.
Let equality and freedom ring.

Marie and I on our wedding day: December 30, 1995, in Del Mar, California. It was beautiful. We were married at the L'Auberge Resort.

Marie and I are the proud parents of beautiful Vanessa Anna-Marie Green, born February 1, 1997. She weighed 8lbs., 12 oz. and is very healthy and happy today.

Baby Green with Mom and Dad in Palm Springs, California, at the NFL League meetings in March of 1997. We are so happy with our little girl, and we hope to give her a brother or sister within two years, God willing.

Vanessa is the "star" of the Green family.

Who says I am not a fishing professional? I even have my own trading card. The card is legitimate, but I will always be a recreational angler; I love the fun and relaxation.

Above is the 1988 49ers staff that won the Super Bowl. In the far back row, four past and present NFL head coaches are in the picture, Back row: me (third from left) George Seifert (third from right), Mike Holmgren, (first on right),First row: Ray Rhodes (first on right).

Here I am with the 1992 NFL head coaches. There are only five of the 28 coaches still with their original teams. Coaching professional football is a tough business, but a great challenge.

Here I am at the 1994 American Bowl in Tokyo, Japan. Chiefs' head coach Marty Schottenheimer and I are flanking Commissioner Paul Tagliabue. Kansas City Chiefs founder and owner Lamar Hunt is to Marty's right, and Vikings' President Roger Headrick, is next to me. The game was a great chance to travel to the Far East and have a cultural exchange. We won two American Bowl games (Berlin, 1993, and Tokyo, 1994). Next stop, a Super Bowl in the USA?

Meeting with Jim Mora, former head coach of the New Orleans Saints. NFL coaches have a strong bond and mutual respect and it's never based on your win-loss record.

In 1993, Richie Pettibone was the head coach of the Washington Redskins. Richie waited years for his shot at the top and only got one year before he was fired—like I said, it's a tough business.

Greeting former San Francisco 49ers coach George Seifert after a game. George has one of the best defensive coaching minds in all of football. He's too young to stay retired. Hopefully he'll be back coaching in the NFL again.

Jimmy Johnson retired from coaching the Dallas Cowboys, but now is back to lead the Miami Dolphins. Like George Seifert, Johnson has two Super Bowl Championships on his resume and the rings to prove it.

I enjoy every minute of the time I spend with children in the Twin Cities community. That's one of the best aspects of being in a high-profile job.

Bill Cosby was kind enough to pose with Marie and Me when he came to the Twin Cities for a PACER Foundation fundraiser. Bill is a great humanitarian, and is always giving his all for mankind.

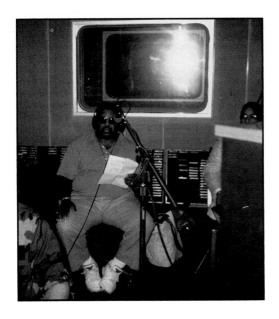

Here I am in Tokyo at the Dakota Air Base doing a live jazz show that was heard thoughout Southeast Asia. Jazz and music in general is a large part of my life and one of my favorite leisure activities.

The CD cover for Sunset Celebration. Working with so many talented, hungry musicians was a great experience. Even though we didn't sell as many albums as we'd hoped, the project was praised by music critics. The style is contemporary rythmn jazz with smooth, soulful vocals.

Here I am in my Viking practice gear on the field. Do you think I am catching the ball or tossing it to someone? It's a nice shot, so I won't tell you.

I love coaching the Vikings. The fans, the players and the Twin Cities have all meant so much to me. I would like nothing more than to bring a Super Bowl Championship to Minnesota and Vikings fans everywhere.

changes might seem. Before Roger and I met in Dallas, I talked football and philosophy to the college coaches assembled. I got on stage and took charge. It was flattering after the program when legendary head coach Eddie Robinson of Grambling came up and told me he liked my speech and my presentation style. When the afternoon session was over, Roger and I met in a hotel across from the convention center in Dallas. This meeting also went well.

In the Twin Cities, the speculation was totally about the status quo. Pete Carroll was going to get the job. The team would get a slight shake-up, but the organization would mostly stay intact. Everyone would be safe and happy. But Roger had other plans. I left the meeting with the idea that he was prepared to offer me the job. I gave Roger my attorney's telephone number.

I felt confident enough that I was a serious candidate that I thought it would be wise to let people in California know what could happen. I did something unusual for me—I called Mark Soutau, a reporter at the *San Francisco Examiner*, an afternoon newspaper. On Tuesday afternoon I called to tell him about my discussions with the Minnesota Vikings. I emphasized that I didn't know whether I'd get the job, but said there was mutual interest on both sides. This was a surprise to Mark because previously I showed no interest in the NFL. Well, there's no sense in having an interest in an NFL coaching job if the league isn't seriously interested in you. I talked to the reporter with the understanding he could run his story Wednesday afternoon. I knew it would be picked up then by the Bay Area radio and TV stations on Wednesday evening, and thus it would not be a complete surprise if the opportunity presented itself.

Things went according to plan. That evening I went out to dinner with two coaching friends who also were in town for the convention —Carl Hargrave, who I'd known since he was eight or nine years old in Iowa City, and John Fontes, a former college buddy from our Iowa Hawkeye days who was an assistant college coach. I had told my attorney that we were going to be at dinner, and if anything came up, he should page me at the hotel.

We had dinner at a big spaghetti place which featured a woman swinging on a swing. We didn't understand the restaurant decor, but I joked that apparently the dinner wasn't over until the fat lady swings. Actually, the dinner did come to an abrupt halt. We were halfway through our meal when I got a page: "Would Mr. Dennis Green please come to the telephone?" Carl and John asked what was going on, and I answered, "I'll let you know if it's a deal." It was, in fact, my attorney Ray Anderson. "Roger Headrick is serious about the job," Anderson said.

Ray and I talked about the money. I thought the Vikings' negotiating offer was too low, but I didn't consider it a deal breaker. "See if we can get more money," I told him. "At any rate, we'll be knocking on his door within two years requesting a new contract." Ray Anderson agreed.

Ray asked, "How do you want to proceed on this?"

I explained that I had an important team banquet on Thursday at Stanford, and didn't want to say anything that night to take the spotlight off the players. "What you can tell Roger is that we need to look at the figures, counter offer the contract, and come up with a better figure," I said.

I went back to the table and announced, "It looks like I might get the head coaching job with the Minnesota Vikings." Both guys were excited and stunned because they had no idea that I was interested in the job.

From that point on, the coaching grapevine was buzzing with talk about Roger's interest in Dennis Green. Ray called to alert Roger that the word was spreading, so he could prepare for some inquiries. That night we went out on the town and really enjoyed ourselves. There was a calm that came over me as I lay down around 1 a.m. After all these years of ghost chasing and wanting to be a head coach in the National Football League, my time had come.

Year after year I saw guys get jobs that weren't considered good matches. They were all qualified, but the question is, were they a good match? Why hire a coach with a great running background if you wanted to throw the ball? Why hire a coach noted for offensive football if you first need to improve your defense? Likewise, why hire a defensive specialist if you need to score more points and put more fans in the stands?

I was convinced that the Minnesota Vikings and I were a good fit, and that's what I told Carl and John. For once somebody in the NFL was desperate enough to go outside the box and hire the best man for the job.

When I woke up the next morning, I was still filled with excitement. It was January 8, and I had a clear-cut plan on how I could secure this job and make sure that the negotiation between Roger Headrick and Ray Anderson went well. In the same sense, I wanted to make sure that if I was going to take this job, it would fall together in good fashion.

There were the obvious questions. Yes, I was happy at Stanford. We had some outstanding players. In fact, in 1996, there were 19 players still in the NFL that were on my 1991 Stanford football team. Stanford had a lot of talent coming back for 1992, so I wasn't bailing out of a shaky situation. In fact, I felt strongly that we had an opportunity to go to the Rose Bowl and claim a top-10 national ranking. We had that much confidence in the type of players we had. There is no doubt I would miss California.

Along with the opportunity, there were some risks involved. I heard much about the great quality of life in the Twin Cities, which I've come to embrace. I also heard about Minnesota Nice, which I admit left me a little skeptical. Most people are sincere and genuine and the kind you like as your neighbors. I had heard players speak about a lot of the problems that they had with Minnesota Nice. The media could be harsh, some even downright mean. Some players felt whenever a prominent athlete had a problem, it was blown out of proportion. They expressed that Minnesotans aren't as willing to accept outsiders as they claim to be.

On the Vikings business front, I didn't think you could have an organization have so little change without it being intentional. I was concerned with the perception that Pete Carroll was one of the family and I was an outsider. But I knew my main focus would be on putting the best football Minnesota Viking football team on the field and letting the rest of those issues work themselves out.

I felt confident that there would be no last-minute snags. Even though the contract was still not 100 percent completed, I started making contingency plans. I flew back to California and met Wednesday night with Stanford athletic director Ted Leland and university president Donald Kennedy and told them that there was a good chance I would be leaving by week's end. Also, on Wednesday I told my family. I didn't want them surprised by reports in the paper.

I met with my staff on Thursday morning, then talked to the players and made sure that they had a chance to express their feelings. Some of them wanted me to stay and continue the process we started and get a Rose Bowl championship. I also talked with several alumni. Many of them were upset that the situation had gotten to this point. If we could have agreed on my contract renegotiation in December, as intended, leaving Stanford wouldn't have been an option.

However, the big bombshells were going on in the state of Minnesota. Bill Walsh's statements to reporters in California on Wednesday that I was the frontrunner irritated the factions in the Viking organization and in the Minnesota media who were pushing Pete Carroll. When Carroll revealed that he had not talked to Roger in more than five days, it gave the impression that he might not get hired. Certain reporters were seeking assurance from Roger that he had not yet made a decision, and Wednesday's news gave them a reason to put more pressure on Roger. Over the previous few weeks, the Twin Cities media were listing the following candidates for the job — Carroll; Bobby Ross, who wound up going to the San Diego Chargers; Chuck Knox, who would go to Los Angeles; Richie Pettibone, who was a defensive coordinator for the Washington Redskins; and Tom Moore, who was a coordinator for the Minnesota Vikings. They didn't mention Hal Schnellenberger, Bill Parcells, and, of course, me.

Thursday morning I visited with my attorney again. He felt we were very close to ironing out final details. We wanted a salary package with bonus incentives. If we were not going to be paid a lot of money going in, then we wanted a chance to get rewarded for success.

The Minnesota Vikings bragged about Metrodome sellouts, but that was exaggerated. In fact they had very few sellouts unless their opponents brought their own fans to the game. They had to use a ticket buyout system, set up with a local corporation, to ensure that fans could see home games on television. If they sold only 56,000 of the 62,000 seats, General Mills would purchase the remaining 6,000 out of a pool of money that was set up as part of the Metrodome lease. The General Mills ticket money, expected to last 20 years, was drained in less than 10 years.

I was willing to take some risks with my contract, and agreed to bonuses based on attendance and for winning the Central Division. The won-loss incentives have paid off, but the attendance clause hasn't. People who fault me for the lack of sellouts should check the facts— there has been a steady decline in Viking ticket sales starting in 1984, two years after the team moved to the Metrodome. Consider the crowds for Bud Grant's two farewell games—when he retired in 1983, there were 51,565 fans on December 17 to watch the finale vs. Cincinnati. After he came back and retired again in 1985, his last game on December 22 vs. Philadelphia drew 49,722.

A lot was happening Thursday night at the banquet. It was held on campus for the first time in a long time. It was very intimate and exciting. We kept it small intentionally. Some of our top alumni supporters were there, but we wanted the banquet to be about the players and their families, the coaches and their families, and administrators and their families who were actively involved. Stanford football in my years was all about players, coaches, administrators and alumni all working in the family, and feeling good about the season.

Despite the speculation that I was on the verge of leaving, the banquet mood was still very positive. The program was about the players and the price they paid to be successful. They understood that if any of them had an opportunity to go into the National Football League, they would seriously consider it. That allowed me tell the crowd simply that indeed an opportunity for me to be an NFL head coach had come up, and it was something I was investigating very thoroughly.

All of a sudden a feeling of calm came over me. I was going to have an opportunity to go out and show what I could do. The deal became official that night and it was time to get to work.

The next morning I got to Stanford around 5:45 a.m. for a previously scheduled 6 a.m. player meeting about winter conditioning. Everyone sensed what was about to happen—I would tell my players and staff I was going to take the job with the Minnesota Vikings. People were happy for me. Many felt this was an opportunity that was long overdue. Stanford had a lot of outstanding assistant coaches who were qualified to succeed me as head coach—including Willie Shaw, a defensive coordinator; Ron Turner, an offensive coordinator; Brian Billick, the receiver coach; and Tyrone Willingham, the running backs coach. They all understood what it took to be successful at Stanford, and I would have recommended any of them.

After saying a lot of goodbyes, I left to catch an 8 a.m. flight to the Twin Cities. I was flying first class again. I hopped in my truck and hurried to the airport on a relatively quiet Friday morning. It felt like going to work. Someone was assigned to pick me up when I landed in Minnesota at 1 p.m., and take me to Winter Park for a 3 p.m. press conference.

Until then, some of the opponents of Roger Headrick hoped that Roger would not bring someone in from the outside. If they could get through the weekend, they could remount their attack. There were articles written on why Pete Carroll would have been the best choice the Minnesota Vikings could make. But it was too late. Dennis Green was on his way. I was in the air, the press conference was set, and I was going to be the new football coach of the Minnesota Vikings.

I landed and was greeted by Steve Rollins, the team's head of security. By coincidence, I played football with his brother, Brian Rollins, back at Iowa in 1969 and 1970. Viking intern Jeff Robinson, who played for me at Northwestern University back in 1985, also was there to welcome me. A media crowd was waiting as I came off the airplane—cameras were everywhere. But we hopped on a cart and took off; the interviews would have to wait until the press conference at the Vikings facility.

# 11

# GOING TO WAR

*"Got an old saying from my minister. Everybody wants to go to heaven, but nobody wants to die."*
—Dennis Green, talking about
paying the price to achieve success

For the first time in 25 years, when Bud Grant was lured down from Canada, the Minnesota Vikings hired somebody outside the organization as head football coach. This time it was a guy with a San Francisco 49er flavor who wasn't afraid to make changes. A lot of people weren't taking it very well.

I was introduced at a Friday afternoon press conference at the cafeteria of our Winter Park facility. The room was packed. Roger and I took our seats in front of the team banner. I found it odd that very few if any owners were in attendance. They underestimated Roger.

I made brief comments about how excited I was to be the head coach. I had an appreciation for the National Football Conference having been in the system with the San Francisco 49ers. I mentioned the fact that the 49ers had won many Super Bowl championships. My hope was to bring a Super Bowl championship to the state of Minnesota. I spoke of what I feel is my aggressive and take-charge style and goal to build a great offensive tradition to match the past Minnesota defensive tradition.

The questioning turned nasty. The dean of Twin Cities columnists asked me, "Just when DID you accept the job?"

"Well, I am here now, and it shouldn't matter when it was finalized."

"Oh, it does," the columnist responded, "because Roger Headrick lied to me." The columnist went into a tirade on live radio, and the footage was played for TV, all because he wanted his close, personal friend Pete Carroll to get the job.

It was a short honeymoon for Dennis Green and the Minnesota media. I think I set some sort of professional sports record—I was getting ripped during the first few minutes of my initial press conference. Even though my background and proven record of success said otherwise, it looked like I would have to prove myself to certain people all over. It didn't set a very good tone for my relations with the media in Minnesota.

I sometimes wonder if my cool reception had to do with being a black man. I had a newspaper write that the only reason I got the job was because I was African American. There were nine NFL head coaching jobs open in 1992—apparently no African American should have gotten any of those jobs. Others suggested I got the job because the commissioner pressured Roger Headrick to hire me. Nothing could be further from the truth. Such stories were a total insult, and only a true bigot would come up with ideas like that. Since 1992, there had been 31 NFL head coaching jobs open, and only three went to African Americans. So much for NFL pressure.

An African American was not the head coach when the Vikings failed in the past. Favorites in three of the four Super Bowl games, they were outscored a combined 95-20 and never won the championship. Some believed that if Bud Grant couldn't go to the Super Bowl and win, then no African American could.

Minnesota has been rated one of the best places in the nation to live—if you are white. The Institute of Race and Poverty, a McKnight Foundation, funded a national study that painted a different picture for African Americans. Subtle or blatant racism implies that a black person needs permission to be ambitious or to seek top-level jobs. I didn't understand that. I was a citizen of the United States of America; I had the same rights and opportunities as anyone else. I should be appreciated for having the same ambitions as anyone else.

I wasn't afraid to prove myself, but I was surprised that in those first few months, some didn't even want to give me a chance to succeed. There were comments that I was a poor choice, and I was compared to Les Steckel, who was fired in 1984 after his first and only season resulted in just three victories. One reporter said I would not even match Steckel's three victories. I ignored such criticism and went to work.

One day during spring mini-camp, I watched as the players finished their stretching exercises, broke down for group drills, and jogged leisurely to their respective fields. I blew my whistle and I called them back. "From now on, all players, will run from drill to drill," I said. I made the players start practice over. The next day a Viking player was quoted in the newspaper that I was "a college coach with a lot of stupid, rah-rah ideas." It didn't surprise me. Some tried to put me in the same mold me as Steckel, who was labeled as more of a Marine drill instructor than a football coach in his short career in Minnesota, and said my coaching career here would be just as disastrous. It doesn't take very long to figure out what happened to those players—they weren't on the new team. I wouldn't tolerate crybabies on the team.

As for being a "rah-rah college guy," numerous NFL players come from my Northwestern and Stanford teams. My background with the San Francisco 49ers as an assistant coach was with a team that had won four Super Bowl championships, four more than the Minnesota Vikings' all-time total. The San Francisco 49ers also beat the Vikings five times in a row.

I didn't come to Minnesota to be intimidated by some people with their own agendas. I was a 42-year-old coach in his first NFL head coaching job. I was not going to follow old patterns or stereotypes. I wasn't trying to sound arrogant. I didn't underestimate my challenge.

My emphasis was two-fold. One, football was a business and we ought to be good at it. Two, we should be willing to work and enjoy what we do. Ideally, the two should go hand in hand. To turn a losing situation around, you have to start with a thorough and honest assessment of what it is you are inheriting. I spent a lot of time studying the roster and looking for the keepers.

The Vikings were labeled underachievers. There were some terrific players on the team, such as guard Randall McDaniel and wide receiver Cris Carter. I was up-front when I took over the Vikings. I felt we were a team on the rise. But we could only reach our potential with a team concept. My objective was fewer stars, better chemistry and more victories.

The person in charge has to possess two things—a clear plan on how to rebuild, and the courage to make the plan work. The head coach establishes the daily routine, and sets the tempo. I planned to inaugurate the new rules the first day of spring mini-camp.

New criteria like making players run from drill to drill, and making them repeat their calisthenics were small things, but it would send a clear message. What was good enough before, wasn't good enough anymore. It helped players understand that a thorough and honest assessment of team attitude was underway to separate the winners from the whiners.

I shared my strategy in a book by Time Warner called *Game Plans for Success*. I was one of 10 past and present NFL coaches selected to participate, joining Mike Ditka of the Chicago Bears; Chuck Noll, formerly of the Pittsburgh Steelers; Joe Gibbs, formerly of the Washington Redskins; Bud Grant, formerly of the Minnesota Vikings; Bill Walsh from the San Francisco 49ers; George Seifert from the San Francisco 49ers; Norv Turner from the Washington Redskins; Marty Schottenheimer from the Kansas City Chiefs; and Tom Coughlin of the Jacksonville Jaguars.

The *Game Plans for Success* was all about identifying winning strategies for life and business as perceived by 10 coaches. My contribution was about turning programs around. In 1990 and 1991, the Vikings were a team loaded with big-name, high-salaried players, but they were not winning. The Vikings lacked discipline and didn't play hard each week. They had good credentials—many appearances in Pro Bowls —but too many guys settled into a comfort zone where they worked just hard enough to get by. The result was occasional instead of consistent winning. To jump start the team, I had to correct the team's attitude.

For a meeting with Vikings president Roger Headrick, I put this chart together on June 1, 1992, five months after accepting the job as the Minnesota Vikings head coach. My first priority was to spend a few months learning as much as I could about the players, then make a realistic evaluation of where the football program and team were at that time. This was necessary so I could be decisive in what recommendations would have to take place. It was clear that change was necessary—otherwise Jerry Burns would still be coaching the Vikings and Mike Lynn would still be the general manager. But this was June of 1992, not November of 1989.

The S.W.O.T. chart helps you assign factors by specific categories: S (strengths) vs. W (weaknesses), and your O (opportunities) vs. T (threats). As you can see in the chart below, I did not pull any punches in this meeting with Roger. Companies that have the best results are the ones who are realistic about their personnel across the board and are willing to do something about their weaknesses.

We took our "strengths" and tried to build on them. Our "weaknesses" were clear-cut. The team was underachieving in 1990 and 1991. The Vikings were picked to win the NFC Central Division, because the team had veterans, talent, and the third-highest payroll in the NFL. Rarely does a team picked to go 13-3 and finish first, go 6-10 and finish last. We needed to be tough enough to bring about the necessary changes. Talk is cheap, so our bite would have to match our bark. For the most part, it did.

The "opportunity" was turning around a team that had missed the playoffs two consecutive years. The "threat" was the resistance to change. This was by far our biggest obstacle. We faced resistance from my first press conference back in January 1992 and are still facing resistance today. In 1992 and 1993, there were players leaking information to the media, as unnamed sources. Then some of the media would put the worst negative spin on what the players said. You had employees spreading lies to the owners. A few of the 9% owners were then and still are leaking confidential  information to the media.

## FACTS V. FEELINGS
## 1992 ANALYSIS OF MINNESOTA VIKINGS AFTER FIVE MONTHS

**STRENGTHS**     1. New and committed president. 2. New and committed coaching staff. 3. Coaches are willing to make realistic evaluations of our talent. 4. We have some solid players.

**OPPORTUNITIES**     1. Overhaul coaching staff and system. 2. Make player personnel changes. 3. New approach can create new fan base. 4. Teach reality. 5. The fans are ready for a team that represents the state. 6. Some teams will underestimate us.

**THREATS**     1. Resistance to change. 2. Trying to get job done with too many Mike Lynn holdovers. 3. Someone talks to the media about confidential matters. 4. Lip service only to change. Some  sit back and expect failure. Somewhat unorthodox front office staff.

**WEAKNESSES**     1. Failure to clearly face the team's underachievement. Attitude exists that everything is OK and change  is not needed. 2. Inflated payroll is not in line  with earned team accomplishments, and hurts our options. 3. Are we tough enough to force changes? 4. Team image outside the organization has not been positive. 5. Loyalty may be questionable.

## IV. WHAT IS OUR DEFINITION OF SUCCESS?

A.    1992
1.    NFC playoff appearance
2.    Top-5 NFC total offense
3.    Top-6 NFC total defense
4.    Top-6 NFC special teams composite

B.    1993
1.    Win NFC Central Division
2.    Top-5 NFC total offense
3.    Top-5 NFC total defense
4.    Top-5 NFC special teams composite
5.    Increase home attendance and national TV appearance

C.    1994
1.    Win NFL world championship (Super Bowl)
2.    Top-3 NFC total offense
3.    Top-4 NFC total defense
4.    Top-4 NFC special teams composite
5.    Increase home attendance and national TV appearance

D.        Our goals are SMART
• Specific        Clear cut
• Measurable      Reality, accountability
• Attainable      Dedication, playing hard, team work
• Realistic       Dallas, San Francisco, Detroit are mentally tough.
                  We can reach that level
• Timely          Let's stop babying the players — 80% of them
                  don't want it or need it. Only 10% of the
                  remaining 20% are salvageable. Make roster
                  moves NOW.

I expected some resistance by the players and some criticism from the media. I wasn't worried about that. Being the head coach of a football team is not a popularity contest. Whether you were hired to turn around a faltering football team or a faltering corporation, you could not lose sight of the reason you were hired. A head coach's No. 1 responsibility is to represent reality. That could mean changing personnel, the physical plant, or turning the whole operation inside out.

Work schedules might have to be changed, and shifts juggled to improve production. Workers, in this case players, had to know what you were doing. They needed to expect that while things were going to change, those who remained would see that the changes were for the better.

I made an effort to get out into the community and talk with people. I spoke to every Rotary Club in the Twin Cities. I wanted to hear what they thought about the Vikings. Also, I wanted to let them hear my plans first hand. What I heard was mostly frustration. That did not surprise me, because 5,000 people canceled their season tickets after the 1991 season. One man said he could accept losing, but it aggravated him when the players didn't even seem to try. I promised him that would change. We might not win every week, but there would never be a question about our effort.

The hostility did not come from everyone in the Twin Cities. Many of the everyday people believed Roger Headrick hired the best available man for the job. In my travels around the Twin Cities, people everywhere were wishing me the best of luck with genuine smiles on their faces. Their message usually was: "Coach, it's gonna take a lot of work. You'll have to kick a lot of butts. You better have a lot of patience, you better be mean and tough, you better be hard-nosed." The perception was this was a spoiled football team, and given the talent on hand in 1990 and 1991, the 6-10 and 8-8 records were embarrassing.

Repeatedly, I told our supporters that winning stemmed from commitment, and commitment begins with attitude. If you take over an operation with a lousy attitude, you have to address it before you can solve other problems. I was very aggressive in that regard when I was hired. The team had a negative image. There were so many cliques on the team, it wasn't a team at all. There were jealousies over salaries, some of which took on racial overtones. I had to sort out this internal mess before I could start with the Xs and Os of football.

The first season we released some players, including Herschel Walker. I had hoped Herschel would stay, but he felt he needed a fresh start. We had an excellent training camp, a solid draft even though we did not have any first-round draft picks. We started playing solid football from the start. We had the best preseason in NFL history—in four preseason games, we never gave up a touchdown and outscored foes 140-6. We held two teams to one field goal and had two shutouts, while

averaging 35 ppg ourselves. We did this while barely playing our starters.

However, even with that impressive preseason we still had only
48,113 for our first home regular season game vs. Tampa Bay, which
was 2-0 at the time. This was a disappointing crowd and the game was
blacked out on local TV. The next home game was vs. Chicago. We were
3-1, but we drew only 60,992, and at least 10-15,000 were Bears fans.
We won, to climb to 4-1, but our next game vs. Detroit drew only 52,816.
This was a clear indication to me that some of the negative things said
in the media about our chances for success under my regime were
having some effect.

All we worried about was playing football, and our preseason
gave us some momentum going into the season. We went on to win
some good football games against good teams. We began seeing the
fruits of our labor. The players got closer and the atmosphere was
happier and more productive. The team began to look, act and feel like
a team. The highlight of my first season was a 21-20, come-from-behind
victory over Chicago in the Metrodome. We scored three TDs in the
final 14 minutes of the game, and Viking offensive tackle Tim Irwin was
quoted saying, "In the past, we would have turned on each other. Today we turned on the Bears." I knew then that we were on our way.
Championship teams are successful because of cohesiveness and unified effort.

With 17 new players on the roster from 1991, we were the surprise team of the 1992 season. We finished as NFL Central Division
champions with an 11-5 record, but lost in the first round of the playoffs. I wound up getting some NFL and NFC Coach of Year awards. I
consider such awards "Staff of the Year" awards. In my opinion, we
were the NFC and NFL coaching staff of the year.

My general rule, everyone doesn't necessarily get treated the same,
but everyone gets treated fairly. I believe in hiring people who are talented and dependable. You'd be surprised how many coaches don't.
Some will take a guy with a big name and never weigh the dependabil-
ity factor. It's not unusual for first-round NFL draft picks, with exceptional physical tools, to bounce from team to team. Some guys simply
are slackers—they have lousy work habits, don't concentrate, and don't
compete.

It comes back to the three D's—desire, dedication and determination. Desire is the essence of living life. It establishes exactly what
you want. Dedication is the price you have to pay to get what you
want. There's always a price. Desire alone doesn't get you into the NFL.
There was time in the weight room, times spent working on technique,
time in film study, that was the dedication factor. If desire was what we

wanted and dedication was the price we would need to pay to get what we wanted, then determination would keep us there. I told players there was no disgrace in getting knocked down, it was simply a disgrace if they didn't get back up. Determination kept you getting up.

We followed up our 11-win first season by returning to the playoffs in our second season as a wild-card team.

Some believed Roger Headrick was a temporary hire as the president of the Minnesota Vikings. That was seven years ago, and Roger is still in the job. In 1971, Frank Gilliam was the first African American hired by the Vikings in a coaching or personnel capacity. Seventeen years later, a second African American was hired—Jerry Brown, who was an assistant football coach here from 1988-91. In those 17 years, the NFL itself went from 25% African American players in 1971 to nearly 67% African American in the 1990s. The Vikings organization wasn't as progressive and was just another Harrisburg Cemetery until Roger took over. In his seven years, the Minnesota Vikings now have 12 African American employees. It's safe to say that if Roger Headrick was not the president, the number would be two, and Frank Gilliam would not be vice president of personnel.

Hopefully my highest moments in the NFL are yet to come and will happen as early as this season. Even though we haven't reached the Super Bowl in my first five seasons, we've had some good moments. Any time you get into the playoffs in the NFL, it's an accomplishment. However, winning a Super Bowl championship has always been our main goal, and we think we have a chance to do that in 1997.

Some specific games that stand out include the 1996 overtime victory at Oakland to stop a four-game losing streak. That gave us some momentum, and we won three of our next four and returned to the playoffs. Another memory came in 1993 when we played Green Bay in Milwaukee, where the Packers rarely lose. Green Bay could have wrapped up the Central Division with a win, while we needed a win to reach, 7-7. It was a cold, windy day, and we persevered and won a 21-17 battle. We came home to play Kansas City the next week and beat them, 30-10. That game probably cost the Chiefs home field for the playoffs, and in turn may have kept them from going to the Super Bowl.

On the flip side, my lowest moment as an NFL coach came on the final day of the 1995 season when we didn't make the playoffs. We had made some good comebacks that season and had a solid playoff shot with two games to play. We had a chance to improve to 9-6 with a road victory over the 49ers in the next to last game, but we didn't quite get it done, and lost, 37-30. We had to come back and play at Cincinnati in week 16. We could still make the playoffs with a win and a Philadelphia win over Atlanta. They were showing the Philly-Atlanta game on TV on the stadium scoreboard during our game. The Eagles, who had already made the playoffs and played with little emotion, were getting waxed. We took a big lead over the Bengals, but as the reality of Philadelphia's impending loss set in, we folded our tents. We shouldn't have, but we did. You always should play to win, and at the end of that afternoon, we didn't.

# 12

# OWNING UP TO A PROBLEM

"*Roger Headrick spent the better part of his first year (as Viking president) in 1991 learning about pro football, how it runs, how it's marketed, where it's going. What he found was that for years the Vikings' success enabled the club to run in the relaxed style of an exclusive businessman's lodge. Before Bud Grant retired, his teams won year-in, year-out. The team sold itself, without needing high-powered marketing stunts. The players had no mobility or bargaining power comparable to that of baseball players, and the payrolls reflected the owners' tight control.*

"*(Former general manager) Mike Lynn could practically run the franchise out of his back pocket. But the new ownership (group) wasn't a football family. It was a consortium. And it took over behind Headrick at a time when players' salaries were escalating. Free agency had come to pro football. So had the salary cap. Everybody was going to lose blue-chip players sooner or later.*

"*The free-agency market got to be a multimillion dollar rummage sale. The swashbuckling Lynns were giving way to the accountants. 'We first had to start setting out an actual budget,' Headrick said. 'The days when you could pull big profits out of pro football were pretty much over. Competition for the buck was tighter. We had to organize marketing plans, sell side products and bring in new fans.'*"

—Jim Klobuchar, in his book *Purple Hearts and Golden Memories, 35 Years With The Minnesota Vikings*, speaking of the issues Roger Headrick faced when he became the team president in 1991

Former *Star Tribune* columnist Jim Klobuchar's 1995 book *Purple Hearts and Golden Memories: 35 Years with the Minnesota Vikings* has some insightful chapters on the team's ownership battles. It really lays out the bad ownership situation the Minnesota Vikings are in now.

Here are some key players:

- Jim Finks, the Vikings' executive vice-president and general manager from 1964-73. He hired Bud Grant and guided the organization to five division titles and two Super Bowls.

- Max Winter, one of the team's five founding owners, who served as team president from 1965-87.

- Mike Lynn, a discount-store executive from Memphis, who was hired by Winter as an administrative aide in 1974 but soon took over the job of general manager, a position he held from 1975-1991.

- Carl Pohlad and Irwin Jacobs, two of Minnesota's most prominent business people, who bought Winter's stock and became 51% owners, but still became entangled in a battle to wrestle control of the organization from Mike Lynn. Pohlad and Jacobs filed a lawsuit against Lynn, claiming an illegal trust was established. After a long stalemate, they sold their shares in 1991.

- Roger Headrick, who lives up the street from Lynn, was hired as president and CEO in 1990 and became one of the 10 primary owners. He remains in that position today.

- And me, the person hired as head coach by Headrick in 1992. I was faced with the responsibility of trying to overcome the Vikings' past mistakes and operate under a board of directors that has not worked together.

(Here's a clarification of the Vikings' current ownership structure as a preface to this chapter: An untrue statement you consistently read is that there are 10 Viking owners who each have a 10% share. The 10 primary owners actually own 9% shares, and a few other people have 1% and 2% shares. Only the 10 primary owners are voting members, though. That unmentioned 10% of the organization could become pertinent as the issue of gaining a 30% majority owner continues to be pursued.)

This story starts with Jim Finks, an admired general manager who enjoyed a great rapport with Bud Grant, among others. Finks went on to a general manager role with both Chicago and New Orleans and was posthumously inducted into the Pro Football Hall of Fame for his career service.

After 10 years as an integral member of the Vikings, Finks went to the frugal Max Winter in 1973 and asked for some company stock as a reward for his efforts. Winter said no. Finks resigned. Winter hired the aggressive Mike Lynn to help with administrative chores in 1974. The ambitious Lynn, who had bigger plans, quickly worked his way into the job of general manager.

The actual ownership battle started in 1984 when Winter, who was phasing himself out of the day-to-day management duties, refused to renew Lynn's lucrative contract. Winter was prepared to cut Lynn loose and find someone else to run the Vikings organization. A desperate Lynn went to the two minority-share owners and basically convinced them to turn against Winter. The threesome came back and told Max to step down as President and Lynn immediately received his new contract as general manager. Even though Lynn owned no stock at that time, he was given complete operational control of the Vikings, while Winter became a figurehead, despite owning 51% of the stock.

Winter eventually went to Carl Pohlad and Irwin Jacobs and secretly sold them all of his shares, which comprised 51% ownership of the team. Lynn, who had put into the by-laws a one-man, one-vote organizational structure, countered by breaking up 40% of the remaining shares and selling them to five new partners. Each owner had an equal vote, whether they owned 5% or 51%. So even though Pohlad and Jacobs held a majority of shares, Lynn controlled two-thirds of the board members.

When Pohlad and Jacobs discovered this, they filed a lawsuit claiming that Lynn's maneuvering amounted to an illegal trust. The internal war among the two camps played out in court for nearly four years. In the meantime, the people involved were still trying to do Viking business.

The National Football League didn't like the situation and encouraged Pohlad and Jacobs to settle the lawsuit. Pohlad and Jacobs, who paid $25 million to Winter for their shares, sold them for more than double that investment. The first story ever to come out said Pohlad and Jacobs got $52-plus million—I've heard it from a knowledgeable source that it's $62 million. It's very hard to get the truth, because too often in this saga people have been untruthful and have deceived the public.

(The Twin Cities media, whether consciously or unwittingly, have helped the deception continue. Besides Klobuchar and *Minneapolis Spokesman* columnist Larry Fitzgerald, I've yet to find one independent news reporter in the Twin Cities who will go out and tell this story completely and accurately.)

Lynn pulled another scam when he put together the group to buy out Pohlad and Jacobs. He didn't rely on his original investors to buy out the Pohlad-Jacobs shares. Instead Lynn recruited some new investors to join his ownership group—he didn't need the investors' money, but because of the one-person, one-vote structure, he needed the additional votes.

In a decision that would haunt the Vikings for years to come, Lynn and the other owners didn't shell out their own money to buy out Pohlad and Jacobs. Instead they borrowed the $62 million from a bank. So in effect, the Minnesota Vikings team bought the shares. It's a scam. Lynn and his partners get a fat loan and pay it off over many years from the team's revenues. As the value of the team goes up, so does their investment. To this day, some operating profits that should be going back into the organization instead are going to pay off the loan, and worse, pay the interest on the loan. Nobody talks about this, but the interest payment alone costs the team $2 million a year.

You tell me who the bad guys are? Certainly, Pohlad and Jacobs turned a nice profit on their investment, but I don't think they're the bad guys. Sure, Mike Lynn and his group got a loan, and borrowed money is borrowed money. That's the American way. I guess if you're lucky, you can borrow $62 million, and you don't have to put any money down. But the annual loan payment of at least $5 million-plus is money that should be drawing interest and being reinvested in the Viking organization and player free agency.

Why did Lynn leave the Vikings in 1991? Nobody really knows. I speculate there was too much animosity between Lynn and the Pohlad-Jacobs group. People didn't trust him. The NFL commissioner also might have encouraged him to step aside. As a booby prize, the NFL put him in charge of the World Football League, but he only lasted one year. He nearly spent them into bankruptcy. Mike's a guy who needs helicopters, limousines and luxury boxes, and that lavish spending temporarily destroyed the World League. Under the NFL chairmanship of Roger Headrick, the World League has since been put back on track and is prospering.

Lynn also negotiated the team's lease with the Metrodome. Apparently, Lynn rewarded himself by building into the fine print a clause that gives him all future revenue from two Metrodome luxury boxes for as long as the building operates. If that's not an unusual perk, I don't know what is. Of course, the same lease that Lynn negotiated is the one the Minnesota Vikings feel is unacceptable. That luxury box revenue isn't the only nice windfall for Lynn. According to Klobuchar's book, when Lynn resigned in 1991 he received approximately $10 million to cover his equity in the team.

Most people think Lynn installed Roger—his Wayzata neighbor —as Vikings president strictly to negotiate the purchase of the Pohlad-Jacobs shares. Roger joined the Vikings January 1, 1991, and 11 months later, the deal to buy out Pohlad and Jacobs was done. Most people thought Roger was just a caretaker. Lynn probably thought that Roger's lack of professional sports experience would make him vulnerable, and Roger would eventually just roll over. It's like the old back-up quarterback situation—Roger would be in there as the starter taking all the heat. Meanwhile, with Pohlad and Jacobs out of the picture, Lynn would sit back on the sidelines, hoping to find his opportunity to come in and "rescue the day." Roger clearly saw it differently.

The beginning of the end for Lynn's chances for a quick return came when Roger forced Jerry Burns' resignation as Vikings' head coach in December of 1991. Roger then took sole responsibility for the hiring of the new coach, shutting out the board of directors in the process. The board actually thought it was going to have a lot of influence, some of them even had their favorite candidate. But nothing bothers Headrick. Even though the media butchers him up all the time, he's unflappable.

Read the last chapters of Klobuchar's team history book, and it becomes clear: It's always been about one thing—money. Who is going to have control of this organization? You know Lynn wouldn't have given up his control voluntarily—he basically was forced out and has been trying to get back in power ever since. Consider the board of directors Lynn installed. They're very wealthy but don't seem to relate to the NFL world. It is a board and an ownership group brought together for the wrong reasons. The members are not all sports enthusiasts, and are involved solely for the financial return. People will tell you that in the current financial climate, a pro football team isn't a place where you can expect a maximum return on your investment. Sports enthusiasts usually invest for the love of the sport and to help the community.

(Maybe the only way the ownership situation will improve is to get more reporters to scrutinize it like Ron Edwards, a local reporter and equal rights advocate, has done over the years. Ron's ability to dig out the truth is a testament to his ability as a legitimate journalist.)

There's no doubt that current NFL commissioner Paul Tagliabue has been very supportive of Roger Headrick and impressed by his ability to keep the Vikings running in the face of this chaos. Roger is very attractive to the NFL because he's in the unique position of being an owner as well as being a team president and CEO. He's a working owner (some in the NFL are not); he has a vested financial interest in the team (not all NFL presidents do); and he's a working president who's well versed on the issues and runs the organization. The NFL can seat Roger on an owners' committee, on a presidents' committee, or both, and know he'll bring a broad perspective.

(Of course even with Roger's strong reputation among NFL owners, the Vikings' fragmented ownership prevents them from having the kind of clout they could. On the biggest issues that affect the future of the NFL, sole owners like Jerry Jones of the Cowboys and Wayne Huizenga of the Dolphins have much more money invested and thus have more at stake. The reality is that Jones and Huizenga now have more influence among the owners than a Minnesota Viking 9% shareholder.)

Amazingly, not only do the Vikings ownership by-laws call for a one-person, one-vote system, they say that approval of any sale must be unanimous. That's one of the reasons you haven't seen a 30% owner emerge. It's hard to get so many people to unanimously agree on anything.

Because the 10 owners don't agree on issues—in some cases they haven't even taken a stand—it makes it difficult for the organization to face complex, strategic issues such as a new Metrodome lease or a new stadium. These are the things that have caused this group to be fractured and indecisive. So now you have Roger, even with the support of the NFL commissioner, trying to lead a group that doesn't act as a united board of directors.

A glaring example of that came in mid-July of this year. Roger had a big meeting with the Metropolitan Sports Committee where he was scheduled to present the case for the Vikings to share a dual-purpose stadium with the Minnesota Twins. Somebody on the board of directors may have leaked the information to a local sports gossip columnist because there was privileged information in his column the morning prior to the meeting. So the Metropolitan Sports Commission officials come to the meeting already knowing the Vikings' strategy—or at least the strategy as seen through the slant of one person—all because someone leaked information of that magnitude.

If you were on any board of directors in America and leaked information like that, first you'd be asked to resign; and second, you'd be sued by the other shareholders for damage to the business. That's not the way corporations do business. If you had one majority owner or a few owners committed to the same goal, you wouldn't have that problem. You can't have loose lips leaking important, confidential information.

In recent years, the NFL relaxed its rule requiring that each team have one person who owns at least 50% of the shares. Now the minimum requirement is for one 30% shareholder. Yet after several years, the Viking owners have still been unable to break the stalemate. Commissioner Paul Tagliabue recently said he won't try to enforce that rule until the Vikings' stadium needs are resolved. Tagliabue has tried to forge a solution himself—he's come to the Twin Cities at least twice specifically to talk to the owners.

Let's not be naive—the Minnesota Vikings are for sale right now. The public just hasn't been informed of that fact. But as long as the team by-laws say a sale needs unanimous approval, don't expect a quick solution, despite the whispers you read in the gossip column.

I think any one of five scenarios could break the ownership stalemate:

- Scenario No. 1: The way everyone has been assuming it will play out is for one of the 10 primary owners to buy an additional 21% from the others and become the lead 30% investor. I don't see this happening, though, for two reasons—first, a 30% owner isn't going to share power with a 9% owner under the present one-person, one-vote structure; and second, unless the present lease and stadium issues are resolved favorably, the team's value will be much lower. I think Roger, for one, might pursue the 30% role, but he won't make a move unless the stadium situation improves. Roger's solid work in Minnesota and around the NFL on important committees has presented other career options for him, too.

- Scenario No. 2: All 10 primary owners agree to cash in their shares and sell the team to an outsider with the stipulation the team must remain in Minnesota for a set period of time. This is unlikely, too, because anytime you set stipulations like that in a sale agreement, you drive down the price you can ask—you've limited the pool of potential buyers.

- Scenario No. 3: All 10 primary owners agree to sell to an owner with no stipulations—in effect, sell to the highest bidder with no say on whether the team stays or moves. Even under this plan, the sellers won't get as much money per share unless the lease and stadium situations improve. You might have trouble getting a unanimous agreement from the present owners, too. The NFL would have to approve the purchase, as well. It appears to me that the Vikings won't get a new stadium, and the team won't even get a new Metrodome lease until the team is sold.

- Scenario No. 4: The stalemate continues for a few years until the NFL forces the issue under threat of large fines.

- Scenario No. 5: Because the other scenarios suggest that a sale isn't imminent, I'm offering myself as a possible 30% owner initially, with the option to purchase the other 70 percent of shares in two years. I have a "Money Mentor" from California who will assist me in making the deal if I choose to do so. My plan, spelled out in the final chapter of this book, has a chance to happen, in part because of a lack of alternative buyers. The owners may come to realize that my purchase offer, though not a blockbuster amount, may be as good an offer as they'll get. The recent NFL trend of paying $200 million to buy a team has been tied to a contingency of a new, community-financed stadium being guaranteed. Without a new stadium, the value of the team and subsequently the value of the owners' shares drop immediately and dramatically.

Meanwhile, Metropolitan Sports Facilities Commission officials Bill Lester and Henry Savelkoul are rigidly enforcing the deal that Mike Lynn signed. For five years, Roger Headrick has been trying to get Lester and Savelkoul to revisit the Vikings' Metrodome lease issue, but they've refused to consider it, even though a child could look at the lease we have, and see that compared to the lease the Twins have, it's not a fair one.

Yet you never see one person in the media say that the Vikings' lease is unfair. Between paying $4 million more a year than the Twins pay for rent and having to pay at least $5 million a year on the ownership loan and interest, you can see why people say we don't operate at a maximum. How could we?

Yes, the Vikings have been selling fewer season tickets every year since the Metrodome opened in 1982—the peak of season-ticket sales. But everyone involved in the Metrodome lease—except the general public—knew that a season-ticket base of 55,000 for the Vikings was unrealistic. That's why to guarantee payment of the bond, they had to put together the General Mills buyout clause. This pool of money also guaranteed home sellouts and avoided home games from being blacked out on local TV. People try to blame the current blackout situation on many things— the head coach, certain players, or the playoff losses. What the public should realize is if not for the General Mills money, most of the games since 1983 would've been blacked out. All of us in the Twin Cities have a stake in the attendance woes. We can either worry about laying blame, or concentrate on solutions. We have to start pulling in the same direction. No one wants to admit to the competition for the dollars by the casino gaming industry in Minnesota. It's a $3 billion a year entertainment entity that didn't exist in the 1970s and most of the 1980s.

If you face reality, you see our actual Vikings' season-ticket fan base has never been 50,000 as some believe, but only about 40,000, which is all they ever sold at the old Met Stadium. If Bud Grant made this argument, people would believe it. But when Roger Headrick tries to make the case, he's ripped by the media. Keep in mind in Bud Grant's last game in 1983—when he retired the first time—there were 51,565 paying customers in the Metrodome for the December 17 game vs. Cincinnati. Those are blackout numbers. When Bud retired the second time in 1985, his last game on December 22 was in the Metrodome and attracted 49,722 paying customers. Once again, the General Mills buyout clause came to the rescue.

In fact, 1995 and 1994 produced the Nos. 1-2 all-time season attendance totals in Vikings' history. My tenure as head coach has also produced the three largest single-game crowds in team history—9/22/96 vs. Green Bay (64,168); 9/25/94 vs. Miami (64,035); and 12/26/94 vs. the 49ers (63,326). And the Vikings aren't the only NFL team to have trouble selling out their stadium. This year, six of the NFL's seven dome teams will have a lot of TV blackouts. St. Louis is the only dome team selling out, and that's in large part because of the wave of enthusiasm of getting a team again.

Let's forget about looking for scapegoats for unsold tickets. I'd like to see us take the high road and go after some entertainment revenue that's never been tapped. We can't rely on the Vikings' fan base of the 1970s to make it work in the 1990s. It's 20 years later. We need to get more of the sons and daughters who grew up using their parents' season tickets to start buying their own tickets for their families. We also need to attract more young people to the games.

It's unrealistic to think that under the circumstances, the 1997 Minnesota Vikings can compete as well as we could if we had that $9 million a year that's going to the loan and what we think are unfair lease payments. The people in the NFL who understand our situation think we've done one of the best jobs of any organization because we have less money to work with. Earlier this year Detroit paid Barry Sanders a $12 million signing bonus. We've never had that luxury—we've never paid more than a $3 million signing bonus. What we've done is make the most of our present situation and say, "We are what we are." We spend less money on our personnel than 90 percent of the other

NFL teams. There's a salary cap list that comes out every year, and we're normally near the bottom in total money spent on player payroll.

There's nothing worse than expectations without commitment. The financial constraints of our Metrodome lease, the interest on the debt and the debt itself means there's at least $9 million a year—$45 million over the last five years—that we haven't had to reinvest in the team. The problem is compounded with the refusal of the ownership to invest new money into the ballclub. Without complaining, we've had to develop new stars to replace guys like Gary Zimmerman, Kirk Lowdermilk, Chris Doleman, Terry Allen, Henry Thomas and Roy Barker—all guys who left for more money and are still playing in the NFL. My challenge now is to develop new stars and somehow keep them with the Vikings when they become free agents. In 1998, we're talking specifically about free agents Robert Smith, Jake Reed and Todd Steussie on offense and John Randle and Dewayne Washington on defense. Without a major change in philosophy and an influx of money, we'll lose these players like we have the others we mentioned because of the owners' lack of financial commitment. That's no excuse for us not to do our best, and we won't use finances as a team alibi as long as I'm here. But until our ownership situation is settled, we're going to face some fundamental problems.

In virtually every large city in the nation, there's debate about the community role in building or improving sports stadiums. It's certainly an emotional issue in Minnesota. I hope we have an open mind and are wise enough to avoid repeating the mistakes of the past.

The University of Minnesota football program made a big mistake going off campus and moving into the Metrodome. When the brick house went down, so did the U of M's best chance at campus-wide support. College football should be played on the college campus. Half of my coaching career was spent in college athletics, and I can say there's not a school in the country that took football games off campus that is now successful in attracting students to the games and attracting the ideal football atmosphere.

In hindsight, we now know we could have spent much less to renovate the Met Center and keep the North Stars here than it has cost to bring back an NHL team. How many millions more are we paying for the new St. Paul arena and the price of an NHL expansion franchise?

The concept of the Metrodome wasn't necessarily a mistake, but frankly, the cheapness of the project put us where we are today. In hindsight, the $50 million budget, small by today's building standards, left us with a lot of headaches 15 years later. When you look at the Hoosier Dome in Indianapolis, it's truly a multi-use facility that houses the NFL scouting combine and a convention center. If people here would have had the vision and followed up with the commitment to build onto the Metrodome, you wouldn't see a Minneapolis Convention Center at the other end of downtown today. Now we have a domed facility that primarily houses sports and a few concerts. And you have three tenants—the Twins, Vikings and Gophers—who are unhappy.

The public needs to be told the truth: if the Twin Cities and surrounding region can't support the four major professional sports of football, baseball, basketball and hockey; plus Division I college programs at the U of M; plus a Senior tour stop, an LPGA tour stop and major charity fundraisers in golf, let's just say it. I personally think we can.

Sure, winning helps in the short run. But winning alone won't solve these important issues. The Twins' 1991 World Series victory had a carryover effect of just one season, and their attendance has dropped since 1993. What we need is for a lot of people to come together and do a better job of listening. If that happens, I think you'll see that all of our professional teams will be here for years to come.

I think the debate has been framed the wrong way. It's being characterized "A threat of the community bailing out billionaire owners with stadiums for millionaire players." The reality is the Twins and Vikings are Minnesota's teams, and we all have a stake in their success or failure. The Vikings, now in their 37th season, are a community treasure, not unlike the Children's Museum, the Guthrie Theatre or Lake Harriet. Even if you don't have an appreciation for football and never attend games, the Vikings are still important to our economy and to our quality of life. We need less politics and more partnerships. It would be terrible if the Twins or Vikings left this area.

Twin Cities newspaper columnists are quick to take the local teams, athletes and coaches to task if they don't perform well. It comes with the territory. It would be refreshing, however, if they would be as consistently aggressive and thorough in covering the stadium topics. Nobody seems to want to hold the two "Dr. Nos" (Lester and Savelkoul) accountable for refusing to consider the inequity of the Vikings' lease compared to the Twins' lease. If our deal was similar to the Twins,' the Vikings would have saved about $40 million over the years, money we could be reinvesting in our organization. The Metropolitan Sports Facilities Commission should pursue the sale of the old Met Center land if it needs more money in its coffers. What the commission is doing now is preventing progress.

Yet some in the local media don't listen to people in a position of authority on the subject— like Roger Headrick or Paul Tagliabue—and instead will print information from their unnamed sources who are afraid to put their names with their opinions. The public doesn't know the motives of the unnamed sources who put out information contrary to Roger. At least the public knows Roger's intention—he's trying to run a multimillion dollar business, while at the same time preserve the Vikings' special relationship in this community. He has to improve the Vikings' revenue streams so we can be competitive on the field in the new NFL economy. He also wants to give the team shareholders a reasonable return on their investment.

I would love to play in a new stadium. If done right, well designed, state-of-the-art stadiums can be wise investments for the teams and the community. But if the plan for a dual-purpose facility for the Twins and Vikings doesn't happen, the next best thing would be to get a new lease and renovate the Metrodome.

Without improvements, don't be surprised if someday the Vikings decide it can't work any more in Minnesota. I offer this only as an observation, because in 1997 there are no plans to leave. The Vikings have never said, "Help us or else..." On the other hand, the Twins have said they'll leave if they don't get a new stadium. Here are some things to consider in this local stadium discussion regarding team movement:

- No baseball team has moved from a city since 1972. With all the recent baseball expansion, there is currently only one state in the country even talking about courting a major-league team—North Carolina. I learned as a young man on the streets of Harrisburg that everyone who says "bye" is not gone.
- There's no room to build a new Memorial Stadium on the U of M's Minneapolis campus, and universities don't move to other cities. So where are the football Gophers going to go?
- If this community doesn't get behind and financially support the things needed to help the Vikings survive here, the team will look at all of its options. Where would the Vikings go? In the last four years alone, three NFL cities have lost four teams—the Los Angeles Rams went to St. Louis; the Los Angeles Raiders went

back to Oakland; the Cleveland franchise moved to Baltimore; and the Houston Oilers moved this year to Tennessee. As many as four communities are waiting to bring NFL football to their cities— Los Angeles and Cleveland are looking for an NFL team in a big way, and when you think internationally, you have Toronto and Mexico City primed to pursue an NFL team.

Football is by far the most popular spectator sport in the country. The Minnesota Vikings have been an integral part of this community for a long period of time. As much as the public may not want to hear it, the Vikings' stadium situation is one that eventually needs to be solved. Just because there have been stadium mistakes in Minnesota's past, doesn't mean we should compound the mistakes now by ignoring real problems today.

# 13

# DON'T BELIEVE THE HYPE

*"I know what I think. If we're going to have a new coach, I hope it's Lou Holtz."*

—Wheelock Whitney, member of Viking
ownership group reacting to rumors
in November 1996 that Lou Holtz would replace
Dennis Green as the Vikings' head coach.

*"I won't play for Lou Holtz. I won't play for a college coach. I don't like that guy. I want to play for Denny Green."*

—Vikings linebacker Jeff Brady reacting to
rumors in November 1996 that Holtz would replace Dennis Green as the Vikings' head coach.

My 1996 season with the Minnesota Vikings was marked by an extraordinary number of challenges and battles, on and off the field. The adversity peaked during a late-season drive to make the playoffs for the fourth time in five years. After a flying 4-0 start, we hit the bumpy part of the season. A disappointing November loss to Seattle sent us into a four-game losing streak. But what followed off the field —when Lou Holtz abruptly resigned at Notre Dame and the Vikings and I were swept into the story—was probably the most bizarre development in my 25 years of coaching football.

I have never been fired from a job in my life. It's not something I'm afraid of and it wouldn't be the end of my world. My priorities in life are family, religion, friends—and then my job. A job is simply what you do, not who you are. So I didn't have this fear of being pushed out during the bizarre 1996 season. I had two years left on my contract then. If they chose to fire me, my response would have been short and sweet: "Gentlemen, my agent, Ray Anderson, will be in touch with you in regard to the method of payment on the remainder of my contract. If he does not get satisfaction, you can expect a real battle with what I call the Green all-star law team of Bob Weinstine, Joe Friedberg, Peter Watson and Leland Watson, who are regarded among the best lawyers in Minnesota. Goodbye."

As a backdrop to the season, the Vikings were never healthy all season. We lost Ed McDaniel, one of the NFL's most explosive linebackers, to a season-ending knee injury in training camp. Then future Hall of Fame quarterback Warren Moon injured both ankles in the first game of the season. The season-ending knee injury to running back Robert Smith in our eighth game was probably the biggest jolt. He was leading the NFL in rushing, on pace for a 1,500-yard season, as he averaged 99 yards a game in our 5-2 start.

The momentum built during our 4-0 start, which included an exciting home victory against Green Bay, slipped away. By the time we faced the Oakland Raiders on November 17, we were 5-5 and had lost four games in a row. Injuries had decimated our team, and our lack of front-line depth was apparent. We were coming off our worst performance in my five years as head coach, a 42-23 loss at Seattle, so we were anxious to get back on track. We knew in our hearts it was one of those defining moments of a season—it was either win now or quit. No Viking team I've coached had ever thrown in the towel on a season. We knew what we were up against.

On the day after the Seattle loss, I put in a phone call to one of my former assistants, Tyrone Willingham, who was in his second season as head coach at Stanford. Tyrone was a great running backs coach for me and is on his way to being a great head coach. Unfortunately, Ty's team was struggling just like we were. There was no whining in our conversation. Both of us knew what our individual situation needed. Tyrone said his team was not listening this year. They were still basking in the glory of the previous season, when they finished 7-3-1 in the regular season, received a bid to play in the Liberty Bowl, and Ty was named the PAC Ten Coach of the Year. Ty said now that they were 2-5 with four games to play in the 1996 season, his players had no choice but to start listening. He told me of his speech that spelled out a goal of four straight wins to finish with a winning record. The Stanford players must have started listening, because they won all four games, received a bowl bid, and went on to finish 7-5. His players responded and did everything they were capable of doing. You can see why Ty is such a winner and has such a bright future in coaching.

My situation was different. We were not a healthy team. The players were giving 100%, but some were not effective. After the Seattle loss, I told our players in the locker room, "Only 100% healthy players will play and win for us next week in Oakland." I meant it, too. We started seven players who had never started for us before. They played great under one of the most difficult circumstances ever in the NFL. It has never happened before, and I hope it never happens again to an NFL coach.

As we prepared for the Oakland game, a news story broke on Thursday, that Lou Holtz, the Notre Dame head coach, was going to resign the day after an expected victory over Pittsburgh that Saturday. The rumor maintained that Holtz would make the announcement the following Tuesday and that he would leave college football to pursue his dream of retuning to the NFL—as the head coach of the Minnesota Vikings. That's right. The report said I would be fired and Lou would take my job. (Two owners were later identified as making inappropriate contact with Lou Holtz without the authority to do so. This has been the NFL's biggest fear in this unusual ownership group that included nearly 15 people—too many people to control. This was another time when some in the group were out of control.)

For the days leading up to the Raiders game, versions of this story were printed in every newspaper and on every major TV sportscast in the country. I told my team, "The media is wrong. They have been deliberately misled by powerful people with underserved influence over the press. I am still the captain on the bridge of the ship, and I plan to stay that way." I also fully realized that a loss that Sunday to Oakland would surely prompt some of our owners to turn up the heat on team president Roger Headrick to fire me. The same owners who, I later learned, made inappropriate contact with Holtz, without the authority to do so. I faced an uphill battle on the field and a personal battle with owners who were willing to sabotage the Vikings' season in order to create a situation where they could hire their friend.

As I look back on the Holtz resignation and the false rumors of him taking my place as Vikings coach, I'm struck by the sheer strangeness of the episode. It's rare that a coach ever resigns in mid-season, and almost unheard of when a coach doesn't give a reason for leaving. Especially when you're talking about a coach and school as visible as Lou Holtz and Notre Dame. In retrospect, I can't believe the national media got suckered into this story and ran with it. I don't like things that interfere with our players' ability to earn a living and their ability to perform. As a football coach, I don't like it and I resent it. I'm a career coach. This is what I do for a living. I don't like innuendo that someone can take my job or someone wants my job.

Remember, the story didn't start in Minneapolis or in the Fox TV studios in Los Angeles or at TNT studios in Atlanta. It started in South Bend, Indiana, the home of Notre Dame. From there it took on a life of its own. It was bizarre from the start. While the episode left a lot of people looking pretty foolish, realistically, it was most damaging to Notre Dame, which lost out on an $8.5 million payout for participating in the Bowl Alliance. The Irish had a relatively easy schedule to close the regular season and had to finish 9-2 to make a major bowl. Since Notre Dame doesn't share bowl revenues within a conference, it always pockets a huge payoff at bowl time. But in the aftermath of Holtz's surprise resignation, the team later lost an overtime game at Southern Cal. The Irish were shut out of a January 1 bowl and chose not accept another lower-paying and less prestigious bowl bid.

Not only was there a manipulation of people, but a lack of consequences for those who acted irresponsibly. People intentionally mislead the public and used the media as their vehicle. Rudy Martzke of *USA Today* wrote that everyone in the media was used, and said the rumor of Holtz replacing me as Vikings coach had no credibility. Peter King of *Sports Illustrated* and other national writers, in my opinion, also felt they were used by people either trying to help Holtz or bring me down in Minnesota.

In my opinion, the timing of Holtz's resignation, the way it stretched out, and the subsequent rumors were intended to create chaos and a lack of confidence within the Vikings team. The resignation didn't have anything to do with our football team and who we were playing that week. It surely didn't have anything to do with trying to motivate Notre Dame, which was playing Pitt. I'm not putting Pitt down, but it only won one game all year. It couldn't have had anything to do with recruiting, because the serious recruiting season hadn't started yet. I think it was all designed to disrupt and contribute to the decline of the Minnesota Vikings.

I don't know all the inside thinking at Notre Dame, but it appears that once Holtz hinted in public he might be leaving, the school didn't try to talk him out of it. Notre Dame moved quickly and talked to two potential replacements in the following days—Gary Barnett of Northwestern and Notre Dame assistant Bob Davie. There was no turning back. A fast, explosive rumor had turned to fact; the train was rolling. Lou Holtz announced his resignation on Tuesday, November 19. I'd never heard a coach of his stature resigning and not giving a reason.

The conclusion everyone in the media immediately reached was that once the Minnesota Vikings—then in a four-game losing streak—

officially fell out of the playoff race, Dennis Green would be fired and Lou Holtz would be named head coach either for the rest of the 1996 season or starting in January 1997. Some reports even had Vinny Cerrato coming back to be the Vikings' general manager, Marc Trestman back as the team's offensive coordinator, and Lou's son Skip leaving Connecticut to join his father's coaching staff. The stories all quoted "reliable sources." A column by a local newspaper columnist was headlined, "Vikings must win rest for Green to keep his job." The story said the only way I would return as Vikings' head coach was if we won our final six regular-season games. (We went 4-2).

The media, influenced by "unnamed sources" with their own agendas, built a circumstantial case based on:

- the unusual timing and manner of Holtz' resignation;
- the fact that Holtz coached two seasons at the University of Minnesota before going to Notre Dame;
- the fact that Holtz had close friends in the Viking ownership group;
- the speculation that Holtz always wanted to get back to the NFL, where he coached the New York Jets to a 3-10 record in 1976;
- and the uncertain prospects for the Vikings, who were 5-5, in a four-game losing streak and facing tough games ahead at Oakland and at home vs. Denver.

It seems to me that the media should be able to make a distinction between what "could" happen; what "will" happen; and what "won't" happen. Rumors like this don't get on every major TV show as fact unless they're planted by people the media feel confident are telling the truth. The reports aired not just on CNN sports, ESPN, and ABC sports, but even on Headline News.

Then on Sunday afternoon during the Fox network football telecasts, a few hours before our Sunday night game vs. Oakland, Fox aired a report that said a "good source" confirmed that one of the Viking owners had already purchased the necessary 30% of the shares. That would open the door to push aside Roger Headrick, fire Dennis Green and bring Holtz in as coach. Of course, it was a boldfaced lie. Yet Fox had the confidence to go on the air with that large of a story on a Sunday when they have their biggest national audience. Irresponsible reporting like that, and the cowards who planted the story without putting their names on the record, made it harder to go out and play football that night and win.

I didn't see the Fox report first-hand, but heard about the report when a national writer who I trust called me for a comment. I didn't say anything to my players that day, but the next day I touched on it. We had only one agenda on a cold, windy, rainy night in Oakland —to beat the Raiders and end the losing streak. What a game it was. Our defense came up big and didn't allow a touchdown, as the Raiders' only score came on a 56-yard interception return. We outgained them in total offense, 445-237 yards. We built a 10-0 lead when Brad Johnson hooked up with Jake Reed for an 82-yard TD pass on the last play of the first quarter. Leroy Hoard rushed 20 times for 108 yards to help us control the ball for nearly 40 minutes of the 72-minute, overtime game. Although we never trailed, there were times in the second half when other slumping teams might have caved in. Oakland won the coin toss in overtime and took the ball, but our defense stopped them on a big third-down play near midfield. Our players gutted it out and we won on Scott Sisson's 31-yard field goal.

What amazes me is the fact that when the story died out and was proven wrong, no one was held accountable, no one wanted to revisit the subject. I guess when you're made to look foolish, you don't want to bring it up. People sold our players short. Sure, we had shown a tendency to stumble, but we've also shown an ability to get right back up. It's been a trademark of our program. And that's what we did by pulling out a victory in overtime.

Of course, had we lost to Oakland, the rumor would have picked up even more steam. A loss would have meant a five-game losing streak. Even though we still would have been alive in the playoff race at 5-6 with five games to play, Roger Headrick would have been under intense pressure to fire me. Roger has stood up to that pressure before. Of course, many of the articles flat out said that unless Roger could put the ownership deal together to become the lead investor, the board would fire him, too.

On Wednesday, November 20, one day after Holtz held a 75-minute press conference yet never said why he was leaving Notre Dame, my attorney, Ray Anderson, was anything but vague. He sent a clear message to the Vikings Board of Directors, via a letter to Roger Headrick that read:

> *Dear Roger:*
> *Greetings.*
> *Finally, as Denny's legal counsel, it has gotten to the point where I am compelled to say, enough is enough!*

*Accordingly, I have advised Denny seriously to consider taking legal action against the Vikings Board of Directors and/or some of its individual members on multiple counts. Indeed, the events of the past week, particularly the roles of some of your board members in this Lou Holtz drama, wreak of bad faith. Once again, there appears a clear and nasty intent on the part of some of your board members to do whatever it takes to run Denny out of town.*

*Roger, please know that Denny and I believe you are doing everything within your power to control your board as it relates to interfering with Denny's ability to effectively do his job. It appears, however, (your) task is seemingly impossible.*

*Thus, this letter is intended to serve notice to your entire Board of Directors and its individual members that they need to back off. Now.*

*Very Truly Yours,*

*Raymond E. Anderson*
*President and Attorney at Law*
*Anderson-Reynolds Sports, Inc.*

It was gratifying, though not surprising, to see the reaction of the Viking players to the rumors of my impending firing. Brad Johnson, who signed a new contract last season, said, "If Dennis Green isn't coming back, I'm not coming back." He planned to explore the free-agent market instead. When the Holtz story played out, Johnson was quoted as saying, "I enjoy who I play for, and that's Denny. It's a distraction for everyone, especially during the season, especially when everyone loves playing for Denny. He puts us in the best situation as far as winning. The losses we have haven't been his fault. It's been the players and how we've been playing."

One lesson in this is that owners often underestimate the importance of continuity to an NFL football team. Continuity means so much to NFL players. The difference between 1977 and 1997 is like night and day. Players can become free agents today, so continuity of coaches and teammates is important. If a player feels the coach will help him become a better player, he wants to stay. If he knows the system, likes the system and feels it's one that's well suited for him, he'll stay. And if he feels he can win in that environment, he'll stay. But if those elements aren't in place, he'll explore the free-agent market. If you get rid of the head coach, everything I just mentioned changes.

The owners who acted this recklessly just don't get it. They don't understand, No. 1, how difficult it is to win. Everyone wants to go to the Super Bowl, absolutely, but we've been consistently in the hunt, despite the fact we have spent considerably less money than most NFL teams. Commissioner Paul Tagliabue said it's "amazing" we've been as competitive as we've been, considering the lack of funding on personnel. Our biggest weakness with the Minnesota Vikings is our limited resources to pay the huge signing bonuses to free agents. Contracts are guaranteed in pro baseball, pro basketball and pro hockey, but not in pro football. Of the marquee professional sports, football also is the most physical, the most demanding and offers the shortest career window. So the only sure long-term incentive for a football player comes with a big signing bonus. Even though we are limited in our ability to realistically pursue new free agents, one thing we were able to do in 1997 was to keep our best guys here.

Fortunately, I always had confidence last season that my team would bounce back. Our players responded, not because they felt threatened, but because they were ready to bounce out of a slump. We took several guys who had been playing but weren't 100% healthy and sat them down. It wasn't working for us. We replaced them with some guys not as talented but who were healthy and would play to the best of their ability. It was a risky strategy in some respects—in the NFL your first instinct is to say players should fight through injuries.

After the Oakland game, the focus shifted from me to Lou Holtz, why he was really leaving, what he would be doing, and the inappropriate contact by the two Viking 9% owners. Lou Holtz did send me a letter after some time had passed. He said he didn't know how the rumor got started.

Our football program moved on to our next game against the Denver Broncos, who came in with a 10-1 record. We suffered a gut-wrenching loss to the Broncos—on a tipped pass caught by my former Stanford player Ed McCaffrey with :19 to go, a pass we should have intercepted. But we bounced back with three consecutive wins to earn a playoff spot in week 15.

We have been one of the best teams in the NFL during the month of December, and when that month kicked in, so did the Vikings. We made the most of our rejuvenated team and made our push, topping Arizona, Detroit and Tampa Bay. After a loss to Green Bay to close the season, we unraveled against Dallas in the playoffs, losing 40-15 for a very disappointing end to the season.

I think we all learned some things in this long, trying season that might help us break through in 1997. We know we need a stronger running game to be competitive in the playoffs. We know we need better depth in certain areas.

The critics jumped on the playoff loss. There was new speculation and rumors that I would leave to become the Oakland Raiders head coach, or that I would yet be fired in Minnesota. Some still had Lou Holtz primed to return, since the New Orleans Saints job he actively pursued went to Mike Ditka. I think Cris Carter summed up our situation well following the loss to the Cowboys when he was quoted as saying, "Do we want to be a championship team or just a team that makes the playoffs every year? We need to upgrade the talent. We don't need to upgrade the coach... If Denny Green was not a good coach for this team, I would say it. I would say it is time for us to move in another direction. But there's no way anybody is going to do a better job with this team than he has done, given the other circumstances he's had to deal with... I'm not mad about it, but somewhat disappointed that we're in the fifth year of his program, we've made the playoffs four times and there's even a discussion about (Green's job security)."

I sent the following letter to Roger Headrick on January 21 to try to clarify my feelings on the events of 1996 and my outlook for 1997:

*Dear Roger:*

*While I apologize for the formality of a letter, I thought it would be important to clarify certain issues with respect to my relationship with the Minnesota Vikings.*

*First and foremost, I want to emphasize my commitment to the Minnesota Vikings. I intend to live up to both the letter and the spirit of my employment contract and do all I can to build a strong team with Super Bowl capability.*

*It's my sincere desire to enjoy a long and successful career in Minnesota, and I have no interest in pursuing any other job opportunity. As we have discussed, however, I believe recent issues, misinformation, innuendo, media leaks and other matters have had a deleterious impact upon both me and the entire Vikings organization.*

*When I was approached by you to consider the position of head coach of the Minnesota Vikings, I was immediately cognizant of the challenges facing the organization and was determined to bring the state of Minnesota and Viking fans everywhere their first Super Bowl championship.*

*For reasons which I trust you will both understand and appreciate, however, I believe that certain issues which have recently arisen—including specifically, but not exclusively, the alleged contact and purported hiring of Lou Holtz as coach, false reports of my going to the Oakland Raiders, and the recent false report in the Minneapolis Star Tribune newspaper of a purported Board of Direc-*

*tors' vote of 6 to 4 regarding my continued employment here—
have had a serious and damaging impact upon my career.*

*Of equal importance, however, is the damage this apparent
lack of unity and teamwork among our owners is creating in regard to how the organization is viewed around the NFL.*

*Over the next three weeks, I intend to sit down with each mem-
ber of the board who is willing and reaffirm my commitment to
work with them in the building of a championship team. I want to
be able to frankly discuss public relations, how I and members of
the team can assist in the sale of season tickets, and the continued
involvement of coaches and players in helping any way we can in
the community. I also will discuss the upcoming 1997 NFL draft
and free agent issues.*

*I look forward to visiting with you on this.*

> *Sincerely,*
>
> *Dennis Green*
> *Head Coach*

I take what I do for a living very seriously. In the last six years, I
have run across people who take what I do lightly. As long as I am
fortunate enough to be the Vikings coach, I will keep fighting. That is
the foundation that trailblazers in our society have laid out. I will be
true to it.

# 14

# YOU ONLY HAVE
# ONE REPUTATION

*"Everyone should have the right to keep their personal life private. If the attacks that I've endured could happen to me, they can happen to you. When that happens, we are all headed in the wrong direction."*

—Dennis Green, speaking on One-on-One national syndicated radio show February, 1995

*"Some people in the Twin Cities media hate my guts. That's OK, because I don't like their guts much either."*
—Dennis Green, January, 1995

On the opening day of our 1997 training camp, my first responsibility was to go to downtown Minneapolis and meet with a breakfast club of sports boosters known as the Dunkers. Not dunking ala basketball, but dunking as in donuts. The group started years ago as businessmen getting together and dunking donuts in their coffee as they socialized and listened to a panel of speakers. It has since grown into a prominent networking group.

On this particular day, it was a chance for our contingent to speak to the Dunkers about Minnesota Vikings football. I attended with longtime friend Frank Gilliam, our vice-president for player personnel. He recruited me and coached me at the University of Iowa. One of our featured guests was Randall Cunningham, our newly-acquired free-agent quarterback, who at one point had been one of the best quarterbacks in the NFL. Randall missed 1995 with an injury and was retired in 1996, so he's trying to get back into the game as our No. 2 quarterback. We also brought along our No. 1 draft pick, rookie Dwayne Rudd, who really went beyond the call of duty that day. It's unheard of for an un-signed player to show up for a publicity event like that. He didn't sign his contract for another four days.

We arrived a little early, and rather than standing around shoot-ing the breeze for too long, I rode the elevator up to the 12th floor to kill a little time. I always like looking out windows—that's one of my fascinations. I'm kind of a railbird and a people watcher. As I looked out the window this day I saw a construction site on the corner of Second Avenue and Seventh Street. There was a wrecking crew tearing down a building that's in an older part of downtown Minneapolis, right across from the WCCO Radio building. Even though the wrecking crew was working slowly, you obviously could see its results. The operator of the big crane and ball would bring it, swing it, it would shake a little bit and chip away at the edges of the floor. Eventually the building would all give way.

To build a structure this size, it takes patience, a lot of engineer-ing and a lot of people—200 or more at one time. It goes up brick by brick, window by window. Yet here was a crew of no more than six people that would tear down something that took all that time, skill and effort to put together. And the crew could do it in a matter of days.

On that day, starting my sixth season as head coach of the Minne-sota Vikings, I clearly saw an analogy between this building in ruins and the reputations of visible people in the community. We've reached an era with the media in our society where a false allegation can end up in print, on the radio, television or the Internet, and in a matter of hours and days can try to tear down a career that many times took 25-30 years to build. People with their own agendas will use rumors, innuendo and even outright lies to destroy careers. It's no coincidence that most of the people making the allegations don't hesitate to tarnish my reputation but themselves are afraid to put their own name with their comments. If we aren't careful, the problem is going to get even worse in the 21st Century.

In a series of stories that ran in the Twin Cities media in 1995 and 1996, my reputation was irresponsibly damaged by several people. The charges came from people seeking money or revenge; were fueled by disgruntled people trying to bring me down; and were reported by many people who simply don't like me.

Here is all you need to know about these issues:

- I've never sexually harassed anyone in my life.
- I did make mistakes in my previous marriage. I learned from them, and I'll never make those mistakes again. It wasn't fair to my former wife or to my children. Since then, of course, I met Marie and I am happily remarried.

I'm sorry if any mistakes I've made in any way reflected poorly on the Minnesota Vikings. I have always worked very hard to insure that any personal issues don't affect my ability to do my job.

Many times things aren't what they appear to be. If you ever find yourself falsely accused—and I wouldn't wish that on anyone—you resent how it plays out. You resent that some in the media rush to proclaim who's good and who's evil. All you can do is get a good attorney to protect your rights and stay focused on your job. It also helped me to have a mentally tough boss like Roger Headrick, who didn't rush to judgment and wasn't afraid to stand up to critics after he stayed in my corner. After he learned all the facts and understood the motives of the people in both cases, Roger found the allegations to be bogus.

After I was announced as the Vikings' new head coach, I received a letter, dated January 10, 1992, from a women who was a mutual friend of mine in California. (This same woman years later would falsely accuse me of harassment.) She wrote in 1992 to congratulate me on my hiring and express her feelings about our friendship. The half-page letter began: "Coach—I can't tell you how much I appreciate your friendship/our relationship these past few months. You will <u>NEVER</u> know how much fun I had." The letter concluded: "I'll always remember you. If you can get me to VIKING land, I'll be thrilled. Otherwise, best wishes for a wonderful new beginning in your lives."

About five weeks later, the same woman sent a resume and a cover letter to my attorney/agent Ray Anderson in Atlanta, dated February 17, 1992, seeking a job with his company. She hoped that Ray would hire her and assign her to work in the Twin Cities in sports marketing representing me. She used my name in the first sentence of her letter as a reference.

Do these letters sound like the feelings of someone who is being or has been harassed? Why would someone want to leave California for Minnesota to be in the proximity of someone if she really felt uncomfortable around that person?

This woman moved from the Midwest, where she had lived all of her life, to California in 1991 and worked for Stanford for a period of 12-14 months. She did not work for me and she did not work in the Stanford football office. From what she told me, she left Chicago for the wrong reason. She came to Stanford to continue a relationship with a male friend, but he moved for a new opportunity after only five months. She told me that the only reason she left Chicago was to be with that friend, and she said she simply wanted to return to the Midwest.

She mistakenly thought our friendship would bring her back to the Midwest and guarantee her a job in some capacity with me. When it became clear in 1992 that there was no job for her here, she became upset with me. By coincidence, she was a friend with a woman in the Twin Cities who at the time was sports editor of a major newspaper. Thus, she joined forces with people in Minnesota who I was already in a battle with and anonymously spread false information that damaged my reputation.

On Super Bowl Sunday, you have mixed feelings as an NFL head football coach. All but two of the 30 NFL teams feel disappointed because they aren't still playing. Yet it's a special day in your profession, and you take pride in being associated with the NFL, its many world-class athletes, its great fans and sponsors and the tremendous atmosphere of the playoffs and this championship game.

For me and many hard-working and loyal Viking employees, our 1995 Super Bowl Sunday was spoiled by a Twin Cities newspaper with a questionable sense of timing. The newspaper ran an overblown story above the fold on page one of its primary news section. This story tried to portray Roger Headrick and me as evil tyrants, and tried to portray the team and the organization as one in chaos. It was a total hatchet job on me on a day where football is on everyone's minds. There was virtually no balance to the story, which relied on comments from unnamed people, former players and from other disgruntled former employees. It tried to portray assistant coaches who had left for promotions as people fleeing a sinking ship. If you believed the story, you'd think the Vikings would never win another game.

This came from the same newspaper whose senior columnist marred my introductory press conference as Vikings coach in 1992. The same newspaper which in 1997 had another columnist—before this book was even finished—in effect declare that the public isn't smart enough to decide whether or not a Dennis Green book is worth reading.

I reached a boiling point in the wake of the January newspaper story and taped a short, blunt statement in response. My brief comments weren't scripted by spin doctors, but were an honest reaction from an angry, frustrated human being.

A few weeks later, the same newspaper printed the false allegation of sexual harassment against me, tarnishing my reputation but allowing the false accuser complete anonymity. The same woman who had sent the friendly congratulatory letter to me on my first day on the job suddenly changed her tune after she was laid off from her job in the Stanford athletic department. She later filed a claim against Stanford for wrongful dismissal based on sex discrimination by the university. That claim was denied by the Equal Employment Opportunity Commission (EEOC). She then threatened to take Stanford to court for wrongful dismissal. After getting nowhere with that tactic, she threatened to include false allegations naming several employees, including me, as having harassed her.

I was put in a no-win situation regarding public relations considerations. I've always believed that if you try to defend yourself against charges that paint you as guilty until proven innocent, all you're going to do is keep the story alive and compound the damage. In trying to protect your rights, you often lose, even if you eventually win. In my case, I resisted the urge to try to defend myself to every newspaper, TV and radio station or to try to seek vindication. I said what I had to say—that the allegations were false—and that was that. I think that's the best way to handle an explosive subject like that. All you can do is proclaim your innocence. The people who believe you don't need an explanation. The people who don't, probably never will, anyway.

It was unfortunate if part of the story eventually became my reaction to the allegations, instead of whether or not they were true or even pertinent. If I had to do it over, I don't think I'd react any differently. I didn't think the media was being fair with me, so I don't think you can look for assistance from people who are being the most biased.

Life isn't a popularity contest, and people who constantly try to please others and suck up to people in the media never succeed. By the nature of his job, an NFL coach attracts critics and often makes enemies. But contrary to what many in the media try to make you believe, I have many friends and supporters in the Twin Cities. People embrace me when I'm out in the community. A lot of Minnesotans have always been in my corner and have believed what I said right down the line. I have appreciated that support. People who know my philosophies and share my love of different styles of music, for example, are the type who tend to support me win or lose, and don't jump on and off the bandwagon.

On the other hand, people who don't like me will believe any negative rap someone in the media puts out there. I could spend a lot of time and money trying to polish my image or in some cases change the impression that some people have of me, but I don't believe in worrying about things I can't control. I know who I am and what I've accomplished throughout my life to reach where I am today. I'm not perfect, and have never claimed to be, but I think I'm a positive person who works hard and tries to do my job to the best of my ability.

I'm probably more active in the way of charities and community work than any head coach in the NFL. I didn't just pick that up here in Minnesota, I brought it with me. I know what it means to have a single parent or have no parents, and to live in the housing projects, and be in the inner city, and that helps me relate to many youths. I have total faith in the Boys and Girls Club of Minneapolis to play a positive role in providing programs for young people in this community. I've met some of the Boys and Girls Clubs' terrific volunteers and donors, and can say we need them now more than ever. I don't like to preach, but I think we need to put some positive messages out, especially to young people who see a whole bunch of negative in their lives. But I don't do community work to impress people or to try to sell tickets for the Vikings, and I'm not like a politician seeking photo opportunities. I volunteer hoping to make people's lives a little brighter and knowing that it helps me appreciate my own good fortune.

There are more than two dozen new and existing community programs for 1997 involving significant commitments from Viking players and coaches. Besides my work with the Bus Green Music Team, the Green Academic Teams and Special Olympics, some of the Vikings out in the community include Robert Smith (NFL Math Bowl/hospital program), Derrick Alexander (Young Achievers), Brad Johnson (elementary school visits/various public service announcements), Cris Carter (Boy Scouts/Special Olympics/Super Challenge), Pete Bercich (Red Sock Gala), Andrew Jordan (MADD Advisory Board); Todd Steussie (Family Umbrella Network); Ed McDaniel (United Way/ACES); Dewayne Washington (Ronald McDonald House); Jeff Brady (juvenile diabetes); Duane Clemons (Leadership—Franklin School); Randall McDaniel (Hands-on YWCA); and Randall Cunningham (Minneapolis Urban League).

Being able to help raise money or raise hopes in the community has always been more important to me than trying to get someone in the media to like me or accept me. What's true is the fact I don't like some media people in the Twin Cities, and a lot of them don't like me. Ultimately, I don't worry about what they say or write. It has nothing to do with the job I'm going to do.

This apparently frustrates some of my local critics—I've been told by national reporters that my Twin Cities critics get upset when I ignore them.

From the first day I came to Minnesota, a lot of people viewed me as an outsider. Some in the Twin Cities media consider themselves to be the sentinels protecting the gates of Minnesota. They determine who comes in and who doesn't. I don't expect to be here my whole life, they do. Right off the bat, we have some differences. I got along fine with the media in Chicago when I worked at Northwestern. I got along fine with the media in California when I was at Stanford and with the 49ers. I've always gotten along with the national media—they've made it clear they will be balanced and fair in their reporting.

But I have to wonder if there's something unique about the Minnesota media. It's clear to me that there's a reporting double standard and a "holier than thou" stance involving my personal life. Some in the media have scrutinized me more thoroughly than any previous Vikings head coach, and more than any other coach in the Twin Cities. If the one newspaper is consistent, it will write a page one Sunday story this offseason on the Minnesota Twins and their six consecutive losing seasons similar to the postseason story it ran on the Vikings in January of 1995. They could probably find some traded or released players and perhaps some former coaches, and second guess a lot of decisions by the front office and the manager.

One thing you'd expect to have in the media of a community this size is balance or diversity in opinion. If you have five primary sports columnists in an area, you'd expect to find one who thinks the Vikings are doing a terrible job, one who thinks the Vikings are doing a great job, one who thinks Headrick is great and Green is a jerk, one who thinks Green is great and Headrick's a jerk, etc... But that independent thought is missing here. It's like these people are trying to impress each other with how tough or negative they can be. It's almost like they have one agenda—get Dennis Green out, get Roger Headrick out. It's an agenda that's worked on a lot of people so far. Ask Christian Laettner. He was a two-time NCAA champion and All-American at Duke, but when he came to Minnesota he met those same media sentinels at the gate who refused to accept him. He was so unhappy, he welcomed the trade to Atlanta, and has performed well there.

Part of the problem is that you have too many people in the media who listen to powerful people with undeserved influence. Many times the reporters and columnists will say or write something that, 1) they're not sure whether it's true, or 2) don't care if it's true, or 3) know it isn't true, but say it anyway. They do this just to stay on the right side of some powerful people.

The ones who irk me the most are the guys in the media who don't do their homework and don't tell the facts correctly. There have been many distorted, untrue articles about players and coaches. And the way the media treats Roger Headrick is incredible. It makes me question how a community can really put up with it. Too many people in the media take the easy way out. They don't have the guts to come down to training camp or come to our Winter Park headquarters regularly and actually report first-hand on what's happening. It's easier for them to interview each other or rely on information from unnamed sources as fact. You wouldn't have a political reporter not come to the statehouse; you wouldn't have a court reporter not come to the courthouse; but we have some people in the local media who are either too lazy or too intimidated to come to training camp or to practice. Yet they still try to portray themselves as experts on the Vikings.

Certainly in all NFL locker rooms there are moments of tension between the media and the players and coaches. But in my opinion, in a lot of cases the reporters and columnists are the ones who created that situation of conflict in the first place. There's no player in the NFL who's going to deal with a media person's cheap shots. Why would they? That runs contrary to the pride you have, the pride that makes you the athlete or the coach you are. Talking to the media is supposed to be part of your job, but you can do that without talking to certain people. People in the media going after coaches is nothing new—it goes on in every professional team and most major college football and basketball programs. Some reporters or columnists seek that reputation. There have been guys in NFL cities who brag that they got a coach fired. I don't think they had that much influence—the guy got fired because he didn't win enough games.

Another thing that's odd about some of the more prominent members of the Twin Cities media is their obsession to be part of the story. The newspaper columnists and radio and TV people show up everywhere in other mediums. It used to be a newspaper guy was a newspaper guy. Now the columnist or the TV anchor is on the radio three times a day, or hosts a three-hour show each day, or is on morning radio. Then they show up on the local Sunday night TV sports shows, or on the weekly cable TV roundtable. If one of these people doesn't like you, he or she can rip you as much as three times a day in print, radio and on TV. This also leads to some hypocrisy involving some of these multi-media types. Some of these same people will rip athletes and coaches for their outside income and endorsements, and are quick to say that athletes and coaches have big egos. Yet it's OK for them to feed their own egos, pad their own wallets and try to become celebrities themselves. One Twin Cities columnist, who's in a minority because he doesn't do free-lance work outside of his newspaper job, wrote a column on this subject a while ago that criticized his multi-media brethren. He correctly said that some of them now have two or more jobs that they do poorly.

Some people took something I said in my first press conference in 1992 and blew it out of proportion. It was often stated that the Minnesota Vikings were underachievers prior to my arrival. In the press conference that announced my hiring, the big question that kept coming up was about how I would deal with problem guys on the team. I'd just started studying the Vikings personnel. I hadn't coached most of the guys, so I wasn't in a position to be talking about personalities and laying down the laws the first day. But the questions wouldn't go away. It was "This guy doesn't like to practice..." and "That guy doesn't think he's getting the ball enough..." and "This guy is considered selfish."

Speaking off the cuff, I answered, "Hey, I'm the new sheriff in town, and if people want to play for this team, they're pretty much going to have to accept that." I was prepared to make some tough and —if necessary—unpopular decisions as I set out to rebuild the team.

But I think that whole sheriff thing was overblown by some guys in the media. The sheriff image might have fueled a perception that I'm a mean guy or a ruthless guy. Ask young people I come into contact with or people in the community I meet, and they find me to be friendly and easy-going. Ask my players and coaches, and I think you'll find that they like to play for me or work with me. They know I'm tough when I have to be, but they'll tell you I'm fair. I have a tough job that sometimes calls for a tough posture.

I try to avoid showing anger, because I don't think it reflects the kind of person I am. People who stay angry often become bitter, negative people or excuse makers. I consider myself a positive person. When I've been wronged, I'll be honest in my assessments, but I emphasize that I'm not a crybaby. I can take any hits I get. If I couldn't, I'd have switched careers a long time ago.

Another area where I think you get half of the story involves some of the early personnel moves I had to make when I came to the

Vikings. Contrary to what's been written and said, in 99 percent of the cases, I'm the one who talks to the player if we release him. I'm also one of the hundreds of coaches who'll tell you it's the worst part of coaching.

Wade Wilson had been the quarterback under Jerry Burns immediately before I was hired. We decided not to offer him a new contract. I didn't break the news in Wade's case because his dealings had always been with Jeff Diamond on contract matters or with Burns as his coach. I'd never coached Wade, and we had no relationship. It seemed the right thing to do to have Jeff Diamond talk to him because it was an issue that his contract was up, and we weren't going to resign him. Some teams rely on the player personnel people to break the news to guys who are released, and their head coaches aren't involved. But in virtually all the cases here, I do the cutting.

Any time you come in and try to turn a program around, you're going to hear a lot of complaining. That's just the way it is. The decisions you have to make aren't meant to be cold-hearted or cold-blooded, but this is a business. Players have shorter careers but make a lot more money. That's the tradeoff. It would be great to be able to reward a veteran player who contributed to a team's success and continuity with an extra year on the roster—even if that means a year past his prime. That was possible years ago. With today's salaries, it isn't. It's extremely competitive, and your objective as an NFL coach is to win. There's no way with so many people to please that all your decisions will be popular.

If you're an armchair quarterback and you're not held accountable whether a team wins or loses, it's easy to have an opinion. You don't have to make a choice between, say, a player who's 23 and single, and a guy who's 30 and maybe has four kids. The single guy may be able to hook on with another team, and maybe the 30-year-old can't. Maybe the single guy doesn't need the money as badly. Maybe the single guy is eligible to go on the practice squad and make $50,000 and the 30-year-old can stay on the roster and make $400,000.

When you start thinking that way as an NFL head coach, however, you've got a problem. The bottom line is, who's a better player and who's going to give you a better chance to win? Once you start to look for other reasons to keep people, the list never stops. And the reasons never cease. Both the 23-year-old and the 30-year-old know what the deal is. They might hope you will cut them some slack, but you don't cut slack in this business. You get the best players playing at their best to give you your best chance to win. It's my job to figure out who the best players are. Sometimes a player won't admit it—it's always easier to seek sympathy—but deep down, from the day he strapped on a football helmet, he knew he would be judged solely on what he did on the football field.

Some of the more tasteless and clearly personal attacks on me have come from a Twin Cities morning radio show that makes mean, negative commentary to get ratings. I've never met the guy who runs the show. He's never come to our training camp or practices. He doesn't know me. He doesn't know any of the players, either.

You know what? The players don't care to know guys like him, either. Why should they? A guy who has spent his whole career developing himself to be a football player couldn't care less about guys who make their living on the negative side of the highway.

If the critics think they can break the players or me, they're wrong. I coached football for 20 years before I came to the Minnesota Vikings. If I don't coach the Vikings one more day, I'll coach somewhere else, so why should I care about somebody who clearly doesn't understand the concept of honest or fair reporting or commentary? It isn't worth paying attention to someone who makes his living making fun of people. Perhaps our community has to take responsibility for patronizing the loudmouths who make fun of others. Isn't that one of the things you learn the first day of kindergarten—don't spit, don't kick and don't make fun of people?

I understand that criticism and scrutiny come with the territory and are nothing new. George Washington and Abraham Lincoln were criticized—and publicly stated their resentment about it many times. Today any public figure, whether he or she is a football coach, schoolteacher, or corporate leader, will be scrutinized. I realize I'm not the first person and certainly won't be the last who has conflicts with the media. I don't think Carl Pohlad wants to sit down with a local newspaper after its stories ripped him this year. Ask Minnesota Governor Arne Carlson, who in 1996 wrote a guest newspaper editorial on fairness, if that same newspaper is fair, and be prepared for an earful.

The stakes are so much higher today in major-college and professional sports that coaches no doubt have less job security. Yet I'm not going to worry about the critics or worry about things I can't control. I know that to build anything, you have to have solid ground to start. I know my foundation is solid and it gives me confidence that I know how to coach football. I know I can take a football team and lead them to victory. I've done it before and hopefully I'll do it many more times. I don't know how to be insecure about the game of football. It all comes down to my commitment and expectations.

My commitment to football is very strong, and my experience speaks for itself. Football is a game I love and understand. My expectations are simply to win—that's what it's all about. My desire to win became clear back in my college playing days when for the first time in my football career, I was part of a team that didn't have consistent success.

I can step back and put everything into perspective. Now I'm at the pinnacle of my career. I'm also a relatively young man—I'm 48 and I feel good. I feel good because of confidence. The NFL has had a lot of coaches who've only lasted one year, and some have lasted only two years. Many of those same guys waited their whole careers to get a shot at being an NFL head coach. Nobody could say these guys weren't ready to be head coaches, it's just that either things didn't work out, they weren't able to adapt to their situation, or they had bad luck. Any one of those three can get you. I'm not in that category. I'm in my sixth year as the Vikings' head coach. We've won a lot of games, certainly a lot more than we've lost. I've been in some of the best and biggest games on Monday Night Football and on Sunday night football. We feel confident we can perform on the football field.

We've had our share of injuries and we've battled through adversity. We've had four-game losing streaks and came back to have a four-game winning streak. We've been there, and there's no bogeyman out there that we fear. We feel confident we can match up with the very best.

Some in the media have said that the Vikings' lack of playoff success in my first five seasons puts pressure on me to win in 1997 to keep my job. There are only two people who put pressure on me—myself and Roger Headrick. As far as pressure I put on myself, I've been in football for 35 years, 25 of that in coaching. I understand what it takes to win and what it means to win, whether as an assistant coach or as a head coach. My priorities are to make sure my players feel I've given them the opportunity to win and be the best player they can be. The other person who could put pressure on me is Roger, my boss.

Everyone has a boss. Roger's expectations are high—they should be. He's seen us win games and he knows we have the potential to play against the very best. He understands that you can't control everything in a competitive game like football. He knows if we don't win, it's not because of poor preparation or effort.

I don't let myself dwell on my playoff record. An analogy I'd use is Robert Smith—he's been injured parts of the last four seasons, but I think Robert could be healthy the next four seasons. I take the same approach to the playoffs. We have not played well enough to win our playoff games. In some of those cases, we weren't healthy enough when we got to that stage in the season. We'd used up all of our energy to get there. We've had all kinds of strange things happen in those games, too. Twice we've had guys running for a touchdown only to get the ball knocked out of their hands. But that's part of football. The bottom line is, regardless of the situation, we haven't played well enough to win.

Yes, we've lost all four playoff games we've played in my five years as head coach. Bud Grant lost all four Super Bowls his teams played in. Does that mean he shouldn't be in the Hall of Fame or is a poor coach? My approach is we'll win the next four. I guess 4-4 wouldn't be too bad. I'm still not going to care about the detractors. We will always hit the field and do the best we can. I'm not going to get caught up in looking for something to complain about. That's the difference between me and crybabies—a crybaby always has something to cry about. A lot of Twin Cities media members behave like crybabies.

When we beat Detroit at home in our second game of the 1995 season, NFL Properties had a film crew following us that day. They are masters of catching the excitement of the moment. The speech I gave at the end of the game in the locker room was taped and shown later in their season highlight package. What I said was, "Only babies get what they want all the time, and they have to cry to get it. I said we didn't have any crybabies in this room." And we never will.

We go out and play the best we can. When that game's over, we prepare for the next one and line up and do it again. When the season's over, if we don't reach our ultimate goal of winning a Super Bowl championship, God willing, we'll come back the next year and try it again.

# CAN'T WE ALL JUST GET ALONG?

*(After a 15-13 win over Green Bay in 1993)*

*Dennis Green*
*Coach Vikings*
*Minneapolis, Minn.*

*Dear Coach:*
    *Thanx 2 u & that other burr-head - running back Terry Allen 4 failing to cover that 3 1/2 point spread against the Packers. That cost me a humanoid monkey - a pretty good buck ... and your n-gger was 2 tired to score (according to that stuttering n-ggers self acclaimed failure).*
    *I played against as good of Army teams as the Packers are 2 day & was never 2 tired 2 score when it counted.*
    *I just hope double tragedy befalls you & your p-ssy running back & that your families are stricken by fatal, tragic & dire consequences.*

*Respectfully yours,*
A K.K.K. Fan

*(After a 28-17 loss in Philadelphia in 1992 that dropped Minnesota's record to 9-4)*

*Green - You f-ckin' n-ggers you'll never be a winner! You f-ckin' n-gger - you'll never be a Bud Grant! He beat good teams - you cain't. You cain't beat anyone with record 500 or better. Your offense suck'd & your defense suck'd in Philly. Don't be stupid and show 49'er's everything you (you may see them in post season you loser).*

*P.S. — n-ggers can execute, but they cain't coach - Vikings suck....
play for the coach you loser.*


*(After a 6-3 win over Pittsburgh in 1992—the Steelers' only home
loss that season—that improved the Vikings' record to 10-5 and
clinched the NFC Central Division title)*

*Green - Nice Offense! You and your f-cking n-ggers couldn't score 7
pts against Pittsburgh! You haven't beat a club over .500 all season.
You f-ckin' n-ggers suck! We need white coaches and players.
Bring back Bud! At least he got us to the Super Bowl. We want to
win a Super Bowl, comprende?*

—A few of the anonymous letters
received by Dennis Green

I am baffled by America's inability to deal with equal rights. Are
you trying to tell me that the color of someone's skin or their religious
beliefs are supposed to determine how we should interact and treat
each other? You have to be kidding me. People are people. There is only
one mankind that inhabits this one earth, and we better start thinking
like one people.

As a product of the equal rights era of the 1960s and a direct
beneficiary of its realities, I am tired of racist, sexist, and religious hypo-
crites. People have been duped. I don't know if they are deliberately
ignorant or just have to believe this notion of superiority. I have lived
my entire life believing that all people are equal under the eyes of the
Lord. My friends have been of all races and religions. What difference
does it make?

If we could pass a world rule to go in effect immediately it would
say: Don't discriminate—it is against the law, and from this point forward it will be enforced. My parents taught me the difference between
racial prejudice and racial discrimination. Prejudice involves feelings,
while discrimination involves actions. There is little that you can do
about someone else's prejudice. But discriminatory actions are another
side of the coin. I will fight these actions whenever I can. I also will
never accept the fact that I was, will be, or could be denied an opportunity on the grounds that I'm the descendant of African American and
Native American Grandparents

Every coach in the National Football League receives critical letters, almost always unsigned. Not only does the mail come when you lose, but sometimes it comes even if you win and don't cover the point spread. Some of it is laughable, some of it is weird. Then there are the hate letters on this chapter's opening page that are in a class of their own. I'd never received such garbage in my coaching career until I became an NFL head coach in Minnesota. I've only read some of the racist mail I get—the stack is very high. But I read some of it every once in awhile to remind me that there are people out there waiting for me to fail.

It also makes me realize that all African Americans will face struggles until America learns to deal with race. I'm not the only one saying it—President Clinton has made racial healing one of the focal points of his second term. The U.S. economy at its best condition in more than three decades—the stock market is at an all-time high, investors are making more money, businesses are making higher profits. But until we learn to deal with race, and figure out how to ensure equal rights, equal opportunity, equal access, then we're going to leave a significant aspect of our society behind.

Any demographics will tell you that America is changing, and we're not going to be able to hold on to things in America the way they were 50 years ago. In 1997 we must face certain realities:

- Races are being blended;
- A white American in this country will be in the minority as early as the year 2020;
- In the largest and most powerful states in the country—California, Texas, New York and Florida—white Americans are already in the minority.
- I think we need to return to concepts like "do unto others..." and "There but for the grace of God go I." We need to resist the people who try to create fear by pitting blacks against Latinos, or white Americans against Asian Americans.

A philosopher named Hegel wrote a thesis called the Hegelian Dialectic. It's based on the principle of forcing change through deceitful misinformation and fear. This three-step attack consists of a Thesis, Antithesis and Synthesis. The thesis: Create a problem using fear, half-truths, innuendo and rumors, transmitted by dishonest, unethical people with influence. The antithesis: Get the assistance of people working on the inside to leak confidential or private information to people on the outside, eventually getting people in the media to spread the information to a wide audience. The synthesis: Offer a solution to the "problem" they in fact created—fire or replace an individual, for example, and bring back the favorite son. In my case, some people who have never accepted me or have been comfortable with me have used these propaganda methods of the Hegelian Dialectic in an attempt to discredit me and get me fired. It is also used to influence public opinion on issues.

In my opinion, a prime example of the Hegelian Dialectic is the Los Angeles football stadium issue. Back in 1980, the Rams left the Los Angeles Memorial Coliseum to play their home games in Anaheim, out in Orange County. The Rams organization didn't want to be seen as abandoning Los Angeles. They didn't want to admit that Orange County simply offered a better deal. They justified the move by using misinformation and fear:

- Put down the Coliseum as old and run down and paint the neighborhood as an unsafe, crime-ridden area.
- Use the media to spread the fear to the community. Get former ticket holders and other NFL teams to paint the Coliseum as unsafe.
- Announce that because of the negative climate, the Rams have no choice but to move.

Even though USC still plays its games at the Coliseum, the publicity surrounding the Rams' departure has hampered growth in that area. And even though the Rams have since moved to St. Louis, the fear created isn't helping Los Angeles' ability to attract a new team.

Another example of the Hegelian Dialectic is the debate on Special Education in New York. Let's follow the formula:

- Every city in America is hurting for public education funds. But there are forces in New York that have decided the city is spending too much to educate children with special needs. So, they keep beating the drum that there will not be enough money to educate the "normal" students.
- Next, they rally their key cohorts and feed the newspapers, airwaves, and then editorials trying to convince the citizens that this policy is wrong and not beneficial to their own students. They say if this policy continues, average citizens will have to pay more in taxes to support these few students requiring so many special needs. They use the ultimate threat of higher taxes as a fear tactic.

- Then they offer their solution for this situation—mainstreaming. They push this approach not because it's what best for students with special needs, but because it will save money.

Instead of calling for more money on public schools—or spending existing funds more wisely—people try to use special needs children as pawns and turn the debate into special needs vs. public schools.

I think some people have tried to use the tenants of the Hegelian Dialectic to get me out as the Vikings head coach. While they don't come out and reveal their agenda, they've tried to use the media to plant stories and create fear that Roger Headrick and I are some kind of evil, insensitive, incompetent people. The underlying message is that the team needs to bring back Mike Lynn and Bud Grant.

People who use fear tactics like those of the Hegelian Dialectic try to shape public debate and hide their own group's ulterior motives. The strategy is designed to polarize groups, pitting one against the other. The attack on Affirmative Action is another clear-cut example of this. Understand the solution and who offered it, and you will clearly meet your adversary. Even if Affirmative Action attacks don't affect you personally, some future attack on equality will.

Unfortunately, we've always had hate, prejudice and fear in our society. One thing I find disturbing in the 1990s is that talk radio is much more aggressive and provocative than during the 1980s when I was head coach at Stanford (1989-91) and Northwestern (1981-85).

In some instances, talk radio has inspired hate in this country. (I'm not alone in my belief that the Twin Cities community has its share of vicious radio hosts and callers, too.) Some of the things that are said on radio are totally derogatory. When that line of decency is crossed and the criticisms become personal, inflammatory or untrue, then you greatly increase the likelihood of producing an irrational response from people on the edge.

One of the hate letters I received began by saying that a certain Twin Cities columnist "was right." I would never suggest that even my harshest critics would condone this stuff, but I wonder if they ever consider the effect their words have on the kooks out there. The message they try to convey in their column or on the radio isn't necessarily the same message the hatemongers hear or read. The kooks think it's OK to call me a "nigger" and "a dumb nigger coach." If I were a white coach, their venom wouldn't have racial overtones. I can deal with hate letters because I understand that they are written by cowardly and ignorant people. But I hope we see the day when my three children—or the next black head coach of the Minnesota Vikings—won't face this kind of hate.

I can remember an incident back in Harrisburg in junior high during gym class. We were playing on an outside field, when all of the sudden several police cars pulled up with their lights flashing. They stopped class and had everybody line up. Then they told the white students to take two steps back. Then they marched down the line of black students, closely eyeballing each one of us. It turned out there was an armed robbery the night before, and the two suspects were black. They brought a witness to our school, but they didn't seem to find who they were looking for. I don't know if they did this search in any other classes, but it was pretty humiliating.

In many ways, the University of Iowa was a well-integrated university. But we often were reminded that we were a few in the midst of thousands. In the final analysis, the university was very unprepared to meet all our needs. We expected that our dignity as unique and valuable persons should have gone beyond our worth as modern gladiators. Many of the black players had begun a secularized midweek prayer meeting in one of the dorm rooms. Our music wasn't always well received, though—we once heard anonymous screams in the dormitories like "Turn down that jungle music." Those things simmered and helped push us toward the eventual decision to boycott the 1969 spring practice.

The University of Iowa was not alone. In retrospect, I can totally understand that there were adjustments to be made on both sides of the situation. The university and our white teammates were experiencing a large dose of culture shock, too. In 1967, we African American players came in as a strong, unified and aggressive group of young people who saw ourselves as fulfilling America's promise. We finally had reached the day that no matter what race or religion you were, if you had the talent, worked hard and got good enough grades, American universities would have an athletic scholarship for you. We were there to collect on that promise. It didn't come without some anxiety on everyone's part. The returning players soon realized that things would change. For many of them, starting jobs would be lost. There were seniors expecting to start who found themselves playing behind a sophomore African American. It was tough. It wasn't talked about at the time, but the tension was there.

One thing I really dislike is segregation in any form. I don't like segregated schools, I don't like segregated churches, I don't like segregated graveyards, I don't like segregated organizations and institutions. I don't like segregation, period. One thing I believe in is integration. I find it interesting that Microsoft, the wealthiest company in the history of the world, has based its whole philosophy on integration. The company has created software that can operate with other computers and with other software. Even though we're talking about machines rather than individuals, people can learn to live and work together. If there's one key word for the 21st Century, I think it's going to be integration.

I owned a fish tank when I coached at Northwestern. I had always wanted fish, so when I got my first head coaching job and had my first big office, I went out and bought a tank. When I went to the fish store to stock the tank, I asked for various species, including angel fish and goldfish. The clerk interrupted me and said, "You can't have those two kinds in the same tank. Angel fish like one water temperature, and goldfish like another. You'll end up killing off one of the species." I didn't accept that idea. I ended up buying all different kinds of fish and putting them together in one tank. I had as much diversity and variety as I could get, including South American species mixed with American river species. Fish, like people, have two choices; they can live together or they can die together. My fish chose to live, and they did so together for many years. We all can learn to adapt if we understand that our quality of life is at stake. Maybe we won't be as comfortable at first, but we'll get used to the new environment.

In our society, we have too many people trying to convince people they'd be better off living in one particular area. The explanation they've given for it, in my opinion, has always been pretty racist. People adapt. They always have and always will, unless the excuse-makers convince them otherwise.

I have always given credit and praise to the many citizens—black and white—who have shown the willingness to fight for issues they believe to be their birthright. In the past few years there appears to be a challenge to the rule of equal rights and equal opportunity. The new diversity had been under attack by many cowards hiding under the shield of "No special treatment." The misguided try to convince the feeble minded that some minority group has been getting an unfair advantage or a preferred starting place. This presumed preferential treatment was attacked under the umbrella of Affirmative Action.

I am proud and grateful that some of the leading universities joined together to take a stand for diversity and a stand against the small, weak-minded individuals who sell exclusion and noncompetition. The Association of American Universities took out a half-page advertisement in the *New York Times* on April 24, 1997. This association consists of 62 leading North American research universities. The group printed its mission statement in regard to diversity:

"We want to express our strong convictions concerning the continuing need to take into account a wide range of considerations—including ethnicity, race, and gender—as we evaluate the students whom we select for admission."

These universities have the courage to tell the truth about admissions. There have always been numerous categories of special admittance—notably the sons and daughters of alumni, professors and other employees of the universities. Unfortunately these categories include few minorities because of past hiring, exclusion and membership policies. So we have discriminatory policies of the past still affecting the present. When you add in student organizations, teams and clubs that have a special place in the fabric of the university—from the football team to the marching band—you see a clear pattern of student admission based on what the particular school sees as a priority. This pattern is what I refer to as selective admissions and selective expectations.

What the studies will show is that the graduation rates for these universities that have been active in diversity are the same as other schools. Providing more for one segment in America does not translate into less for another. There is enough to go around.

I don't think that we'll ever get ahead in America until we stop worrying about our communities' racial makeup and start focusing on shared values. And those values are almost always the same. I know they were the same when I was growing up. Everybody wants a safe place to live without crime and violence. Whether you make $10,000 a year or $100,000 a year, everybody deserves safe environments where they live, attend school, work, worship, shop and spend their leisure time. Whoever commits a crime, whether they do it in a poor socio-economic neighborhood or an upper-class neighborhood, should be punished equally.

The human spirit says that all people want to succeed. I've never heard a young person say, "I want to grow up to be a killer or a gangster," or "I want to grow up and sell drugs," or "I want to grow up and be on welfare." But opportunities haven't always been equal. When you look at why someone is doing well, maybe it's because his father made $100,000 when he was growing up. When you look at why someone is struggling in life, maybe it's because he didn't know his father, and his mother could only earn $100 a month sewing.

If we want Americans to prosper together instead of drifting apart, it's imperative we demand good public schools that prepare our children for college or a career. I lived in a working-class neighborhood in the inner city of Harrisburg. The public schools were small and crowded, but we received a good education because that's what we were there to do. That's what we were seeking when we moved out of the housing projects to a better place. And then you sought what anybody would want—to purchase a house and have a stable property value. If you don't have a stable property value, then you don't have a tax base. And if you don't have a tax base, then your public schools will suffer. If we all share these goals and values, then what difference does it make what race or religion you are?

I remember sitting in a seminar with the president of General Mills. He explained that his company wanted diversity throughout its workforce because it didn't have any racial or religious restrictions on who it wanted to eat Cheerios. He said if General Mills expects everyone to buy Cheerios, then everyone who could be involved in the design, production, selling, receiving and vending of the product should reflect that diversity.

I support the need for diversity in gender, too. I attended a concert this summer featuring the great Lee Ritenour and composer/pianist Dave Grusin. Lee's drummer was a woman named Hillary Jones, and she's among the new wave of females in that industry being hired for her ability.

I recall sitting in an NFL meeting with seven owners and seven general managers—some of the wealthiest and most successful business people in America. The issue of hiring was addressed and the point was made that the lack of opportunity for African American coaches was a function of a white network of executives hiring people they've known and worked with. The way it was categorized summed up one of the underlying issues: One person said, "Maybe we've made a mistake by hiring only people that we're comfortable with."

We need to eliminate the notion that people are comfortable or uncomfortable with a certain skin color. That mistakenly suggests that blacks are supposed to feel more comfortable with all black people but wouldn't be as effective working alongside white people. And vice versa for whites. I can show you some white people, who, if you saw them walking down the street you'd run for cover. And I can also show you just as many black people like that. The point is we're all just people who should be defined by our character instead of our skin color.

I grew up in an era where neighborhoods could literally change overnight. The demographics in Harrisburg said that all the black people lived uptown. And if they didn't live uptown, then they lived in the Howard Day Homes, a federal housing project built for the African American neighborhood. (There also were the Herbert Hoover Homes, a housing project on the south side of town in a white neighborhood. No one talked about the projects in the white neighborhood. I grew up with an impression that only black people needed housing projects. My perception changed when I attended junior high school and met kids from different neighborhoods.)

When a Harrisburg family living in the Howard Day Homes wanted to improve their standard of living, they moved into the Hill neighborhood. Traditionally in our country, when a black family moves in, we've had what we've come to call the abandonment of the inner cities. White families who believe the perception that their property value will decrease, respond by moving into a different neighborhood. So when the black folks move in there on 12th, 13th and 14th streets, then all the white folks move up to 18th, 19th, and 20th streets. All of a sudden a whole neighborhood can change overnight from all white to all black within two or three or four years of time.

Too often when a black family moves in to a primarily white neighborhood, real estate opportunists go around to all the white people in the neighborhood and tell them, "Your neighborhood value is going down, you better get out now!" They use this fear tactic to convince them to sell—traditionally for less than the property value. Of course, they turn around and sell the house—often for more than its actual value—to an African American family trying to escape an even less stable neighborhood.

The NFL has to do a better job in its equal opportunity hiring practices—there's not one person in the league who would deny that fact. The league has new ways to pick its players, but the same old way to pick its coaches.

When Ray Rhodes and Tony Dungy were named head coach of the Philadelphia Eagles and the Tampa Bay Buccaneers, respectively, in recent seasons, they joined me as the NFL's second and third active black head coaches. Three out of 30. We must question if this is considered real progress in an era when more than 67% of the league is composed of players who are African American. It's not a case of jobs never turning over, either. Since 1992, there have been 31 head coaching positions available.

On a positive front, there is a growing presence of qualified African American executives in front-office positions with a number of NFL teams. Also, with the addition of Jacksonville and Carolina into the league, the NFL can now boast of having black men in minority ownership positions.

But there's a consensus that football lags behind other professional sports—especially the National Basketball Association (NBA)—in naming blacks to head coaching positions. I went to New York this June to assist in a presentation to a panel of top NFL team personnel. Commissioner Paul Tagliabue assembled owners Jerry Richardson of Carolina, Bob Kraft of New England, Dan Rooney of Pittsburgh, Mike Brown of Cincinnati and Jeff Lurie of Philadelphia; general managers George Young of the New York Giants, Ron Wolff of Green Bay, Bill Polian of Carolina, Bill Tobin of Indianapolis and Rick McKay of Tampa Bay; vice-presidents Michael Huyghue of Jacksonville and Bob Grier of New England; and coaches Jim Fassel of the Giants, Tony Dungy of Tampa Bay and me.

I introduced the following chart of current and potential head coaches, divided into nine particular categories. If you study the charts below, you see that 14 of the current 30 head coaches are at minimum second-chance head coaches. That's not necessarily bad—I could conceivably be a second-chance head coach myself someday. But it's important that the top assistant coaches be cultivated and considered fairly, instead of just the ones on F and G.

I won't list who I think the best assistant coaches are because I'd probably leave many worthy names off the lists. With the years these assistants have put into the NFL, no one can convince me that they are unknown commodities. I'll continue to encourage the NFL to help open doors for African Americans in all areas of the game.

## Current NFL Head Coaches (30)

**(A) Returners,**
**First NFL Chance (13):**

**(B) In Second NFL Chance (9):**

Dom Capers, Carolina
Dave Wannstedt, Chicago

Joe Bugel, Oakland
Pete Carroll, New England

**(A) Returners,**
**First NFL Chance (13):**

**(B) In Second NFL Chance (9):**

Tom Coughlin, Jacksonville
Bill Cowher, Pittsburgh
Tony Dungy, Tampa Bay
Dennis Erickson, Seattle
Jeff Fisher, Tennessee
Dennis Green, Minnesota
Mike Holmgren, Green Bay
Ray Rhodes, Philadelphia
Barry Switzer, Dallas
Vince Tobin, Arizona
Norv Turner, Washington

Bruce Coslet, Cincinnati
Lindy Infante, Indianapolis
Jimmy Johnson, Miami
Marv Levy, Buffalo
Ted Marchibroda, Baltimore
Marty Schottenheimer, KC
Mike Shanahan, Denver

**(C) Unretired (2):**
Mike Ditka, New Orleans
Dick Vermeil, Philadelphia

**(D) Newest Hires-First Chance (3):**
Jim Fassel, NY Giants
Kevin Gilbride, San Diego
Steve Mariucci, San Francisco

**(E) Changed NFL Jobs (3):**
Bill Parcells, NY Jets
Dan Reeves, Atlanta
Bobby Ross, Detroit

**(F) Ex-Head Coaches,**
**Now Assts. (13):**
Bill Belichick, NY Jets
Rich Brooks, Atlanta
Dan Henning, Buffalo
Les Steckel, Tennessee
Ray Perkins, Oakland
Rod Dowhower, NY Giants
Rich Williamson, Carolina
Al Saunders, Kansas City
Art Shell, Atlanta
Jim Hanifan, St. Louis
Wade Phillips, Buffalo
Bud Carson, St. Louis
Rick Venturi, New Orleans

**(G) Ex-Head Coaches**
**Waiting (5):**
Rich Kottite
George Seifert
Jim Mora
David Shula
Sam Wyche

**(H) Top White Assistants**

**(I) Top Black Assistants**

Fill in your own choices for H and I. The past tells us that 50% of new head coaches come from the above assistant lists. Let's make sure both H and I are used in the future, because both groups have earned the opportunity and are qualified.

What our society needs is more understanding of each other, more open minds and more stories of hope. I think the way Tiger Woods has burst onto the professional golf scene has been great for our country. Of course, he's a Stanford man. Tiger was just coming on campus when I was leaving Stanford to coach the Vikings. Wally Goodwin, who was golf coach at Northwestern during my tenure there, also was Stanford's golf coach during Tiger's recruitment, and I remember him talking about this blue-chip recruit. Tiger was about 16 at the time and a great student, which made Stanford even more excited. The university didn't have a top-10 golf program at the time, but we were close, and I think Tiger knew we could reach that level.

Tiger is such a great competitor and his golf game is so sound. He's a thinking man's player, but he's not afraid to go for it. He's created so much excitement. People talk about Tiger's impact on golf, but he's got a chance to be a special force in society. The great thing about Tiger is that he has a chance to bring a whole generation of young people along with him. In generations before, the successful guys like Bill Russell, Wilt Chamberlain and Jim Brown had showed them, "Hey, maybe I can go to Syracuse to play football" or "to Kansas to play basketball." Young people can see Tiger's "can-do" attitude and dare to be great. He's showing young people that they don't have to live in the suburbs or take $100-an-hour golf lessons. You can achieve the same things in golf that you can in basketball or football if you're willing to put in the work and aren't afraid to dream.

In the meantime, here are 10 things people should remember:

1)   Black people pay taxes, too. Even though the unemployment rate (1995 census) for blacks was 11.6% compared to 4.6% for whites, and just 13.7% of the 34 million blacks had a college degree, compared to 30.6% of whites.

2)   The "good old days" were not good for all Americans. Even in 1995, the per capita income for blacks was $10,982 and $19,759 for whites.

3) Celebrating 50 years since Jackie Robinson integrated professional baseball is really a reminder of how recently baseball got out of the institutional racism business.

4) Baseball Hall of Fame pitcher Bob Ferry proclaimed in 1947 that if Jackie Robinson were white, he would not have been considered big-league baseball material. The truth is Jackie was a great athlete in football, basketball, track and baseball.

5) There were no written rules that prohibited Negro players from playing in Major League Baseball before 1947.

6) Diversity offers opportunities to hear, express and synthesize new points of view.

7) In 1981, there were 14 million children in America living under the poverty level, and it's no coincidence that today in 1997, 16 young black American males die every day due to homicide. I was lucky to be born in 1949.

8) I believe in equal rights. Sometimes I see the term "civil rights" and think that it's redundant. There's nothing civil about discrimination.

9) There is an entertainment reality that verifies everyone's money spends the same.

10) Rachel Robinson, the wife of the late Jackie Robinson, explained that "Black Americans' survival depends on resilience and indestructible hope. The hope that things will get better. I believe this."

# 16

# NFL ISSUES

"As a member of the NFL Competition Committee, I've strongly supported the present system of four preseason games and 16 regular-season games. I've always felt young players need the extra time to get ready for the season and to help their transition to a new system.

"However, the fans are adamantly opposed to the current four preseason games, and it will give way to change. An 18-game regular season is on the horizon for the NFL. I think the current format of four preseason and 16 regular-season games eventually will change, dropping two preseason games and adding two regular-season games."

—Dennis Green, offering one of his insights into the future of the National Football League

Before the issues of expansion and realignment are dealt with, the NFL has two priority issues—a new TV contract and a new collective bargaining deal with the NFL Players Association.

The new television contract, set to go into effect in 1998, will greatly affect the amount of revenue that will be available for the collective bargaining talks in 1999. I think the revenue numbers will go way up. Even though some people expect the revenue to level off or drop, I think it'll continue to rise due to the way our economy is sailing along. All indications are pointing up—the stock market, employment, consumer goods, consumer purchases.

Once the television deal is resolved, then we have to reach a new collective bargaining agreement to ensure labor peace in the NFL. We need labor peace because the fans want to see owners and players work it out, regardless of who gets the edge. They'll view both sides as spoiled brats if there's a strike by the players or a lockout by the owners. Everyone involved in the sport—owners, athletes, coaches, executives—are doing pretty well right now, and the average person would frown at any type of stalemate over money.

Pro basketball was on the verge of a strike last year, and baseball had its strike two years ago. We're fortunate the NFL has had labor peace since 1987—10 years now. But the next contract is going to be a tough go. The players make more now than they ever have, but a significant number of them have short careers. The current contract we have now encourages huge signing bonuses. This summer in our NFC Central Division alone, Green Bay's Brett Favre and Detroit's Barry Sanders got signing bonuses in the $10-12 million range. Under that system, you get a few guys making a lot more money, but a lot of guys making the league minimum, too. Look at a team like the Oakland Raiders—they had to re-do 20 contracts this year to try to keep players happy. That pushes the money out even further. That's going to be an issue.

## Realignment

Once we get the TV contract and the bargaining agreement resolved, realignment will be a key issue. I think some form of NFL divisional realignment is definitely going to happen for the good of the game. It's just a matter of when. The problem is that no one wants to give up their traditional rivals. When you look now at the NFC West, you only have one team in the division west of the Mississippi—San Francisco. St. Louis and New Orleans are basically central region teams, and Carolina and Atlanta obviously are on the east coast.

Once you realign, the significance of the AFC and NFC as we know them won't be as endearing. This was faced before when the NFL and AFL merged. The NFL went to owners like Pittsburgh's Dan Rooney who were willing to put the NFL's best interests ahead of their own team. Pittsburgh was willing to leave the NFC and join the upstart AFC. More people like Rooney will again have to step up for the sake of the entire NFL.

I think we need to study our current playoff structure, too. How much longer can we go with the clear-cut domination—at least in the one-game Super Bowl—of the NFC over the AFC? In one of the years Buffalo won the AFC Championship, the Bills had beaten all four NFC teams they had played in the regular season, yet couldn't win in the Super Bowl. The AFC and NFC non-conference records are comparable. But in the one-game, winner-take-all championship game, it appears that the physical nature of the NFC has made it very difficult for the AFC to win. The 49ers are 5-0 in Super Bowls. People think of them as a finesse team, but that's a facade. They've always been extremely physical on defense, and even though they throw the ball a lot, they're physical on offense, too. Look at the Washington Redskins and their Super Bowl success. The Redskins' famous "Hogs" were the first offensive line to receive that status.

Let's say that one day we reach a point of having 32, 34, maybe even 36 teams in the NFL. You could have 16 make the playoffs and eliminate first-round byes. The current system has 12 qualifying for the playoffs, and an expanded postseason field that would keep fan interest high in more cities late in the season. You also add four first-round playoff games to increase revenues. A bold way to go would be to take the 16 playoff teams and seed them No. 1-16, based on their regular-season records and the current playoff tie-breakers. Then No. 1 would host No. 16, No. 2 hosts No. 15, etc... You would still have a Super Bowl champion, but you improve the chance of getting the best two teams playing for the championship, rather than the best NFC team vs. the best AFC team.

The present system hasn't hurt the NFL at all. It surely hasn't hurt the NFL's economics and interest, which are as healthy as ever. But once we expand, we'll be able to consider a better alignment and playoff plan.

A lot depends on willingness to change. There's been a lot of discussion in baseball this year about its new intra-league format. Those who criticize this experiment are using the old economic thinking. Does anyone believe that a fan in a National League city doesn't want to go to his home park and see Ken Griffey, Jr., during the regular season because of tradition? Even baseball is considering a bold realignment, which could happen as soon as 1998, that could flip-flop traditional National and American League teams and base divisions solely on geographic time zones.

Following is my proposal for a realigned National Football League in the year 2000—just three years away:

**East Division**
Baltimore Ravens
Cincinnati Bengals
Cleveland Browns**
Pittsburgh Steelers
Tennessee Oilers
Washington Redskins

**West Division**
Denver Broncos
Los Angeles Mustangs*
Oakland Raiders
San Diego Chargers
San Francisco 49ers
Seattle Seahawks

**North Division**
Buffalo Bills
New England Patriots
New York Giants
New York Jets
Philadelphia Eagles

**South Division**
Atlanta Falcons
Carolina Panthers
Jacksonville Jaguars
Miami Dolphins
Tampa Bay Buccaneers

**Midwest Division**
Chicago Bears
Detroit Lions
Green Bay Packers
Indianapolis Colts
Minnesota Vikings

**Southwest Division**
Arizona Cardinals
Dallas Cowboys
Kansas City Chiefs
New Orleans Saints
St. Louis Rams

*expansion 2000
**expansion 1999

Teams would play an 18-game regular-season schedule with just two exhibition games (more on this to follow). You'd play each team in your division twice; play all but one team from your partner division (East-North, Southwest-South, Midwest-West) and at least one team from the other divisions. A computer would have to determine the exact schedules.

For the playoffs under this format, 16 of the 32 teams would qualify, and there would be no first-round byes. Teams would be ranked by record and the current tie-breaker system Nos. 1-16. The team with the best ranking would be the host team, with No. 1 vs. No. 16, No. 2 vs. No. 15, etc.

## Expansion

Expansion is another issue that is probably going to happen in the next two to seven years. Cleveland has been promised a team by commissioner Paul Tagliabue, and he'll make good on his promise. I think you'll see them playing as an expansion team in 1999. The city is building a downtown lakeshore stadium that's expected to have the same appeal as Jacobs Field, and will be state of the art for the NFL. The state of Ohio loves football and they've responded to the loss of the Browns with a determined plan. Ohio has the great Hall of Fame connection in Canton, and supports the nationally ranked Ohio State program well.

I expect the Browns to be placed in the AFC Central, where Cleveland has a great tradition. Now whether that means the Baltimore Ravens stay in the AFC Central or go to the AFC East will be determined. In 1997, we have six five-team divisions in the NFL. If Cleveland is added as an expansion franchise, it will mean 31 teams. Either one division will have an extra team or some new configuration will be needed.

The next expansion franchise to begin play would likely be Los Angeles by the year 2000. I know that's a long time away, and Los Angeles football fans would love to get a team sooner, but too many questions have yet to be answered.

The issue for Los Angeles is the venue. People who support the new Los Angeles Coliseum say there's a lot of new construction going on in that area, right near the USC campus, and say the neighborhood is safe and getting more stable all the time. The NFL, I think, has doubts whether people will come to that site and whether other development will come along. I would recommend that Los Angeles put together an aggressive season-ticket drive, led by powerful business people but carried out on a grass-roots scale. If they can convince the NFL that crowds will come, then the new Coliseum will work.

The NFL wants what's best for the entire league. So Los Angeles, it's time to get busy and unite the forces of Mayor Richard Riordan and city council member Mark Ridley-Thomas and show the league you support the plan. Neither the Rams nor the Raiders drew well in Los Angeles. Based on that, the NFL has to take the position that a new expansion team won't necessarily draw enough fans unless there are some new strategies. The way for Los Angeles to change the NFL's position is to secure commitments for tickets and luxury boxes.

It hasn't helped Los Angeles to see the passion that fans of Carolina and Jacksonville have shown since they were selected as expansion teams. The commitment they made to their new stadiums, with the number of seats and luxury boxes purchased, was gangbusters. Los Angeles has to develop some passion of its own for pro football. That could be hard, because there are so many other things to do and so much competition for the entertainment dollar in that region.

Now there's no doubt the impact of Fox TV owner Rupert Murdoch's impending purchase of the Los Angeles Dodgers baseball team could be a factor. Because restrictions have been eased on cross ownership of pro teams, he could be a key player if he chose to get involved on the football side. Murdoch purchased the team, stadium and property in the Dodger deal, and a lot of people feel there's room for a football stadium on that property. With Fox TV right now being in control of so many NFL television games in all the major cities, Murdoch would have a good shot at an NFL expansion team for Los Angeles. I don't know if that's Murdoch's intent, but if it is, it would give him one leg up on Ted Turner in their continuous battle to be the king of communication and entertainment.

There used to be a rule that you couldn't own an NFL team and another pro sports team, to avoid any conflict of interest. But that rule has been eased because of Wayne Huizenga, the owner of the Miami Dolphins, and the NHL's Florida Marlins. The way the rule is now, Huizenga can't own a Minnesota hockey team but he can own a Miami team. As of right now, both Cleveland and Los Angeles have to come up with owners who'll be partners with city-owned stadiums.

Part of the expansion issue involves some current NFL problem cities. Of course, Houston has lost the Oilers to Tennessee. At one point recently there were six other NFL franchises whose futures looked uncertain—Cincinnati, Seattle, Cleveland, Los Angeles, Indianapolis and Minnesota. (See any pattern to the franchises and cities in that group?)

It appears that Cincinnati is going to win approval to build a new stadium. Seattle just got approval for a new stadium. Cleveland got a new stadium and will be in expansion. I believe Los Angeles, one way or another, will be involved in expansion. That leaves two teams—Indianapolis and Minnesota—still needing to upgrade their revenue and stadium situations.

The league wants the Colts to stay in Indianapolis and not move to Cleveland. The other team the NFL is watching is the Minnesota Vikings. The league would like to see our community come together on a stadium situation that reflects the new economies of the NFL as it looks to the 21st Century. They want us to have a stadium that will allow the owners to benefit from their investment, like anyone should expect, and create the kind of income flow that allows a team to compete on the field on an annual basis.

When these specific franchise issues are solved, then the future would appear to be international. Let's say by the year 2005 the NFL is going strong with 32 teams, assuming Cleveland and Los Angeles get franchises back. They easily could expand to as many as 36 teams—which would make an even number with six six-team divisions—if they don't limit it to the United States. Here are some possible expansion sites for 10-15 years down the road:

- Mexico City certainly would be a possibility, with its proximity and the population. Every time Mexico City has hosted an NFL preseason game it has sold over 100,000 tickets.
- Moving into Canada seems like a good possibility, too. Toronto has been clamoring to get a team in the NFL.
- Anaheim/Orange County, California, is another, especially if Disney gets involved in ownership like it is now in pro hockey with the Mighty Ducks and in baseball with the Angels.
- Houston is one of the largest cities in the nation and sits in the most rabid football state in America. The wounds will heal from the Oilers' departure, and don't be surprised if that the community eventually comes back with a new stadium. If not, another Texas possibility would be San Antonio.

## 18-Game Schedule

As a member of the NFL Competition Committee, I've strongly supported the present system of four preseason games and 16 regular-season games. I've always felt young players need the extra time to get ready for the season and to help their transition to a new system. However, the fans are adamantly opposed to the current four preseason games, and it will give way to change. An 18-game regular season is on the horizon for the NFL. I think the current format of four preseason and 16 regular-season games eventually will change, dropping two preseason games and adding two regular-season games. The coaches like the current length of the training camp to develop young players. Plus, there's resistance to change on two financial fronts:

- First, NFL teams rely on the preseason money because they keep all the ticket and concession revenue for those games. We don't start sharing the money with the rest of the league until the regular season kicks into gear. We still charge full price for preseason tickets and the owners use that money to help fund their whole organization.
- Second, more regular-season games will mean paying more money to players. They'll want some adjustment on their contracts for the added work. Adding two games will mean a 10 percent longer season, so player contracts likely will go up about 10 percent. Revenue will have to be found to cover that.

The current approach has been to change how preseason games have traditionally been marketed. The NFL has tried to change the perception of exhibition games, emphasizing that future stars are on display, and jobs are on the line. A Twin Cities columnist floated an idea to use your preseason won-loss record as part of your playoff tie-breaker, to create more interest and more competitive games. But that idea would have little support from players, who don't want to risk injury, or from teams, who want to see young players in game situations, yet don't want to do anything that could jeopardize their playoff chances.

The rash of injuries you saw this preseason will keep the debate for a shorter preseason alive. But the main reason I see a change to 18 games coming will be to provide more value for the fans, sponsors and television networks. The corresponding drop from four to two pre-season games would put more emphasis on mini-camps as well as more outside scrimmages in training camp.

## Indoor Grass

Another change we could see in the NFL's future involves artificial turf. Its benefits are clear in adverse weather, and the turf can be especially friendly to teams blessed with great speed. But when players are polled, they overwhelmingly want to play on real grass. Medical studies also are clear that playing and practicing on artificial turf puts players at greater risk for injuries. The trend in outdoor major college and pro football fields over the last decade has been to tear out the turf and go back to real grass. These state-of-the-art real grass fields have specially designed underground piping to ensure correct moisture, even growth and swift drainage.

For some or all of the seven NFL teams who play in domed stadiums—Minneapolis, Detroit, Indianapolis, Atlanta, Seattle, New Orleans and St. Louis—a new technology could bring back real grass to their stadiums, too. The Portable Assembled Grass Football Field (PAGFF) is an innovative concept I'm proposing, and I think it's the idea for the future. This is a natural grass playing field that is grown in sections on platforms, then loaded onto semi-tractor trailer trucks and taken to the stadium. There the grass-covered platforms are assembled (like Madison Square Garden's court for basketball) on the football field. Then we play the game. Following the game, the platforms are taken apart, loaded up on the trucks and taken back to the growing site. If it is the growing season, the platforms are kept outside where they're watered and revived for the next use. If it's in November or later, then the platforms would be placed in two huge hothouse sheds. The Pontiac Silverdome installed a real grass system for a World Cup soccer tournament over a two-week period a couple of years ago, and this builds on that concept.

The biggest advantage to indoor real grass would be a reduction of injuries and possibly prolonged playing careers, which could save a team money in the long run. If you have $40 million invested in Barry Sanders and several million dollars collectively in other players, you certainly would listen to any plan that might protect that investment. While it might be too expensive for some leagues to even consider, an NFL team has just 10 preseason or regular-season home dates. If the technology is in place and the system can be worked out in the multi-tenant domes, it would seem to be an idea worth trying in the future.

If the concept sounds a little outrageous, consider these points:

- Green Bay actually resodded Lambeau Field last January for the NFL Championship game.
- When rock star Meat Loaf played at the Metrodome, he needed 40 semi-trailers to haul his stage and props around for one night's performance.
- Remember in the early 1980s, only the college teams with lights could play night games or have late afternoon kickoffs. When expanded television coverage came and meant more dollars, the concept of portable lights became attractive. If you could get a night game and be on national TV, you did it. The home team paid the $40,000 rental for the portable lights, and once the game was over, the three semi-tractor trailers with the crane-type lights would drive away from the stadium to the next assignment.
- The players may demand it. They could come back in the next collective bargaining agreement and say they want to outlaw astroturf. They don't want quarterbacks landing on their heads on that hard surface like Troy Aikman did in Dallas.

The technology is ready. This will bring a new excitement to the game. Every community can't build a new stadium—most will have to renovate existing ones. Only a few will have the funds for a retractable dome stadium. So the issue of a hard surface, unpopular with the players and coaches who see more injuries, is not resolved.

One way to ensure the NFL's continued success is to be innovative and creative. Additionally, we would increase the chances of keeping our best players healthy and happy. The cost can be justified as another cost of doing business. I was hoping that an indoor real grass system would have made its football debut at this past season's Super Bowl in the New Orleans Superdome, but it didn't happen. However, I'd love to see the Vikings take a close look at the plan and do it.

## Buoying Interest in Football

Football is the most popular sport in our country today, yet there is a concern that in 1997, fewer boys age 12 and under played the game compared to the number of 12-under youth who played in 1967.

The 10-year-old boy who played football in 1977 is now age 30, and research says he absolutely loves the NFL. With youth participation down at the present time, I think we have to assume that there's a link between early participation in football as a recreational sport and a later love of NFL football.

So the NFL has begun some initiatives to try to improve participation—not only for boys, but for girls, as well. The PLAY Football program is a summer flag football program in inner-cities. Football isn't just a tackling game. We're trying to let young people know that it's fun to catch, run and throw. The NFL is also hosting seminars to show people that with the proper equipment, football is a safe game.

There are very few junior-high football programs today, especially in the inner cities. You've heard me talk about the importance of my junior-high football experience in my life—without it, I'm not sure things would have worked out the same way for me. It's valuable for kids to establish at an early age that they can go out and accomplish something positive in a competitive setting. Hopefully this NFL initiative and other community programs can help keep youth football afloat. Most people who play pro football came from lower economic backgrounds. If you eliminate the youth football programs in some of these rural and inner-city areas, it will affect the number of kids who could eventually get a college scholarship. I came from a situation as a youth where earning a football scholarship was all my friends and I talked about. That was our ticket out.

The NCAA decision to raise academic standards could have an effect on future players. I know, for example, there are a lot of African Americans right now who aren't able to meet those newer standards. That's not making excuses, that's just reality in some of the school systems that these young people have to work and excel in. How the new standards will affect college football, for example, will be interesting. A number of African American young people are going to fall short of qualifying to play major-college football, and in turn miss a chance at the NFL. Those cases are already showing up. People who push for the standards say it's all relative and that nobody will notice any drop in quality. I disagree with that. We need to be careful these new academic standards are not an attempt to purify the game of football.

People who play major college football pretty much come from rural America and the inner cities. Not as many come from the higher socioeconomic areas. I certainly think you have to be concerned about the quality of education kids are getting. But we have to make sure kids are given some opportunity and encouragement, and not just told they're not good enough and denied the access that's been part of the new way of American thinking. The old way in America was before anyone cared about equal rights and opportunity.

As we try to build and maintain interest in the NFL among youth, we can't ignore or take lightly the popularity of soccer. The soccer moms are an organized group and, together with 85 percent of the African American vote, got President Clinton elected. There's no doubt soccer has risen in participation among youth. I think the NFL must always show its game in the right light and also show the effect football has had on the American spirit.

## Replay and TV

Instant Replay, even though it was defeated this year, will return to the NFL, sometime by the year 2000. We've pushed hard for it on the NFL Competition Committee. It will become clear, as we move into expansion and realignment issues, that getting calls correct will be extremely important. From a financial standpoint, there's too much at stake not to have a better system. The technology will be better, too.

Television always has and always will influence how the NFL schedule is set up. I'm not necessarily sure we'll see more prime-time TV games than what we have now. One obvious reason is that you can't play a Thursday night game then play again three days later like in other sports. The NFL enjoys a special place as a Sunday and Monday night event across the country.

Would the league ever consider sliding into Thursday, Friday or Saturday nights to get more television and exposure? I hope not. The thing about the NFL game that's unique is that because there are far fewer games than pro baseball, hockey and basketball, every game takes on more meaning. It's what I call the "Big-Event" concept. NFL football is the topic at office water coolers and on loading docks in this country. Not as many people talk about baseball, basketball or hockey, until you get deep into the playoffs. The anticipation in this country for Monday Night Football is amazing. It's still one of the highest-rated shows on television.

## Salaries

Pro football is indeed in the entertainment business. The reality is that our best players are no different than Tom Cruise or Denzel Washington, Rod Stewart or Luther Vandross, Jerry Seinfeld, Bill Cosby or David Letterman. The NFL  has people with special skills and a unique ability to entertain people. We can yearn for the good old days, when the business of sports didn't dominate the games themselves, but the fact is that when fans buy tickets, corporations buy luxury boxes, advertisers pay to be associated with your product, and radio and television pays to broadcast your games, you have to invest in your team, and that means paying more for players.

For the NFL, we're moving into an era where the very best players will receive a lot of money, but other players will get significantly less. I think you'll see more veteran players being asked to take a pay cut if they want to keep their jobs. It will be cheaper to use rookies and free agents willing to play for less.

This year, we saw Barry Sanders and Brett Favre get the big signing bonuses and lucrative contracts. Brett was the MVP in the league for the second year in a row and MVP of the Super Bowl. I guess he earned every cent of that money.

The NFL offers the shortest career and the greatest injury potential, so its players have to earn their money while they can. And for now in the NFL, contracts aren't guaranteed beyond the current year, unlike the NBA, where teams regularly swallow salaries to cut loose players who aren't in their plans. In general, football has been more responsible in its salaries than the NBA or major league baseball. But even in pro football we've reached the point where we're pushing the limit. We're foolish if we don't learn from the mistakes that owners, agents and players have made in other sports. When it was learned last August in the Twin Cities that Minnesota Timberwolves player Kevin Garnett turned down an initial offer of $102 million for six years, there was a backlash against the player, his agent, his team and I think other Minnesota pro teams, as well.

The pressure to cover the cost of these salaries doesn't have to come from the fans. Corporate sponsorship and network television money pays a lot of our bills. Hopefully our revenues from corporate partners and television will go up, and those costs won't simply be passed back to the consumer.

Right now in 1997, most professional sports are flying high—whether it's golf, basketball or football. I believe in the free-market system—that's the great American way. What we have are players being rewarded because they're popular and talented.

# 17

# OBSERVATIONS

*"Dennis Green is uncanny in being able to find out what the dynamics are on a team. If he doesn't like the dynamics, he changes them.*

*"He changed Stanford from a soft-type football team to a very aggressive, hard-hitting football team...If we had problems over the years, it was that we couldn't stop anybody. Dennis revolutionized Stanford football.*

*"He's a superb corporate executive. A lot of people can X and O you to death, but inside their program is in shambles. With Denny, you get soup to nuts, A to Z. Football is America's corporate game. It's all about organization and motivation."*

—Former Stanford athletic director
Andy Geiger, who hired Green
as Stanford head coach in 1989

As someone who is regularly interviewed in the media and who is a frequent public speaker, I'm often asked my opinions on a wide variety of topics, from the NFL, to college football, to race, to business. I've always felt my core philosophies of life could apply to football, society or the corporate world.

Here are some commonly asked questions and things I've learned and observed in 26 years of coaching:

## Leadership

As leaders, many old-school coaches have a military-like outlook of football. Most of them were coached themselves by the military type and adopted many of those philosophies. I was not in the military, though I recognize how the military and football chains of command are alike. I've always thought of my leadership style as similar to that in a business environment. I understand business, and I think there are a lot of similarities between managing a business and running a football team.

I always wanted to be a head coach. Back in Harrisburg, I was always organizing the basketball games, for example. I'd call all the guys and then I'd call the team from the other side of town. I'd set the time and the locations, and then I'd bring the ball. I've been influenced by the men I've played for. They put an emphasis on success in school and on the field. I learned discipline from them. Once I made the team, they taught me I had to get in shape and stay in shape. Then I had to develop the grittiness to become a winner. They stuck with me as a youngster, taught me to be aggressive and showed me the way to the top.

Being a good leader means being a good example. I really enjoy the challenge of getting to work every day. I love my job and I can hardly wait to get on the field. If something comes to me in the middle of the night, I won't be able to sleep because I'll be so anxious to get started implementing it. I think a challenge is great.

Being a good leader also means being well organized. Organizing is the key to planning. We write down exactly what we want accomplished. Our players know what we want and how we're going to do it. The can take that to the bank. We plan out our pre-season in its entirety. We know exactly what we will do each day and each hour. The players know that on Tuesday, July 29 they will be off the field at 5:30.

The players know where I'm coming from and the pressure is on us to do it. So you have to know your strategy, plan your work and work your plan. Then you have to implement your plan. Some people don't know how to pull the trigger. When crunch time comes, they want to analyze again. No. You've already done the analyzing, the planning and now is the time to implement your plan. Make sure you've done a good job of organizing, analyzing and planning, then do it. You make the decisions when it is decision time. Not later. Pull the trigger.

## Effective Management

I was an assistant coach for 12 of my first 17 years in coaching, and I understand a basic motto: treat others how you want to be treated.

I think I know what my staff wants from me. A good assistant has to want his position players to make a contribution. If it doesn't bother the assistant that the player isn't producing, you have a big problem. The assistant coach is like a department head. He has to want his department to succeed. A football team is like a company. The players are the employees, the assistant coaches are department heads, the coordinators (offensive and defensive) are vice presidents, and the coach is the CEO.

One person cannot do everything alone. There is nothing worse than a head coach who tries to be the offensive and defensive coordinator, the special teams coach, the player personnel manager, the scout and the general manager. Delegating means you have to respect and trust your coordinators. And you have to make sure they know precisely what it is you want and how you want it done. But give them authority to do what they have to do and they will be happy. All of my staffs have been happy because I let the coordinators do their job. I let them coordinate. But I remain the leader. There can be only one head coach, but others have to contribute.

Whether you're a company president or a head football coach, you can't feel threatened by new ideas and approaches. You'd be a fool not to take advantage of what your assistants have brought from other teams. I've had guys on my staff like Gary Zauner, who coached under George Allen, and Tony Dungy, who coached under Chuck Noll. We try to learn from all systems. You have to give your assistants the freedom to seek knowledge and apply it. The key is to make sure everyone is on the same page in goals and philosophy.

It's also unwise to ask someone to be what they're not. One guy might be a "rah-rah" type and another might be a strong silent type. Both can be effective but they have to be themselves.

The first thing I look for in an assistant is loyalty. Talent, intelligence and experience don't come before loyalty. The second characteristic I seek is the ability to work hard. Third, I want a team player, someone not interested in the individual but the team. Fourth, we look for talent.

## Goal Setting

I believe strongly in goal-setting. The biggest thing is to establish goals for yourself and then to accomplish them. That's success. We establish short- and long-term goals for our football team. When I first came to Minnesota, our short-term goal was to win the Central Division, while our long-term goal was to win the Super Bowl.

As a team, we have to take advantage of everything available to reach our goals. That means acquiring players through free agency and the college draft. It also means being involved in player development to improve individual skills. Then our goal is to have a successful training camp, finding the right balance of teaching and training. We don't want the players sick of football when training camp ends. We want them to feel fresh and eager for the season to start. We want them confident that they've been trained well and now know what it takes to win.

## Motivation

The ability to motivate players often relates to your goals. First of all you have to make sure that what you want that person to accomplish is realistic. I can try to motivate you to run through a brick wall, but that's not realistic. Then we have to lay out clearly what their responsibility is. You have to remember that in motivation, you can't want success more than the person you're motivating does. If you are head of a company and the marketing, sales and research areas are all pulling their weight but production is not, you are in trouble. You can't will that production person to produce. You'll have to put someone in charge who wants to produce and be successful.

Of course some people are easier to motivate. One of the first things we look at in evaluating a prospect is how much success a player has had in his career, and what role has he had in his team's success? Has he had a leadership role? Some guys are flat out winners. The team wins when they play and doesn't win when they don't.

I treat all my players even-handedly. But you have to remember that each player is different. Some people need a kick in the behind, while others need a pat on the back. A player may complain to me, "How come you yell at me, but you don't yell at him?" I answer that I am being evenhanded. I am yelling at him to try to help him. I may not yell at another player because I am trying to help that player, too. A true leader must have vision. Thus, setting the goal is the easy part. Whether you are CEO of a large company, president of a small company or head of a department, you have to know exactly what is expected of you. Then you have to know exactly what you want to accomplish. Once you have that set in your mind, you need two things—commitment and expectations.

You have to know what you expect and know what is expected of you. Some people are just in business, they aren't out to accomplish great things. There are organizations in the NFL who aren't trying to win the Super Bowl, hard as that is to believe. There are people in business who don't have basic goals for success, let alone lofty aspirations. So you need commitment and you need expectations.

## Perseverance

It's not always easy. If your spirits are way down, it's not always easy to get back up. My 0-11 debut season at Northwestern was the hardest thing I'd ever been through in coaching football. But I couldn't let the losses diminish my confidence. I also had to resist the human temptation of blaming others or blaming the situation and simply accept total responsibility for the defeats. Some people can't handle failure. By the same token, when you win a championship, you can't let it become an ego thing either. You can't think you won because you were a great coach. You have to keep an even keel. When you do that, you won't get too high or too low.

## Team Players

Everyone in your organization has to accept that there is more to be gained by team success than individual success. We tell our players, "If you seek team success, you will enjoy individual glory. But if you seek individual glory, you won't enjoy team success." The same is true in business. If everyone in a company has success as their objective, that business will thrive. But if they are only looking out for themselves, the company will fail. I ask my players, "What would you rather have, five Pro Bowl appearances or one Super Bowl championship?" You know what the answer be. If your team is successful, you will get plenty of individual recognition.

Everyone has to have a team attitude. If the most talented guy on our team—who is making $2 million a year—shows disrespect to our trainer who is making $35,000, who am I going to side with? The trainer. I won't be afraid to cut a player who shows a pattern of disrespect. This is a team. We can't let a player pick and choose who he is going to respect, even if he is the most talented player on the team. Everyone must be treated with respect.

The head coach has to want to win more than anyone else on the staff, or on the team for that matter. The same is true in business. The president of a company has to want to turn a profit more than anyone else in the organization. The coach has to believe he can win.

## Great Rivalries

One of the things that make sports so unique are the emotions that are felt, not just by the players and coaches but in the stands and the community. Special rivalries are like that. At John Harris High, the big game was vs. William Penn. At Stanford, I was a part of one of the best rivalries in the history of college athletics in our battles with Cal Berkeley. In the NFL, the Vikings' most emotional games have been vs.

the Green Bay Packers, who come into this season as World Champions. I think the Packers have replaced the Bears as the Vikings' biggest rival.

Our biggest challenge in 1997 will be to try to unseat the Packers in the Central Division. Packer head coach Mike Holmgren and I worked three years together with the 49ers. We shared an office and worked in the press box together during games. I have a great deal of respect for him. It was a unique situation because we both were hired for our respective jobs on January 10, 1992—it was my first NFL head coaching job and third overall, and it was Mike's first head coaching opportunity of any kind. I'm not surprised by the success he's had at Green Bay. He's an excellent football coach, very solid fundamentally. He's like Bill Walsh in the fact he's a lot tougher than people realize. He could not have turned around Green Bay without being tough.

Packer fans have never wavered in the support of their team, but they had a long dry spell after Vince Lombardi. Guys who as players and coaches were some of the biggest names in football, like Dan Devine and Bart Starr, couldn't accomplish what Mike Holmgren did in bringing a world championship back to Green Bay. Mike's ability to put everything together brought them the championship. All of our games have been interesting ones and have contributed to making the Vikings and Packers one of the top rivalries in the NFL. We won the first four games against Green Bay, and in the last three seasons, each team won at home and lost on the road for a 3-3 split. So going into the 1997 season, we had a 7-3 record vs. Green Bay.

## Personalities

Mike Ditka, like myself, a Pennsylvania native, has been great for the game of football. His charisma and presence have helped make the NFL the success that it has become. I enjoyed our trip to LaCrosse in training camp to scrimmage the New Orleans Saints and see Mike Ditka across the sideline. He was a Hall of Fame tight end and a very successful head coach with the Chicago Bears. Now he's back in the game, and that's good for the NFL. I hate to see guys retire prematurely. I had only coached against Mike in my first season, and we were fortunate to win both games. His return to the game will increase the competitive edge for the Saints. He can always put a team on the field that has a chance to win. His strong personality alone can keep a team in contention.

While Ditka uses toughness and tenacity to get results, NFL commissioner Paul Tagliabue is a down-to-earth guy who uses intelligence, diplomacy and vision to run our league. He has the most difficult job of any of the professional sports commissioners because there are more teams (30) to govern than any other sport, which means a responsibility to more owners, coaches and players in enforcing the rules, regulations and by-laws of the NFL. I've always been impressed with his background for the job. He had conducted business with the NFL for many years, but was the right person at the right time to carry on the great work of Pete Rozelle and continue to guide the league's increased income, popularity and visibility. There are always those who wanted a former coach or player to replace Rozelle, but realistically, Paul has the NFL on top and climbing as we move into the 21st century.

Some tricky issues are on the commissioner's hot burner—including expansion, team movement and fan involvement. He also has his eye on the future. Research tells him there are fewer young boys playing football today in youth programs, junior high and high schools than at any time in the last 50 years. One of the goals of his new P.L.A.Y. football agenda for youths is to offer football of all varieties to young people in America; touch and flag football for boys and girls, and tackle football. All of these formats can give young people a chance to experience the excitement, teamwork and thrill of participation and give them a chance to develop a love for the game of football.

## NCAA Issues

I spent more than half of my coaching career in college football, and one of the things I've never understood is the resistance to a national championship playoff. The NCAA and university presidents are not being fair to college football, and they know it. I still think there's a lot of jealousy aimed at college football. Men's and women's college basketball have increased in popularity in recent years, and rightfully so. The men's basketball Final Four is the best show in town. It presents a great forum to sell college basketball. I think a Division I football playoff would do the same thing.

I expressed this opinion in Dallas a few years back in 1991 at one of the rare meetings that involved the PAC 10 and Big Ten coaches and the already established College Football Association (CFA). I also predicted the demise of the CFA, and I was correct. It appears to me that football has been under attack for several years now. The NCAA wants less scholarships, less budget, less recruiting time, less practice time, less development time, less spring practice time, but still wants to collect the big revenue from gate receipts, television and bowl games. In some ways I can appreciate the NCAA's one-school, one-vote philosophy. But relevancy is also important. To think a Division I basketball school that doesn't play football would have the same thing in common with Ohio State or Iowa is not realistic. College football is now suffering from the compromise of the flawed Alliance bowl system. The only way to have a national championship is to have a playoff system. NCAA Division I-AA has it; Divisions II and III have it; NAIA has it; all of the NCAA women's sports have championships. Only one sport doesn't have an NCAA-sponsored national championship, and that's football.

Besides the fairness of crowning a true champion, a playoff system of some kind would showcase the game of college football, and of course raise millions of dollars that would be shared in all NCAA schools across the nation. We don't have to erase the tradition of the major bowl games. They can be among the new partnerships that can be formed with playoff games at neutral sites. I think the value of college football has been denied selfishly for too long. A playoff system is the American way. We can have a Little League World Series champion but not an NCAA Division I football champion.

I've heard the academic arguments against Division I football play-offs, but as someone who has coached at Stanford and Northwestern, I think it sells players short to say they can't handle the time and travel commitments. When you realistically look at the travel demands of a college basketball team that might make 20 trips, many in midweek, over five months, you can justify a football team that could make 8-10 trips all season, almost exclusively on weekends. Again, if Divisions I-AA, II and III can do it, there's no reason Division I can't, too.

College football is also under attack on the gender equity front. Who doesn't want equity? The question gets down to how do you achieve fairness and at the same time be realistic about your sources of revenue?

Of course I want equal athletic opportunities for my daughter Vanessa as she enters the educational and athletic systems, just like I wanted for myself 30 years ago.

At Stanford we had a clear understanding that we all were in the same boat. Revenue had to be distributed fairly. That money to pay your bills and support your student-athletes has to come from gate receipts, university funds, or at some universities, state and federal government funds. A sound Division I football program can generate tremendous income and alumni donations for the university.

Hopefully we can find the right balance in gender equity that doesn't encourage bashing of football, and doesn't encourage schools to drop wrestling or baseball to get their ratios in line. It takes the Stanford way where everyone is working together.

College administrators have to be careful when they talk about scaling back football. Realistically, college football's popularity across the country is high, but with all your great intentions, if you water down the product, you risk losing spectators and television viewers. Certainly, college football is about getting an education first and foremost, but it's naive and foolish to ignore the benefits that major-college football teams bring to their campus, community, alumni and the nation. If football does lose popularity and generates less money, people are going to need something else to pick up the slack. Who is that somebody?

People who push for the concept of proportionality—that strictly ties gender equity to equal numbers of athletes competing for women and men—refuse to accept the fact that football is a unique sport for two reasons—1) its great revenue-generating status and 2) the fact there's no counterpart sport to football that a female could compete in, like softball is to baseball. If a school has 85 scholarship players and 35 walk-ons in football, that's 120 males competing. Proportionality advocates, in effect, want to deny those 120 their chance to participate.

In the fall issue of *Sidelines* magazine, Grant Teaff, the executive director of the American Football Coaches Association, shoots down the proportionality proponents' thesis that Division I football programs don't make money. He cited a 1995-96 survey by the Athletic Directors' Association, with 87 schools responding. Total football income generated that year at those 87 schools was $628 million, with football expenses of $328 million, leaving $299 million in profit for schools to spend on other programs. Men's basketball brought in $241 million and had expenses of $149 million, for a profit of $92 million. The other men's sports at the 87 schools brought in $14 million and had expenses of $126 million, for a deficit of $112 million. Women's sports at the 87 schools generated $11 million while spending $182 million, for a deficit of $171 million.

It's not just the financial reasons. I'm bothered to see at most schools that gaining more opportunities for women means reducing opportunities for men. Participation is good for everyone. The whole idea is for young people—women and men—to experience the value of participation. Any time you start cutting numbers of walk-ons or having whole men's programs dropped, it's bad business. I just think we're on real dangerous ground when we start making the issue "More for you has to be less for me." There has to be a better way of doing it.

It's real easy to look at the ones who have the most, like football, and say, "Cut there." But it's silly to think somebody can say they know more about what it takes to run a successful Division I football program than the people who have been doing it their whole careers. The game is popular because you can watch people do things nobody else can do. If  suddenly we deny the players the chance to really perform and be outstanding, their  college experience is diminished and the game of college football will suffer. I just worry that too many cuts will diminish the popularity of football, and that could affect schools' entire budgets for men's and women's sports.

# 18

# WELL ROUNDED, WELL GROUNDED

*"I think the players like the fact that their head coach has a life outside of coaching football. Now, when I ask them to do something, they know I'm not just asking them to do it because I have no life."*

—Dennis Green, on how his passion for music
gives him a nice outlet for his football stresses

My parents bestowed many gifts on me in our brief time together. I'm especially grateful that Dad exposed me to music. Dad believed that if you're well rounded, you're well grounded. Learning to play a musical instrument provided me many of the same benefits as athletics. I learned the importance of practice, patience and hard work. I learned how to work with others in the band. In the process, I gained an appreciation for music in general.

I often wonder today if my Dad knew I would get hooked on drumming when he insisted on my taking drum lessons when I was a kid. The option for Bus Green's kids wasn't whether or not to play. The only choice was which instrument. "Take your pick," was all he said. "All your brothers took music lessons, and you will, too. I don't care which instrument you play. If we don't have it in the closet, then we will find a way to get it for you." Dad required us to try music and marching band in junior high, then let us decide whether to play on in high school or not.

Billy played the trumpet. Playing football was no excuse to keep him off of the Edison Junior High School band. Dad and Mom challenged the idea that you could not be in the band and play sports. The Green boys would do both. Billy already was a tremendous athlete—he eventually would have been a college scholarship player if there were more opportunities when he graduated. But even the star athlete would get a taste of being in the marching band. At Edison Junior High in the 1950s, that meant marching along in a pretty humbling uniform. The hats looked like something worn by the great Czar of Russia during the 19th Century. Throw in tight, maroon high pants and white buck shoes, and you resembled a Buckingham Palace guard in a Pat Boone video.

Bobby skipped junior-high football and was "rewarded" with three years of  marching band. Bobby owned a brown drum that was later handed down to me. Come to think of it, it probably was a hand-me-down to Bobby, too. (I never dared ask my parents.) Bobby was bigger than Billy, and I cringe when I recall that tight-fitting uniform on his lanky body. Bobby hated the marching part of the band the most. We saw him play at every football game and parade. My parents would point and say, "There's your big brother, Bobby." So it was no surprise that Bobby retired from music when he reached high school. His brown drum stayed in the closet until I resurrected it  many years later.

Stan, who played the clarinet, almost made the uniform work. Stan was eight years older than me and combined his music, singing and leadership skills by starting his first rhythm and blues band during his junior-high days. The Thundering Senturies, the hottest R&B band in central Pennsylvania in the 1960s, was in its formative concept phase even before Stan got to high school. Stan was the lead singer, complemented by three backup singers, a lead guitarist, a bass guitarist, keyboardist and drummer. All of the guys in the band wanted to hit it big and were willing to pay the price. In 1963, when their regular drummer enlisted in the Army, they let me play the drums for them at all of their summer performances. I was just 13, and caught the music business bug in a big way.

Greg, who chose the trumpet, also was a three-year veteran of junior-high marching band. In 1961, I brought out the old brown drum that was painted white, and joined Greg in the band. Greg has always been a sharp dresser, and he worked on his uniform and somehow gave it a different look. The sight of me in that awful uniform was another story. Let's just say that if pitchman George Zimmer sold these uniforms in his Men's Wearhouse stores, even he wouldn't guarantee satisfaction. There we were at a parade. Greg made the uniform look just right, while I looked sloppy and uncomfortable. When I was measured for the uniform in September, we didn't anticipate my growth spurts of that school year. When I put the uniform on in late May for the Memorial Day parade, it was so tight it made spandex seem baggy.

The Thundering Senturies experience was exciting and challenging. We played everywhere you could have a gig—in gyms, concert halls, on college campuses and at outdoor venues. Who would guess that 30 years later, I would be back in the music business? My present wife Marie and I helped form a company called Savannah Street Music. Our three-year music company involvement was full of hope, excitement, dreams realized and dreams unfulfilled, relative success and major disappointment. I was chairman, Marie was president and Ben and Kazir, two young and talented Minnesota artists, were the producers.

We had three primary releases and worked closely with more than 30 musicians and vocalists. Savannah Street is a full-service music company that writes its own songs and music, and also performs on the albums. The records are produced in the company's St. Paul studio, too. Major recording projects required that the editing and final mastering be contracted out. We had a stable of young talent—up-and-coming artists who dreamed of making it big—and we formed the Sunset Music Band out of this promising collection of artists.

We met, performed with, and performed before a few of the legends in the music business. In 1995, we opened for the one-and-only B.B. King at an Epilepsy Foundation fundraiser, and later opened at a special party with saxophone superstar Kenny G, one of the top recording artists in contemporary jazz. After listening to our band, Kenny offered praise and encouragement, which was a thrill for our musicians.

Our band released a CD in the spring of 1995 called "Sunset Celebration." World-renowned trumpeter Doc Severinsen performed on two of the songs and was the greatest. We met previously when he was in town as the guest conductor for the Minneapolis Symphony Orchestra. He asked me to perform a few songs with the Orchestra. Sitting there playing the drums in front of a full house of sophisticated music lovers at Orchestra Hall was an unbelievable experience for a kid who got his start with a painted drum. To be on stage with so many talented and committed musicians was a big thrill. My parents probably were smiling down and shaking their heads at the sight. Who would have thought that their little drummer boy would put those music lessons to such good use?

Our Sunset Celebration album featured Twin Cities vocalists Dennis Spears of Moore by Four fame and Cynthia Johnson, who had a big 1980 hit with "Funky Town." The album was received well by the critics, but didn't get the major marketing and exposure to let it find the mass audience we thought it deserved. Contemporary jazz guru Bob O'Connor of San Diego was among the many to play and talk up the album. We tried to get the support of industry people, however, they said they weren't sure if we were jazz, rhythm and blues, or hip hop. We're definitely not hip hop—we like to call our music "rhythm jazz" with smooth, soulful vocals. In New York they call it "cool jazz," in California they call it "contemporary jazz." Over 140 stations in the country have adopted a broader format, known as adult contemporary. It's been around a long time, with guys like Kenny G, Tom Scott, Grover Washington, Jr., and The Crusaders leading the charge. Some traditional jazz people have been critical of some of the artists, labeling it "safe jazz," and saying it's not as challenging. But people like to listen to it because it's good music.

I don't think the major music industry is fair with America. They have pushed rap music so hard by putting so many dollars behind their artists. They don't give young people other places to turn. So much of that business is marketing and endorsing a certain product. If the major companies will only pump the millions of their production dollars into rap artists, and in turn if those are the only artists stations will play, that's the music the children will buy. All music is good, so let's promote all of it.

As a result, some of our country's finest musical artists, particularly from the 1970s and '80s, haven't gotten the financial and promotional support they need, and therefore can't make records. Young people right now, in my opinion, aren't being exposed to the whole gamut of music. A whole generation is missing out on the R&B sound, which has been around since the '50s.

I'm not trying to totally discount rap music. There are some positive things taking place there. But in this "gangsta rap," you hear too much tension. It's not positive. There are too many aggressive and violent attitudes aired. There's not much a society can ever accomplish with violence. I think we need to show our young people they can make it in life, not just because they're a great golfer or basketball player or football player, but because they're an everyday person who can get an education, set goals and pursue dreams. A more positive music format could reinforce that if a person is going through hard times, he's not going through them alone. There is hope.

What we've tried to do with our music on the Sunset Celebration is to emphasize the positive side of life and living, love and relationships. Sometimes it shows people enduring hard times and seeking better times in an upbeat fashion. We try to take the high road.

I loved to work with positive people and situations with potential. My nephew, Stanley Green, wanted to get into the music business.

He was a singer, a performer and played a lot of musical instruments. He took after his father, Stan Sr., of Thundering Senturies fame. Stan Jr. and I met a couple of guys called B-Cube (also known as Ben) and Kazir. Both guys were born in Nigeria, but they had never met each other until they came to the United States to attend the University of Minnesota. They are very talented and helped drive the creative end of Savannah Street Music. I became their executive producer, which meant I provided the funding. When I remind myself that sports is part of the entertainment business, it helps me accept the fact we lost a lot of money with this music venture. By 1995, Marie, my future wife, was president of the company, and we set out to make it big. Our first album was released in 1994, called "Love Cycles." It was a collection of nine songs about being a vulnerable lover. The vulnerable lover went through cycles of love. Stan Jr. performed on this album under the name Milo Green.

In 1994, we revamped our Vikings highlight television show on KARE 11. We went with a live audience—the only live audience television show of any kind in the Twin Cities. The Sunset Music Band played during intermissions and going into breaks. It was a band of some of the top artists in the Twin Cities: David Eiland was our sax man; Troy Norton was on lead guitar; Derrick Russell played bass guitar; I joined Larry Mack on drums; Marie and I worked the percussions. Ben and Kazir played the keyboards; and special guests included Mike Scott on guitar; Sandy Kay on flute and vocals; Allen Glen on vocals; and a group called Coco with Marvin and Bruce on vocals.

We gave the music business our best shot, but it seemed like luck was against us. We produced videos and a hired a financial consultant to find us an investor. About five days before we were supposed to meet our investor, he was asked to be executive producer and the lead investor for the Michael Jordan and Bugs Bunny movie, Space Jam, and we were back to square one. Ken Ross, of New York, did a great job on the Space Jam project, and the R.Kelly song, "I believe I can fly" was its No. 1 song.

The sucking sound that you heard was money going down the drain. We did produce a second video. The guy who helped us most was Larry Lieberman, vice president of Time Warner. We were included on video samplers with Blessed Union of Souls, Monica, the Silver Bullet Band, and The Black Crows. We were marketing, but we weren't selling records.

Late in 1996, after Marie and I were married, we decided to cut back. We had won an award for the best coaches' entertainment show and we were featured on ESPN, FOX and TNT. We were expecting our first child in February of 1997. Marie was born and raised in St. Paul

and my job was here. We had just built a house, so we divested ourselves of the music business and began focusing on raising a family.
Savannah Street Music is still going strong with Ben and Kazir. They are
extremely talented, and have more than 100 songs ready to produce
that would rock the music industry. Ironically, what's holding them
back in the age of so many tense rap music, is the fact that their songs
are positive, upbeat and soulful.

Unfortunately now in the music industry, it seems like the tail
wags the dog. People in charge don't understand what is successful or
why it's successful, they just find what sells and all come up with the
same thing. A few years ago, rap music sold, so that's what the industry
locked into.

I'd like to see more support for some good old-fashioned R&B
music to turn this cycle around again. I grew up listening to groups like
the Temptations, Miracles, The Four Tops and the Spinners. Today's
youths are losing out if they aren't exposed to that sound.

I think it's also important for kids to have a chance to participate
in music. It's so easy in athletics to recognize talent, but a lot of great
potential is wasted in music, particularly in inner-city kids, because
they don't have the programs, the resources or the encouragement to
learn to play an instrument. That's why music programs have been a
big part of my community service focus throughout my career.

I'm glad I was born in 1949 and not 1981. Growing up always
has its challenges, but I think it's much easier today to get into trouble
and slip into despair. If I were 15 today and living in poverty in the
inner city, I might be a hellraiser myself. My Dad and my brothers
would have been activists who weren't afraid to speak out. There's no
excuse for criminal behavior, drug use or hooliganism, but such misbehavior is often rooted in poverty and low self-esteem. Self-respect comes
harder for people with no job and no hope.

I love young people today. I get so dismayed when I see people
come down on them. I get so excited about their potential. They have
it much more difficult than my age group did when we were growing
up when you consider the obstacles—a breakdown of families; the
crime and the violence that threaten our communities; the lack of discipline and respect in schools; and a diminished influence of our
churches. Those issues aren't the fault of our young people. So many of
them are out there doing terrific things, but instead of those stories, we
lead off the TV newscast with stories about a few people who make

the wrong choices. The negativity begets more negativity, and there's more cynicism and less hope in our society.

We're lucky in sports because we're dealing with achievers. We've had a lot of rags to riches stories. We have stories of guys being the oldest one in their family who gets a scholarship and carries the hopes and dreams of his entire family with him as he tries to succeed in football and get his degree. But even sports has its share of heartbreak.

Young people have to learn that anything in life worth having comes at a price. When we talk about what we expect from them and what they expect from us, I like to use an analogy of taking $100 to a bank. You're not going to go back a year later and wonder if it's still there or hope it is. You expect it to be there, plus interest. The bank isn't doing you a favor. Once we get our young people expecting success, expecting opportunities and expecting more from themselves, we'll have even more success stories.

In athletics it's easy to recognize accomplishment because athletic ability is extremely visible. You make the team, get a scholarship, win games. The expectations are laid out right there for you. What we have to do for all young people is to give them something to look forward to in life, something to expect. We have to show them an opportunity and say "It's laying right there— What are you going to do?"

Marie and I are committed to do all we can in volunteer projects to make a positive difference in the lives of inner-city youth. I started before I came to Minnesota in 1992. When I met Jim Crotty, the Executive Director of the Minneapolis Boys and Girls Club, my focus as a volunteer became crystal clear. Jim and I had a lot in common. Both of us grew up in the inner city and relied on sports and recreation activities at places like the YMCA and Boys Clubs to stay out of trouble. I learned to swim at the YMCA and often swam with my brothers in the Susquehanna River. Jim, who was running four Boys and Girls clubs when we met, has been successful in launching innovative programs, as well as the tried and true standbys of basketball, baseball and football. He offered me a role as a board member, which I accepted. This introduced me to a new group of friends who are committed to helping youth. An avid fisherman, I host an annual bass tournament to benefit the Minneapolis Boys and Girls Clubs outdoor programs.

Eventually, I started a music program in conjunction with the Vikings in my Dad's memory and spirit—the Bus Green Music Team. The team is a 20-member drum corps, and there's a junior program to provide lessons for younger kids before they advance to the main team. The Bus Green Music Team plays at every Vikings home game, in area parades, and other events. We drilled some important themes into these young people's heads:

- accept responsibility for yourself;
- don't wait for good things to happen, instead go out and pursue success;
- realize that life is a journey and destiny is a matter of choice.

We also set up a mentoring program with the University of Minnesota Drum Corps. The instructor, Rob Muller, has done an incredible job. He was tough when he needed to be tough, and gave encouragement when needed.

The Team was part of the Kaleidoscope Performing Arts program at the Boys Club. This also consisted of a choir, step team and theater group. I can't tell you how excited and proud these kids have made me. Some kids are talking about playing drums in college. Three years earlier, many of the kids hadn't even considered life after high school. Marie and I made some great friends through this performing arts group —Jan Berman, Kent Hensley, Rhea Isaacs, Susan Lake, Ruthie Roitenberg, Linda Schimberg, Patti Taube, Elizabeth Villafana, Sharon Waller, my lovely wife Marie, and the rest of the advisory board have done a great job of creating the programs.

I've had the privilege to work with the American Red Cross, the Community Bridge Consortium of Maplewood, the PACER Center in Minneapolis, Project Offstreets in Minneapolis, the Second Harvest Food Bank of St. Paul, The Jacob Wetterling Foundation in St. Joseph, and the United Negro College Fund of Minneapolis.

At the 1997 Special Olympics Minnesota Summer games, it was a moving experience for me to see how proud and excited two young ladies were on the awards stand. Melissa, from northern Minnesota, was in tears on the platform. She bent to allow me to put her second-place medal around her neck. She kept saying that her two older brothers would be so proud of her, and she was right. Kelli, another participant, had never been in the games before. I sensed she had dreamed about the victory stand and receiving a medal. She kept asking as she stood on the third-place platform if she was going to receive a medal, too. When I said yes, she would scream, ask me again and she would scream, again.

My experiences in the Special Olympics have been very rewarding in more ways than one. In February of 1993, I was attending a send-off breakfast for the Winter International Games for a Special Olympics event. There was Marie Law. Marie and I had met before in her career as a flight attendant. Her employer, Northwest Airlines, was responsible for our charter flights to away games. Marie was a volunteer for Special Olympics. Our chance meeting led to conversations on volunteerism and adult involvements with youth. I expressed my goals of multiple participation in charitable activities and being able to make a real difference. Marie was planning to start her own company, Creative Consulting Enterprises. I suggested that we discuss the role she could play as a consultant/organizer working with me. Marie was born, raised and educated in St. Paul and was very familiar with the Twin Cities. She is especially familiar with many charitable organizations because her brother, Jim, Jr., who is now 30, has epilepsy and is mentally challenged. Her family has been active with the Epilepsy Foundation, Special Olympics, ARC, United Way and PACER for years.

When Marie and I started working together, she pulled all of my charitable activities together, which enabled me to be much more effective. Her commitment to people who were less fortunate is admirable. In 1994, following the breakup of my first marriage in 1993, Marie and I started dating. We were married in December of 1995.

Since 1994, Marie and I have made quite a team. We've delivered Meals on Wheels to senior citizens, and helped them with their campaign to sign up more volunteers to do the same. We picked up the meals at the Martin Luther King Center in St. Paul, where Marie's grandmother, Lorraine, had volunteered every day for 22 years. Lorraine passed away on January 20, 1995. We and all the dear people at the MLK Center really miss her.

One of the best things about my community service projects is the wide range of people I've worked with and met. I've been fortunate to know Bill Cosby through the years, and he was involved this year in our PACER Foundation benefit to raise funds for young adults with various disabilities. Even with the tragic death of his son this year, Bill kept his commitment to appear in the Twin Cities, and we had a chance to visit briefly. He's still so positive and such a strong influence on me and so many other people, especially young adults. He puts his own personal situation aside when he goes on the road. He's just a tremendous guy. We talked previously when he was trying to help revitalize the football program at Temple, his alma mater. They've gone through some of the same things we went through at Northwestern. He was influential in the hiring of Ron Dickerson, an African American, as head coach. Ron has been working his tail off trying to improve the Temple program. Bill believes in the human spirit. I hear he's talked about two specific ideas for his future—1) the possibility of buying a TV network; and 2) the possibility of buying a professional football team. There's never been an African American as a majority owner in the NFL. The tragic and senseless death of his son, Ennis, could put those ideas aside, however. He certainly doesn't need the money or the aggravation of such high-profile positions.

Like my passion for music and community work, fishing provides me with a great escape. My father started all of us fishing when we were pre-school age. He took us across town where the Susquehnna River flows. It's one of the best smallmouth fisheries in the country. We didn't just fish for smallmounth, though, because we were fishing for food, too. Just about anything we hooked, we kept. The Susquehanna has plenty of hot spots we liked to hit. Some of the best memories I have of my Dad and brothers together involve those fishing days. I try to get back to Harrisburg every summer for at least a week, and I fish as often as I can.

As a Minnesotan, you can't beat the bass fishing, especially if you're as close to Lake Minnetonka as I am. The lake, only 20 minutes from my office and 10 minutes from my home, offers a lot of diversity but plenty of bass. I enjoy all phases of fishing. I enjoy the excitement of early-season fishing when I can pitch spinner baits and topwater lures. I also like wormfishing and plugging, too.

I've been asked how fishing relates to football, and I think there are a couple of connections. First, there's the momentum factor. The hardest points to score in football are the first ones of the game. You hate missing that first, early opportunity to score. We might get close then miss a field goal or have a turnover. Everyone wants to put points on the board on that first drive. Fishing is the same way. You like to get out and start the day well. If you catch a fish on your first few casts, the day seems to go much better.

Another correlation between football and fishing is how you prepare for the different conditions and challenges in each activity. People who love fishing, like football coaches, have to be flexible. Because I have such a limited time to fish, I've become very adaptable. I change with the environment and the species. When I'm in California, I primarily fly-fish because I'm river fishing for steelhead or salmon. I've also moved a lot during my coaching career and have lived in places where the only fishing was in rock quarries or strip pits, and all I did was fish from a canoe. I've even tried ice fishing on the frozen ponds of Minnesota.

With my busy schedule, I have to plan my fishing into my daily routine. From the time the bass season begins in June all the way through mid-July, I'm not under as much pressure as I am during the fall. During the six weeks of training camp in July, we're down in Mankato, about 90 minutes from home, and I'm only able to fish one night a week for two hours. Once training camp ends and the season begins I try to get out on the lake when I can to clear my head. Sometimes if we win on Sunday, I'll fish Monday morning right after my radio show until about 9 a.m. Then I'll fish Friday afternoon from about 3-6 p.m. When we lose, I don't fish at all that week. Winter comes too early in Minnesota, so my fall angling routine is cut short by the time November rolls around.

I'm primarily on the water just to fish. I try to leave work and the stresses of life behind and focus on fishing without outside distractions. In the summer, I'm out on the water some days as early as 5 a.m. and fish until I have to come into work. I occasionally like to sneak out and fish in the late evening hours. I don't stay out all day or go on the three-day fishing trips, though. I consider fishing and playing the drums as my favorite hobbies, and I want them to be fun. The only time angling isn't fun is when you go out and expect to catch 'x' number of fish. I have enough competition in my job that I don't need fishing to become another contest. Whether I land two bass or seven, I'm going to consider it a good day. That's not to say I don't prepare and do some homework. I go out with a certain strategy of how I intend to catch fish, and part of the enjoyment of the sport is mapping out the strategy and carrying out the plan. But if the plan doesn't work, I don't let it bother me. We've all been skunked before, haven't we?

I plan to keep fishing and playing the drums as long as I live. Like my parents I'm convinced that a person who's well rounded has the best chance to be well grounded. I was raised to seek success, and fortunately when success came I had my feet firmly planted on the ground and was never too full of myself.

In 1979, I used that "well rounded" motivational speech on Dwight Clark, an 11th-round draft choice of the 49ers. "The more you can do, the better chance you have to make the team," I told him. Dwight took my advice to heart, and became a versatile receiver and special-teams player. He's enjoyed a long and successful NFL career, first as a player and now in his job as a vice president with the 49ers. I still remind him of my sage advice when we see each other.

# IF IT LASTS UNTIL TOMORROW

*A Sunset Celebration*

*Every sunset brings the hope of a new day.*
*Life's opportunities and challenges are before us.*
*As the day's end draws near,*
*People who recognize the energy of the sun*
*And appreciate its value*
*Come together for the close of a beautiful day.*
*A sunset celebration.*

—Dennis Green

One of the appealing aspects of writing an autobiography is that it helps you appreciate where you've been and makes you contemplate where you're going in life. My walk down memory lane has reminded me how much I've been blessed. It also has inspired me to try to be the best I can be in family, spiritual, community and career matters in the days and years ahead.

In the best-case scenario, as far as my coaching career goes, I'd like to be the Minnesota Vikings head coach for about three to five more years. My ultimate goal in the NFL is to become both head coach and general manager of a team, for approximately a four-year stretch.

Then for the last five years of my career, I would expect to relinquish the head coaching part of the job and finish as general manager. That would get me to retirement at about age 62. I'd like to get the opportunity to work in television broadcasting when I'm out of football. I would like to dabble in radio and other communication formats, too.

Being an NFL color analyst would allow me to stay with a game I've embraced my whole life. I know there will come a point when I won't want to keep up the seven-day football pace like I always have been doing. Marie and I have a young child now, and hopefully Vanessa will have a younger brother or sister, God willing. I look forward to the opportunity to retire and spend more time with my children as they hit their teenage years. If it all works out, I'll be able to devote all my time to my family during the week and still work some on the weekends in football season to keep me in the game. That would be ideal.

I enjoyed my chance to work as an analyst on the Aloha Bowl back in 1984. I've also been flown into New York and worked in the studio during the playoffs of the old CBS Today shows, before Fox got the TV rights. I worked with Terry Bradshaw and Jim Brown. It's always a lot of fun working in the studio on game day. That was pretty exciting —flying into New York first class and staying in the finest hotels and having a limousine taking you back and forth to the airport.

It's human nature for people to want to be liked and appreciated. I think a more realistic career goal for me is to hope I earn people's respect. You will always have detractors and critics who think it comes easy. You always try to learn what you can and move on to the next battle. You can't let criticism have any effect on you. People are entitled to their opinions. I'm happy for them. That's what makes it America. But any coach worth his salt would never allow criticism to play a role in his thinking. You have to believe in what you're doing. You have to plan your work, and work your plan, and you have to stay the course. I've seen coaches who have buckled under criticism and changed to try to please others, but it really doesn't work.

I've always considered myself to be an underdog, a fighter. That's why I ended up taking jobs like Northwestern and trying to get programs off the ground. I think I have the ability and the toughness to build programs. As far as coaching, I'd like to be seen as a guy who's mentally tough and well organized. I think people around the NFL consider the Vikings' football team one of the league's most organized. A good example of our organizational ability is that during training camp, we've traveled to Tokyo and Berlin and regularly scrimmage on the road.

I'd especially like to be known as a guy who loves to win. There's not a person in our locker room who wants to win more than I do. I love the competitive arena. I think the excitement on game days is breathtaking. I love to go out and lay it on the line. I'm not afraid to lose, and I'm not afraid to give it all I have to win, either. That's a point where some people back down—it's tough to put everything on the line and lose.

I'll savor the little things I've achieved in life.

I didn't let Bus and Anna down as a teenager.

I wasn't the best student, but I got my college degree in four years while playing big-time football and working a couple of jobs to support a family.

I worked as a volunteer to get my start in coaching, and earned everything I got as I climbed the ladder.

I've had hundreds of great friendships and relationships with players and colleagues throughout my 26 years in coaching. Hopefully I taught them a couple of things about football and about life as I was learning along with them.

While it wasn't my main goal, I helped show that African Americans can succeed as head football coaches in major colleges and in the NFL.

I've always tried to appreciate fans and people who support us. Whenever somebody tells you "Good job, coach," I say thank you, and really mean it. I'm glad people are proud of our football team and know that in a small way we help improve the quality of life in this area. A pro football team like the Vikings can give people all over the Twin Cities from different backgrounds a common subject. We can celebrate together, and occasionally feel disappointed together. It's a good feeling to be a part of an organization like the Minnesota Vikings that can have such a positive influence on community spirit.

There's no doubt the effect of losing my parents at such a young age played a large role in my distrust of "sure things" in life. The concept of "Here today, gone tomorrow" is something I had to face. Death is very final. But as a 48-year-old man in 1997, I'm really at peace with myself now. I think at times I was on a little too fast a pace, and I've made some mistakes along the way. But now I'm at peace with myself. I'm happily married, I have a new family, I'm still close with my adult children, Patti and Jeremy. Their involvement with Vanessa and Marie is something that makes me realize how lucky I am.

I probably don't tell my children enough how proud I am of them. Patti and Jeremy were delightful kids and are fine adults. Patti was born 10 weeks premature and only weighed 3 lbs, 3 oz. I'm sure that's where she developed her fighting spirit. She is sweet as can be, but has the determination of a lion. She works with MCI.

Jeremy grew up with the "basketball Jones-bug" like so many of our young people. He was an excellent golfer, too, but basketball was his passion. Now that he's an adult, a love for football is shining through. He works as a personnel coordinator in professional sports. He's helped give me a better understanding of the agent representation side of professional sports. I hope someday we can work together in some capacity.

Marie has brought me all the happiness in the world. It's clear to me we were meant to be together. Both of us recognize how fortunate and blessed we are to have our daughter, Vanessa. Marie has always made my older children, Patti and Jeremy, feel that our house is their house, and that they're always welcome.

Our new house was built in 1995 on land that housed an old-fashioned farmhouse and barn. We jokingly refer to our house as a "mini-mansion," but we appreciate that it is so functional. There's an office to let us have a home work environment, and guest room for my children when they come to visit. The neighbors are friendly, and there's shopping, schools and churches nearby. I'm just a few minutes to my Arkansas-built Champion bass boat moored on Lake Minnetonka. When I think of the modest houses where I grew up and the places I lived early in my coaching career, I feel lucky that to be so blessed. With love, this house promises to be a beautiful home.

It's so easy to think about my newborn daughter, Vanessa Anna-Marie Green. Marie delivered Vanessa on February 1, 1997 at 4:44 p.m. For the first time I was allowed in the delivery room. My emotions exploded the day she was born. Tears flowed like a waterfall. My wife did all the real work and suffered all the real pain. We cried together. I knew my Dad would understand if I cried this time. Patti and Jeremy love their baby sister Vanessa. Marie and I are committed to do everything we can to build a good future for our children. That was Bus and Anna's priority, and that's our priority.

With that in mind, a thought occurred to me—maybe I should buy the Vikings. I could leave the team to my wife and children.

Why not? I could buy the 30% controlling interest in the Vikings with an option to purchase the remaining 70% in two years. Wouldn't that be something? Just think—a former inner-city guy from the 'hood whose parents were not allowed to be buried in the Harrisburg Cemetery, would become the team's primary decision maker. I could culminate the purchase at the Vikings' November 11, 1997 board of directors meeting. The present owners should view this as a business proposal, and not a personal attack.

When my turn came to talk, I could start passing out copies of a purchase agreement. I could be the first African American to own controlling interest in an NFL team. Some of the present owners would be stunned, but nobody is very happy right now, anyway. Let's face it, this situation has gone on too long. In fact, if you read what Jim Klobuchar has written, the confusion has existed since 1984. That's 14 years of non-compliance with NFL rules. I would support any deal that Roger Headrick puts forth. But if Roger chooses not to pursue the 30% ownership control, don't be surprised if Dennis Green steps in as a black knight to the rescue.

## One Conceivable Game Plan Scenario:

### PHASE 1:  THE 10% SILENT OWNERS (Phantom)

Tuesday, November 11, 1997, my attorney would contact every individual who made up the 10% minority owners. I would attempt to secure purchase options for their shares. This transaction would be based on their ability to maintain strict confidential negotiations. They would be offered a binding purchase agreement preconditioned on my completing the purchase of 18% interest of two of the 9% shareholders by 5 p.m. on Thursday, November 13, 1997.

Most people don't know this minority ownership group even exists. Time after time, the reports say that the Vikings have 10 owners that each own 10% of the club. Now, these true shareholders who collectively own 10% can strike their own deal. The price would be $1.3 million for each 1% share. This price would reflect the last realistic sale of shares that took place in 1991 of 50% shares for $62 million to a two-person ownership group of Carl Pohlad and Irwin Jacobs. The Pohlad-Jacobs group originally purchased the 50% shares for $25 million in 1986. I would offer cash money—this should encourage them to take the deal. Remember, there is value only if there is a buyer.

### Phase II

With 10 percent already secured, my next move would come Thursday, November 13, 1997, 10 a.m. at the Vikings Board of Directors meeting in downtown Minneapolis. I would distribute copies of a purchase agreement that would secure for me 20% of the 90% outstanding shares of Vikings team ownership.

Dear Directors:

I am purchasing the 9% shares of the two individuals sitting in this room who contacted Lou Holtz, the former Notre Dame head coach, without authority last year and deliberately interfered with my ability to coach the team.

I will not single you out even though most of the people in this room know who I'm talking about. Your solicitation of Lou Holtz was a major distraction on a local and national level. It caused harm to me and my coaches and players, as well as our families. This disrespect for my position as head football coach of the Minnesota Vikings hurt my football reputation and undermined my leadership capabilities.

*As a career coach of 26 years, who can be expected to coach for another 15 years, these two board members may have damaged my future career opportunities. In other words, I AM BUYING OR SUING. My claims in damages are compensable under Minnesota's Tortious Interference law, separate and above the damages ordinarily available for such tortious conduct, as specifically held in Swaney v. Crawley, 157 N.W. 910, 911 (Minn. 1916). Please do not misunderstand or underestimate what I am saying. In my opinion, everyone in this room—including the other eight board members— can be held accountable and responsible for the actions of these two.*

I look forward to your immediate response.

Sincerely,

Dennis Green

Case Type:  Contract

STATE OF MINNESOTA                     DISTRICT COURT
COUNTY OF HENNEPIN              FOURTH JUDICIAL DISTRICT
                                       Court File No:  _____

Dennis Green
                    Plaintiff,
                                                       COMPLAINT
vs.

                    Defendants.

For his Complaint against defendants, plaintiff alleges:

1.      Plaintiff and the Minnesota Vikings Football Club, Inc. (the "Vikings") entered into a contract on _____, 19_____ in which plaintiff agreed to provide head coaching services for the Vikings for a period of seven years (the "contract").

2.      Defendants, who are shareholders and members of the Vikings' Board of Directors, were aware of the contract at all material times herein.

3.      The Vikings are members of the National Football League, (the "NFL") an organization of 30 similar entities, each fielding a football team for competitive play between and among each other every fall and early winter.

4.      Pursuant to the terms of the contract, plaintiff was to use his best efforts to field a competitive football team for the Vikings, for play in the NFL, throughout each of the seven seasons of said contract.

5.      In addition to his scheduled salary, plaintiff's remuneration under the contract provided for bonuses and other additional benefits, which were dependent upon achievements of the Vikings team in each particular season during the term of the contract ("bonuses").

6.     It was further agreed and expected by plaintiff and the Vikings that plaintiff would be further compensated by endorsements, media contracts, personal appearances and other secondary sources arising directly as a benefit from his successful performance under the contract ("secondary compensation").

7.     The NFL, in which the Vikings participate, is the premier professional football league in the United States consisting of 30 football teams playing a competitive schedule of regular and post-season play each fall and early winter.

8.     Included in the organization of the NFL are rules, regulations and procedures which have, as a goal, competitive parity between and among each of its 30 member teams ("parity"). Such parity has generally been achieved by similar levels of talent and skills of the players on each team.

9.     The success of a head coach of any NFL team is generally measured by his ability, in spite of the parity, to lead his team into the playoffs after the regular season, and then successively winning playoff games with the intention of ultimately reaching and winning the Super Bowl, the pinnacle of such post-season play.

10.     Because of parity, the success of the head coach and his team in advancing in the playoffs and reaching the Super Bowl, is as dependent upon the relationship between the head coach and his players as it is on the skill of that team's players.

11.     During the 1996 football season, the Vikings team was sufficiently successful during the regular season to be eligible for the playoffs despite an intrusive situation.

12.     Shortly before the beginning of the playoffs, in late 1996, defendants, without any authority, solicited the services of one Lou Holtz, a former coach of a college football team in Minnesota, to coach the Vikings team (the "solicitation"). Mr. Holtz was available as a coach since he was about to resign from another college team he was then coaching in Indiana.

13.     The local and national media immediately became aware of this solicitation and falsely announced the impending appointment of Mr. Holtz, and the firing of plaintiff, as the Vikings' head coach, notwithstanding the existence of a valid contract between plaintiff and the Vikings and the likely participation of the Vikings in the playoffs later that season.

14.     This conduct by defendants constituted a tortious interference, without justification, of plaintiff's contract with the Vikings in that it made it more difficult and/or impossible for him to perform successfully under said contract, and denied him the benefits he was entitled to thereunder. Specifically, among other things, such tortious interference:

   a. Adversely affected the leadership relationship between plaintiff, as head coach, and his staff and players, rendering it difficult for plaintiff to motivate the players to play up to their competitive level of ability and skill and advance in the playoffs and to the Super Bowl;

   b. Made it impossible for plaintiff to meet performance goals within the contract entitling him to additional compensation including, without limitation, bonus compensation for the Vikings' advancing in the playoffs and to the Super Bowl; and

   c. Impaired plaintiff's value and opportunities for media and endorsement contracts which the parties to the contract knew and agreed was a part of the value thereof to plaintiff.

15.     In addition to the foregoing loss incurred by plaintiff under said contract as a result of defendants' unlawful interference, plaintiff's reputation and value as a head football coach in the NFL, which is incident to and part of the contract, was substantially impaired so that his continuing success and compensation in his field of endeavor, both with the Vikings and elsewhere, has been substantially diminished or rendered so unlikely as to be impossible.

16.    As a result of the foregoing circumstances and events set forth in paragraphs 14 and 15 immediately above, plaintiff has been damaged in an amount in excess of $_____.

WHEREFORE, plaintiff, prays for judgment against defendants, jointly and severally, in an amount in excess of $_____ , plus costs, disbursements and attorneys' fees as allowed by law, and such other and further relief as ordered by the Court.

---

## STOCK PURCHASE AGREEMENT

THIS AGREEMENT is made December___ , 19___ , by and between Dennis Green ("Buyer") and _____("Seller").

## RECITALS

A.    Seller owns _____ shares of the issued and outstanding capital stock of a Minnesota corporation ("the Vikings").

B.    Buyer desires to purchase all and Seller desires to sell all of Seller's shares on the terms and conditions set forth in this Agreement.

NOW, THEREFORE, Buyer and Seller agree as follows:

1.    <u>Transfer of Stock.</u>  Upon the terms and conditions set forth in this Agreement, Seller agrees to sell and Buyer agrees to buy all of Sellers' shares of the capital stock of the Vikings.

2.    <u>Purchase Price and Payment.</u>  The Purchase price for the shares of Seller sold hereunder is $_____, to be paid by Buyer as follows:

(a)     $_____ earnest money upon tender of this Agreement by Buyer to Seller.

(b)     $_____ cash or certified funds payable to Seller at closing.

3.     Representation and Warranties of Seller.  Seller represents and warrants to Buyer as follows:

(a)     Seller has good and marketable title to all of the shares of the Vikings being sold hereunder, with absolute right to sell, assign and transfer the same to Buyer free and clear of all liens, pledges, security interests or other  encumbrances and without any breach of any agreement to which Seller is a party, other than the right of first refusal between Sellers and other shareholders, which shall be Released on or before the closing.

(b)     Seller has no claim for any additional shares in the Vikings pursuant to any  warranty, option or any other oral; or written agreement.

(c)     Seller has disclosed to Buyer all liabilities or claims of potential liabilities against his stock sold hereunder of which he has knowledge.

4.     Closing.  The closing will be _____ at 10:00 A.M. in the office of Buyer's counsel, _____, Minneapolis, Minnesota,  55402.  Said closing may be postponed, at the option of Buyer, from time to time.  Provided, however, closing must occur on or before _____, 19_.  If this transaction has not closed on or before said date, this agreement shall be null and void.

5.     Transactions at Closing.

(a)     Buyer shall deliver to Seller $_____ in certified funds.

(b)       Seller shall deliver to Buyer at closing stock certificates for _____ shares of stock in the Vikings, sufficiently executed to evidence transfer to Buyer of all right and title to such stock free and clear of any security interest, pledge or lien, other than that which is created in favor of Buyer at closing, including the right of first refusal in favor of any other shareholder, which shall be released by all such prior shareholders as a condition precedent to closing.

(c)       Seller shall tender his resignation as an officer and member of the Board of Directors of the Vikings. Notwithstanding this resignation, Seller agrees to cooperate and, if necessary, execute any documents subsequent to closing that involve the organization, minutes or other matters relating to the administration of the Vikings, provided that such execution will not constitute an unlawful act or obligate Seller to make any statement which is not accurate.

5.      <u>Expenses of Transaction.</u> Each party shall be responsible for his/her own expenses incident to this transaction, including but not limited to legal and accounting expenses and related costs.

IN WITNESS WHEREOF, Buyer and Seller have executed this Agreement as of the day and year first written above.


_____

                                          Buyer


_____

                                          Seller

There's no doubt the 9% owners all expect to receive a lot more than $700,000 per 1% share. Therefore, I know the board won't be happy. But after the board's attorney sees that I have grounds for a lawsuit, eventually I could purchase the 18% shares at a price of $700,000 for each 1% share. This would total $12.6 million.

## PHASE III

I would distribute and execute an agreement to purchase Roger Headrick's 2% share of the team. I would then issue a Shareholders Control Agreement among all Viking shareholders providing for Roger's continuing management of the team in the same capacity. Such shareholder control agreement would allow him to control the business and affairs of the corporation even though he had less than the previously required 9%. This was permitted in Minnesota (Mn. Stat. Sec. 302A 457). I would pay Roger $1.3 million for each of his shares. This would total $2.6 million. I would remain the Head Football Coach, become General Manager, and Roger would remain President.

## THE SUMMARY

The purchase breakdown:

|   |   |   |
|---|---|---|
| a) | 10% phantom owners at $1.3 million per % | $13.0m |
| b) | renegade owners 18% at $.7 million per % | $12.6m |
| c) | Headrick's 2% at $1.3 million per % | $2.6m |
|   | TOTAL | $28.2m |

## ACCEPTED

By 5 p.m. Thursday, November 13, 1997, I would have secured 30% ownership of the Minnesota Vikings in shares of stock, purchased for a premium discount price of $28.2 million. The NFL office and other NFL owners who have grown weary of the intentional delay tactics of this ownership group—in violation of league by-laws—would be pleased. The reason a single majority owner was required is simple —the one who invests the most money has the most incentive to run a solid organization.

The former Viking ownership group consisted of people who had invested very little money by NFL owner standards. Relatively speaking, they had very little to lose. They could operate outside the rules that other team owners set up. The owners could have agreed to sell to a friendly buyer from their own group, but if they can't agree on less difficult matters, how can you expect them to come together on something of this magnitude?

## FUNDING

I would secure funding for this purchase through one of the country's leading venture capital companies, like Arthur Anderson. One of the Twin Cities' top financial people, Larry Zipkin, has looked over this bold move and says the plan has possibilities. His company, Equity Financial, handles a variety of financial matters. John Carroll, a financial wizard and Stanford graduate who lives in Houston, is eager to assist on this project. John brings a wealth of information and is a conduit to major sources of revenue in California and Texas.

I realize that raising money is not easy. But my ace in the hole could be my Money Mentor in California, who would be willing to consider providing the funding for this bold move. The formula is simple —he provides the money, and I provide the opportunity and the team.

In NFL history, no team had decreased in value from the purchase price. I would have $10.8 million of equity in the purchase of the 18% shares at the discounted price. Therefore, my plan would be to borrow $28.2 million. The principal would remain a sum in addition to this to establish a reserve equal to the first two years of payments. The two-year reserve would be $12 million, making the amount borrowed a total of $40.2 million. On a 10-year level amortization with interest at 8% per annum, the estimated annual payment of principal and interest would be $6.0 million a year. More importantly, the team is worth a lot more than I would pay for it only if there is another buyer.

Maybe it's time for the guy who cut through the Harrisburg Cemetery and cut through the whites-only turf of major-college and NFL head football coaching jobs to cut through all the B.S. in this ownership soap opera and provide some sorely-needed action.

# Dennis Green's Coaching Resume

| | | |
|---|---|---|
| 1972 | U of Iowa | Volunteer Asst. Coach |
| 1973 | U of Dayton | Asst. Coach |
| 1974-76 | U of Iowa | Asst. Coach |
| 1977-78 | Stanford | Asst. Coach |
| 1979 | San Francisco 49ers | Asst. Coach |
| 1980 | Stanford | Offensive Coordinator |
| 1981-85 | Northwestern | Head Coach |
| 1986-88 | San Francisco 49ers | Asst. Coach |
| 1989-91 | Stanford | Head Coach |
| 1992-present | Minnesota Vikings | Head Coach |

*"It is rare that one individual represents two unique talents: Sound business savvy along with strategic athletic leadership. This person is Dennis Green."*

—Al Golin, Chairman
Golin/Harris Communications, Inc.

*"Do you know this man? He delivered Meals on Wheels to senior citizens and has donated time, money and clothing to the homeless kids at Project Offstreets. He founded the Bus Green Music Team for the Minneapolis Boys and Girls Clubs in memory of his late father, Bus. He supports the Epilepsy Foundation, the United Negro College Fund, Special Olympics, PACER, and he's a member of Children Cancer Research Fund's Benefactors Circle. Because people helped him overcome adversity in his youth, he believes passionately in giving back to the young people of today."*

—Sharon Waller
Author, "Circle of Hope"

*"Dennis Green has given many gifts to every community he has ever lived in. Football enthusiasts at every level have watched him coach the game. This book, however, is one of his greatest gifts because he is sharing himself in an honest and powerful way."*

—Rev. Keith E. Johnson, CEO
Christian Athletes United for
Spiritual Empowerment (C.A.U.S.E.)
Minnesota Viking Chaplain

# Other Titles by Sports Publishing Inc.
## a division of Sagamore Publishing

### Dennis Green: No Room for Crybabies
### Leatherbound edition

Limited edition of 250 leatherbound books signed by Dennis
Green, Harvey Mackay and former players and/or coaches.
**Available only by calling Sagamore Publishing**
**at 1-800-327-5557.**

### The Golden Dream
### ($22.95)
by Gerry Faust and Steve Love

Gerry Faust won more hearts than games. He came to Notre
Dame as the mythical high school coach from Cincinnati's
Moeller High School, such a perfect fit for Notre Dame that it
seemed almost too good to be true. It was.

Faust admits his mistakes, which include the manner in which
he put together his first coaching staff, changing Notre Dame's
offense without considering carefully the type of players former
coach Dan Devine had left him, even feeling sorry for himself.
He explains how he could beat Southern California, but not Air
Force and Purdue.

Gerry Faust took the path he believes God wanted him to take.
Now, he invites you to walk that path with him, see what he
saw, feel what he felt.

## All titles are available at your local bookstore
## or by calling 1.800.327.5557

### Joe Paterno: The Coach from Byzantium ($22.95)
by George Paterno

George Paterno, the brother of Penn State football coach Joe Paterno and color analyst for Penn State football, tells the story about his legendary brother. This book is a combination of two novels - the story about an icon and national legend evoking his life as a young man prior to beginning his journey to fame. The story describes the role effect of Joe's immediate family, his relationship with them, and the importance they played in his future development.

The second part of the story deals with Joe's career after he joined Rip Engle's staff and his subsequent marriage. All of the people who helped and contributed to his legend are brought into focus for the first time.

In essence, the book is about two brothers, close but different.

### George Perles: The Ride of a Lifetime ($22.95)
by George Perles with Vahe Gregorian

In 1983, George Perles took over the reins at Michigan State and after just one rebuilding year led the Spartans to their first Bowl game in decades. George Perles: The Ride of a Lifetime goes behind the scenes to explore the successes and challenges that Coach Perles faced in his career, including the trying finish to his career.

### Bud Wilkinson: An Intimate Portrait of an American Legend ($19.95)
by Jay Wilkinson with Gretchen Hirsch

Bud Wilkinson, Bear Bryant, and Woody Hayes - the names that come to mind when the talk turns to great collegiate football coaches. Wilkinson received the American Dream playing by the rules. No short cuts or quick fixes. As Americans search for success and role models, a retrospective view of Wilkinson offers a road map to the top, and a look at a durable American hero.

## All titles are available at your local bookstore or by calling 1.800.327.5557